Pedagogy and
Culture and Identities

efore th

This Reader is one of a series of three which form part of *Curriculum, learning and society: investigating practice* (E846), a course belonging to the Open University Masters in Education programme. The series consists of the following books:

Learning and Practice: Agency and Identities (edited by Patricia Murphy and Kathy Hall)

Pedagogy and Practice: Culture and Identities (edited by Kathy Hall, Patricia Murphy and Janet Soler)

Knowledge and Practice: Representations and Identities (edited by Patricia Murphy and Robert McCormick)

The Open University Masters in Education

The Open University Masters in Education is now firmly established as the most popular postgraduate degree for education professionals in Europe, with around 3000 students registered each year. It is designed particularly for those with experience of teaching, the advisory service, educational administration or allied fields. Specialist lines in leadership and management, applied linguistics and special needs/inclusive education are available within the award. Successful study on the Masters entitles students to apply for entry into the Open University Doctorate in Education programme.

Details of this and other Open University courses can be obtained from the Student Registration and Enquiry Service, The Open University, PO Box 197, Milton Keynes MK7 6BJ, United Kingdom; telephone: +44 (0) 845 300 6090; e-mail: general-enquiries@open.ac.uk.

Alternatively, you may wish to visit the Open University website at http://www.open.ac.uk, where you can learn more about the wide range of courses and packs offered at all levels by The Open University.

Pedagogy and Practice: Culture and Identities

Edited by
Kathy Hall, Patricia Murphy and Janet Soler

Los Angeles • London • New Delhi • Singapore

The Open University

The Open University
Walton Hall
Milton Keynes
MK7 6AA
United Kingdom
www.open.ac.uk

First Published in 2008

SAGE Publications Ltd
1 Oliver's Yard
55 City Road
London EC1Y 1SP

SAGE Publications Inc.
2455 Teller Road
Thousand Oaks, California 91320

SAGE Publications India Pvt Ltd
B 1/I 1 Mohan Cooperative Industrial Area
Mathura Road
New Delhi 110 044

SAGE Publications Asia-Pacific Pte Ltd
33 Pekin Street #02-01
Far East Square
Singapore 048763

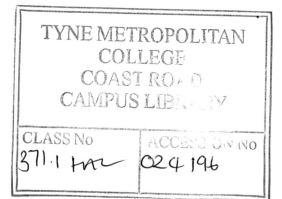

Library of Congress Control Number: 2008920074

British Library Cataloguing in Publication data

A catalogue record for this book is available from the British Library

ISBN 978-1-8478-7367-5
ISBN 978-1-8478-7368-2 (pbk)

Typeset by C&M Digitals (P) Ltd, Chennai, India
Printed by The Cromwell Press Ltd, Trowbridge, Wiltshire
Printed on paper from sustainable resources

Contents

Acknowledgements

We would like to thank the authors who contributed their chapters, as well as colleagues within and outside The Open University who helped with the preparation of the manuscripts. Special thanks are due to the following people for their assistance in the production of this book:

Sally Jones (course secretary)
Fulden Underwood (course manager)
Professor Valentina Klenowski (external assessor)
Gordon Bloomer (critical reader)
Gill Gowans (copublishing media developer)

Chapter 1

From: Alexander, R., *Culture and Pedagogy: International Comparisons in Primary Education* (London: Blackwell, 2001). Reproduced and adapted by kind permission of the author and publisher.

Chapter 2

From: 'Defining Pedagogy' by Patricia Murphy in *Equity in the Classroom: Towards Effective Pedagogy for Girls and Boys*, ed. by P.F. Murphy and C.V. Gipps © UNESCO 1996. Used by permission of UNESCO, with bibliographic references native to the original edition excised.

Chapter 3

From: *Oxford Review of Education,* 33 (4), 2007, pp. 403–422. Reprinted by permission of the publisher (Taylor & Francis Ltd, http://www.informaworld.com).

Chapter 4

From: Wertsch, J.V., Del Rio, P., Alvarez, A. (eds.) *Sociocultural Studies of Mind* (Cambridge: Cambridge University Press, 1995). © Cambridge University Press 1995, reproduced with permission.

Chapter 5

From: *International Journal of Lifelong Education,* 25 (1), 2006, pp. 3–13. Reprinted by permission of the publisher (Taylor & Francis Ltd, http://www.informaworld.com).

Chapter 7

From: Chapter 6 in Wenger, E., *Communities of Practice: Learning, Meaning and Identity* (Cambridge: Cambridge University Press, 1998). © Cambridge University Press 1998, reproduced with permission.

Chapter 8

From: Gonzalez, N., Moll, L.C. & Amanti, C. (eds.) *Funds of Knowledge: Theorizing Practices in Households, Communities and Classrooms* (New Jersey 2005: Lawrence Erlbaum Associates), pp. 89–118. Reproduced with permission.

Chapter 9

From: *British Educational Research Journal,* 28 (3), 2002, pp. 399–418. Reprinted by permission of the publisher (Taylor & Francis Ltd, http://www.informaworld.com).

Chapter 10

From: *Teacher Development,* 9 (2), 2005, pp. 185–200. Reprinted by permission of the publisher (Taylor & Francis Ltd, http://www.informaworld.com).

Chapter 11

From: Chapter 8 in Lankshear, C. & Knobel, M., *New Literacies: Changing Knowledge and Classroom Learning* (© 2003, published by Open University Press). Reproduced with the kind permission of the Open University Press Publishing Company.

Chapter 12

From: *Gender and Education,* 9 (1), 1997, pp. 9–30. Reprinted by permission of the publisher (Taylor & Francis Ltd, http://www.informaworld.com).

Chapter 13

From: *Assessment in Education,* 14 (3), 2007, pp. 281–294. Reprinted by permission of the publisher (Taylor & Francis Ltd, http://www.informaworld.com).

Introduction

Kathy Hall and Patricia Murphy

This book is one of three readers examining relational views of learning, pedagogy and knowledge. Adopting a sociocultural approach it takes pedagogy as central to learning, regardless of where that learning happens or the nature of the learning being promoted. Pedagogy involves understanding ways of participating in practice, people's opportunities and lack of opportunities to participate, and the positions people take up and are given within activity, opportunities and positions, which in turn signal identities and emerging, new ways of being in the world.

Many texts dealing with pedagogy tend to treat it as only pertaining to teaching in schools and often only address techniques and strategies pertaining to a domain of knowledge, such as mathematics. So pedagogy becomes bounded and gets defined narrowly. Understood from a sociocultural perspective, pedagogy is also and crucially concerned with what is salient to people as they engage in activity and develop competence in the practice in question. It takes account of two phenomena and their dynamic relationship: (a) the social order as reflected in, for example, policy and its associated cultural beliefs and assumptions; and (b) the experienced world, as reflected in both the enactment and the experience of the policy, including the beliefs underlying the approaches used in its enactment and the beliefs mediating how it is experienced. The parallels in curriculum can be thought of as being at three levels: curriculum as specified (the social order, the policy), curriculum as enacted, and curriculum as experienced (the experienced world). Pedagogy, from a sociocultural perspective, has to be concerned with these three interrelational aspects of curriculum. In this sense, it is concerned with the relationship between practice and the cultural, institutional, and historical contexts in which the practice occurs (Wertsch, 1998). What is fundamental is the relationship, how the social world, the individual as agent, and the practice are interconnected. People's ways of knowing, their histories of participation (Holland et al., 1998) and the ways in which these mediate ongoing activity in education and workplace settings are facets of a sociocultural perspective that are highlighted in this view on pedagogy.

This deeper and broader notion of pedagogy, which is not confined to a particular place, setting, age or stage, draws attention to the identities which are variously valued, reproduced and transformed as people participate in activity. Whether the practice is in relation to becoming a reader, a learner of mathematics in school, a teacher, an architect, a hairdresser and so on, how the cultural practice is mediated by one's lived experience becomes significant for one's ability to demonstrate oneself as competent and be recognized by others as competent in a given practice. Pedagogy involves an appreciation of the significance of experiences and mediational aspects as key to supporting learning. Wenger (1998: 149) says we define who we are by where we have been and where we are heading – the past and the future, he says, give meaning to the present. Knowledge of learners' histories of participation is a resource that teachers and mentors can draw on to understand and shape the meanings that learners construct in settings in the present.

Culture is a contested term in research but in a sociocultural perspective, culture is generally thought of as emerging as people interact and engage in activity together. It is not simply a product of practice, rather it is ways of being in practice. The routines, reifications, values and concerns that people make meaning of in an education or work setting are part of culture, and a sociocultural perspective on pedagogy would direct us to attend to those routines and practices for they give insights into how to support learning and transform identities. Seeing culture, not as fixed, but as something that changes as people, practices, communities and institutions change means that the telling issues for pedagogy are not about pedagogical approaches that essentialize non-dominant groups or even about how people adapt to their context or how contexts adapt to people, but rather how transformation happens both in the participants and in the contexts of their participation (Gutierrez and Correa-Chavez, 2006). In this sense, the focus of attention is on institutional practices of which individuals are a part, the resources available to them to participate, and relationships that they make and are available to be made, rather than on the identification of individuals as problems. Such a take on culture does not deny the merits of knowing about the valued practices of groups but it does challenge the idea of teaching or mentoring prescriptively according to broad, underexamined generalities about groups and assuming that what is known about a group fits all individuals in that group (Gutierrez and Rogoff, 2003). The notion of a culturally responsive pedagogy (Moje and Hinchman, 2004) is used by socioculturalists to refer to how learners' ways of knowing and experiences can be used to challenge and reshape curriculum for the benefit of all parties involved, especially for those who have been traditionally marginalized. Although we include some here, we did not find many studies, especially in the UK, of culturally responsive pedagogy that demonstrated positive identity transformation in our searches for this book. This is clearly an area that merits further exploration by sociocultural researchers.

The first section of the book contains five chapters that offer conceptualizations that are relevant to a sociocultural perspective on pedagogy. Chapter 1 is an edited excerpt from Robin Alexander's seminal book *Culture and Pedagogy: International Comparisons in Primary Education* (Alexander, 2001), in which he defines, explores and distinguishes notions of pedagogy, curriculum, didactics and culture. Pedagogy is an overarching concept for Alexander encompassing curriculum as enacted in the classroom. Although he is not writing from a sociocultural perspective, his contribution includes some key ideas that are part of a sociocultural perspective on pedagogy, in particular, his concern with curriculum enactment as well as with the curriculum as specified. Of particular significance is the way Alexander's international study allows him to demonstrate the similarities and differences across institutional policies and practices in the different countries, which provides insights into how participants in the different countries draw on 'cultural scripts' to construct notions of valued knowledge, success and learning. Chapter 2, written by Patricia Murphy over a decade ago, is quite a different chapter, both in its significance and its empirical basis, as it was a preface to an international book exploring effective pedagogy from a gender perspective. Of interest for the book is that the chapter defines pedagogy in a way that is complementary to a sociocultural perspective and is applicable to both schools and workplaces. Murphy recognizes all three levels of curriculum acknowledging the social order or collective and the lived world. Murphy's interest in what learners and their teachers bring to settings – their subjectivities – reflects a concern with the appropriation of the social order by teachers and children, but in relation to their histories of participation and identifications. These identifications emerge in settings which are informed by teachers' pedagogic, epistemological and ontological beliefs and are experienced by students. Hence, Murphy moves us towards the view that pedagogy and practice are distinct, in that they operate at different levels of the social order.

Michael Eraut, in Chapter 3, sketches out a framework for describing and supporting professional learning in the workplace. In doing so, he argues that sociocultural and cognitivist theories are complementary and he proceeds to draw on both perspectives in developing his framework. The assumption of complementarity of cognitivist and sociocultural perspectives is a dominant view among many influential theorists, although it is difficult to reconcile his eclectic orientation since the perspectives he is trying to merge stem from categorically different views of mind (McCormick and Murphy, 2000). However, Eraut begins to describe learning in terms of participation and he identifies aspects of overt guidance for learning, that is, pedagogy. The significance he attaches to the building of relationships with others in the workplace link with the sociocultural notion of learning as a movement deeper into practice (Wenger, 1998; Boreham and Morgan, 2004). In uncovering the blurring between informal and formal learning (Lave, 2008), based on a vast amount of empirical research, Eraut raises important points that move thinking towards a sociocultural view. In Chapter 4, Barbara Rogoff, a socioculturalist, offers a conceptual framework that captures and allows for the description and analysis of the dynamic nature of pedagogy. Defining and applying the developmental processes of apprenticeship, guided participation and participatory appropriation, her sociocultural framework allows for the contributions of individuals and their histories of participating in related practices, along with those of their social partners, together with the broader cultural/institutional context in which individuals act. In other words, it has the potential to take account of the social order and the world as experienced and their constituent nature. The feasibility and elegance of her framework stem from the potential foregrounding and backgrounding of three different planes of analysis, namely institutional, interpersonal and personal, without losing sight of their dynamic relations. Pedagogy, as part of the social order, emerges through policies and structures, say assessment and accountability systems, on the institutional plane, be it in an educational or workplace setting, and this mediates the interpersonal plane in the context of enactments where beliefs on the part of teachers, mentors and other participants about how to support learning emerge in practice with consequences for how people are positioned. At the intrapersonal plane, we can begin to illuminate the experienced curriculum that is mediated in the interaction between people in activities and influenced by their histories of participation and what is cued as legitimate to do, say, and become in the settings.

The last chapter in this section by Solomon, Boud and Rooney gives us a sociocultural way of looking at learning in the workplace. It challenges the divide between learning and living (Lave, 2008) in picking up on and explaining why the informal/formal divide is not helpful in a sociocultural perspective. Their chapter raises important challenges for the analysis of Eraut's ideas above. In bringing together and pondering the learning occurring in the social/leisure and workplace spaces, they invite ways of rethinking how, for example, we understand home–school, everyday–specialist activity, playground–classroom, and other distinctions that are often made across contexts. Where Murphy referred to identity work in the context of school subjects – a critical pedagogy stance – Solomon et al. open up the ongoing identity work that is undertaken as people negotiate and manage identities in the spaces made available to them.

The four chapters assembled in the second section of the book together with the three in the final section address in various ways the issue of cultural bridging. They show the pedagogic processes and challenges in the transformation of identity, attending to such

ideas as bridging, reshaping knowledge and the consequent repositioning of the participants, as well as curriculum and knowledge. Based on a longitudinal ethnography,
Chapter 6 by Kathy Hall illustrates how pedagogy involves consideration of what children bring with them to the classroom and not only what teachers do. It is an account of
how one boy, with others, maintains himself as 'cool teenager' and of how this salient
identity mediates what is available for him to learn both within and without school. In
demonstrating the unavailability to him of a successful learner identity in primary school,
together with the emergence of a potentially new positive learner identity in secondary
school, the need for a culturally responsive pedagogy is highlighted. Chapter 7 is a conceptual piece taken from Etienne Wenger's ground-breaking study, *Communities of
Practice* (1998). Here he develops the connection between identity and practice, showing
how identities are multifaceted because they emerge within the complexity of relations of
practice. Particularly relevant to pedagogy is his notion of identity as a nexus of multimembership. He is referring to the ways in which people reconcile their different forms
of belonging in different communities of practice into one identity. This is far more than
a straightforward matter of learning new information or making discrete choices, rather
it involves resolving between different forms of individuality that are important in different communities of practice, an idea which opens up the complexity of pedagogy and the
need for mentors and teachers to be attuned to the potential reconciliation work undertaken as learners engage in practice and negotiate tasks.

Chapter 8 is an edited excerpt from a chapter by Norma González and her colleagues entitled 'Funds of Knowledge for Teaching in Latino Households', in which the research team
describe a project which sought to build on learners' histories of participation. In order to better understand and support learning in classrooms, they shifted their gaze to households and
communities and tapped into the resources available there, the intention being to examine
existing teaching approaches and introduce innovative ones based on the repertoires of knowledge they found in those households. Their relationships with community members were
based on reciprocity and respect and since they were searching for resources, they found
resources, and as such were able to dispel myths about, for instance, deficits and poor educational backgrounds among the Mexican immigrants with whom they worked. Chapter 9, by
Kathy Hall, Kamil Özerk, Mohsin Zulfiqar, and Jon Tan, is an edited version of a study which
sought to understand the nature of human action and intentions in supplementary schools in
the context of the positioning of the former with mainstream schooling. It addresses aspects
of the social order and the experienced world. Despite the apparently more rigid and traditional approach adopted by the volunteer teachers in the supplementary schools, pupils and
teachers experienced themselves as people with opportunities to construct a different and
more positive set of meanings, values and constructions of self to those available to them in
the mainstream. Pupils experienced learning environments that were conducive to the reclamation of individual and collective senses of identity and power. This emphasises the significance of probing subjectivities and being open to the potential of different pedagogical
approaches and sets of relationships to be differently productive of meaning.

Literacy learning happens to be a theme within three of the four chapters in the final
section of the book, although they were all chosen because they offer a sociocultural perspective on pedagogy and they exemplify the constitutive nature of the social order and the
experienced world. The multiple nature of identities, positioning and the transformation of
identity are made visible in relation to enactments and experiences that attest to the importance of recognizing learners' ways of knowing. Chapter 10, by Patricia Murphy and

Gabrielle Ivinson, provides an insightful account of how pedagogic strategies, assumed to address sex group differences in achievement such as single-sex grouping and gendered seating, shape what counts as knowledge in English settings in secondary schools and as such determine what gets assessed. The emphasis on such strategies, their case study date demonstrates, meant that teachers attended to students' attributes at the cost of the English texts they were creating, a finding that led them to conclude that teachers need to be mindful of how their strategies are mediated by the social representations of gender, as well as the demands on students of managing gender identities within the public sphere of the performing classroom. Chapter 11 is an edited chapter taken from a book by Colin Lankshear and Michele Knobel (2006) entitled *New Literacies: Everyday Practices and Classroom Learning*. It is based on a project which was designed to build on students' ways of knowing within information and communication technology, to promote mature participation and the production of an authentic produce from the students' perspective, and to enhance critical literacy practices involving new technologies. The analysis points to the positively transformative potential for students and teachers, and for curriculum, of a pedagogy that incorporated the interests, purposes and subjectivities of learners.

Chapter 12 by Bronwyn Davies discusses how people become gendered through cultural tools made available to them in the culture, and she goes on to present a case study of a classroom in which a teacher supports the boys in his class to see themselves as literate in ways that might typically be shunned by boys in the pursuit of hegemonic masculinity. Along with the importance of opportunities to extend agency and choose from a wider range of possible masculinities, her chapter reveals the significance of equipping learners with the reflexive knowledge that would enable them to critique the various discourses that are available to them. Primarily about the social order and policy enactment, the final chapter by Harry Torrance touches on all three levels of curriculum in post-secondary education and training. What emerges from Torrance's analysis is that the recent trend towards explicitness and criteria compliance reduces opportunities for moving deeper in practice. His evidence propels us to attend to 'local communities of practice' where judgments are negotiated and made meaningful by and for the members of those communities.

References

Alexander, R. (2001) *Culture and Pedagogy: International Comparisons in Primary Education.* Malden, MA: Blackwell.

Boreham, N. and Morgan, C. (2004) A sociocultural analysis of organisational learning, *Oxford Review of Education*, 30 (3): 307–25.

Gutierrez, K. D. and Rogoff, B. (2003) Cultural ways of learning: individual traits or repertories of practice, *Educational Researcher*, 32 (5): 19–25.

Gutierrez, K. D. and Correa-Chavez, M. (2006) What to do about culture, *Lifelong Learning Europe*, 11 (3): 152–9.

Holland, D., Lachicotte, W., Skinner, D. and Cain, C. (1998) *Identity and Agency in Cultural Worlds.* Cambridge, MA: Harvard University Press.

Lankshear, C. and Knobel, M. (2006) *New Literacies: Everyday Practices and Classroom Learning* (2nd edition). Maidenhead and New York: Open University Press.

Lave, J. (2008) Everyday life and learning, in P. Murphy and R. McCormick (Eds) *Knowledge and Practice: Representations and Identities.* London: Sage.

McCormick, R. and Murphy, P. (2000) Curriculum: the case for a focus on learning, in B. Moon, M. Ben-Peretz and S. Brown (Eds) *Routledge International Companion to Education*. London: Routledge, pp. 204–34.

Moje, E. B. and Hinchman, K. (2004) Culturally responsive practices for youth literacy learning, in J. Dole and T. Jetton (Eds) *Adolescent Literacy Research and Practice*. New York: Guilford Press.

Wenger, E. (1998) *Communities of Practice: Learning, Meaning and Identity*. Cambridge: Cambridge University Press.

Wertsch, J. (1998) *Mind as Action*. New York: Oxford University Press.

Section 1

Thinking about Pedagogy

1

Pedagogy, Curriculum and Culture

Robin Alexander

[…]

What is pedagogy?

[…] It would be as well to clarify the difference between teaching and pedagogy, for despite the fact that the terms are often used interchangeably, there *is* a difference. In brief, teaching is an *act* while pedagogy is both act and *discourse*. Pedagogy encompasses the performance of teaching together with the theories, beliefs, policies and controversies that inform and shape it. […] Pedagogy connects the apparently self-contained act of teaching with culture, structure and mechanisms of social control.

This, I think, is different from the exploration of the notion of pedagogy by Watkins and Mortimore. Noting – properly – a tendency for discussion of pedagogy in the UK to dwell on the teacher, they insist that any definition of pedagogy must also take the learner into account and to that end offer as their own corrective 'any conscious activity by one person designed to enhance learning in another'.[1] This, however, is not far removed from my definition of *teaching*, and what it does is to place outside the domain of pedagogy those theories, beliefs, policies and controversies alluded to above and to reflect a characteristically British gulf between theory and practice. In the Watkins and Mortimore account there is 'pedagogy', 'research on pedagogy' and 'practitioners' views of pedagogy' or, if you like, pedagogy as practice and – free-standing, free-wheeling and not necessarily connected with it – pedagogy as theory (for the ideas of researchers and those of teachers are all species of theory).

It was Brian Simon who asked many years ago why there was no pedagogy in England, by which of course he meant not that at that time (the early 1980s) there was no teaching but rather that pedagogic discourse was confused, anecdotal and eclectic rather than coherent, systematic and purposeful.[2] When he revisited his question in the mid 1990s, he held to his original explanation that the problem stemmed mainly from the nineteenth-century public (i.e. private) school view that education should be concerned with 'character' rather than the intellect, a view which also kept the study of education out of Britain's two senior universities until the latter part of the twentieth century.[3] It was for the so-called 'provincial' universities to make the running in the academic study of education. […] However, elsewhere Simon showed how as the 'foundation' disciplines of educational studies 'became more rigorous and

From: Alexander, R., *Culture and Pedagogy: International Comparisons in Primary Education* (London: Blackwell, 2001). Reproduced and adapted by kind permission of the author and publisher.

inevitably academic, the historic neglect of pedagogy was accentuated' adding, significantly: 'By pedagogy is meant the *theory and practice* of teaching'.[4]

The divergence of education theory and the practice of teaching is a well documented aspect of the development of teacher training in the UK during the twentieth century. It was exacerbated by the arrival of the BEd degree in 1965, the desire to make teacher training academically respectable and the attendant departmental structures in colleges and departments of education, which generally relegated 'method' to the lowest level of the institutional hierarchy.[5] After a brief period of convergence under the umbrella of 'professional studies' during the 1970s and the 1980s, largely fostered – it must be said – outside the universities in what were then polytechnics, under the auspices of the Council for National Academic Awards, theory in teaching was not so much neglected as officially banished. For during the late 1980s and throughout the 1990s, right-wing luminaries such as O'Hear, Lawlor and Woodhead mounted a strident and successful campaign against the notion that the act of teaching warranted any kind of theoretical underpinning,[6] and their view was supported by the Conservative governments of 1979–97. In 1991, Secretary of State Clarke spoke scathingly of 'barmy theory'.[7] Significantly, in the light of Simon's reference to the ambience of the public schools, Clarke's attack was made at a meeting of the public school Headmaster's Conference. At the Conservative Party Conference the same year, Prime Minister Major damned all those who dared question right-wing orthodoxy as 'progressive' (which by then had been toppled from its 1960s pedestal and become a term of abuse):

> We will take no lectures from those who led the long march of mediocrity through our schools … I will fight for my belief. My belief is a return to basics in education. The progressive theorists have had their say and, Mr President, they've had their day.[8]

From 1997, the Conservative Government's Labour successors were more than happy to sanction the continuation of this 'discourse of derision',[9] usually through their chief inspector and a compliant press rather than directly.[10]

For a while, the Council for the Accreditation of Teacher Education (CATE), the government advisory and accrediting body established in 1984, successfully resisted being tainted by this discourse, but in 1994 they were summarily disbanded and their successors, the Teacher Training Agency (TTA), capitulated. The TTA reduced teaching to a set of competencies or 'standards', and teacher training to the task of demonstrating to OFSTED's inspectors that these were complied with. The possibility that teaching was problematic in other than a strictly instrumental sense was not to be entertained. Teachers, by 2000, were expected to confine their questioning to children. Thus, in this all-important arena, British anti-intellectualism demonstrated its longevity.

For good measure, the TTA then appropriated the word 'pedagogy' itself. In 1999, Anthea Millett, the then head of the TTA, urged schools to talk about 'the issues of pedagogy and competence, excellence and failure in teaching methods', adding:

> Pedagogy is a word rarely used in education in England … I am always struck by how difficult teachers find it to talk about teaching … They prefer to talk about learning. By contrast, they can talk with great clarity about matters such as the curriculum, assessment and testing, classroom organization, examination structures – almost anything except teaching itself …[11]

A notion of teaching that excludes curriculum, assessment, classroom organization and *learning*? If she had looked more closely at the European antecedents of the term 'pedagogy', Millett could have avoided this muddle of categories. But then her real message was not about pedagogy at all: it was about performance management and teachers' need to comply with government thinking on just those matters – curriculum, assessment, examinations – that they refused to stop talking about. For whereas in 1991, Education Secretary of State Clarke had said 'Questions about how to teach are not for Government to determine',[12] his successor's controller of teacher training prefaced her comments above by warning that 'pedagogy is not, and should not be at the whim of individual teachers to determine in their classrooms'.[13]

Pedagogy and didactics

The case of pedagogy outside England looks somewhat different. The sites for our Russian field-work were negotiated on our behalf by a 'pedagogical university' which, although it trained teachers, did so in a way which was far from narrowly instrumental, and in continental Europe generally pedagogy is a prominent and respected intellectual field (especially in Germany). It is also very broad: Watkins and Mortimore cite a Swedish definition of pedagogy as a 'discipline [which] extends to the consideration of health and bodily fitness, social and moral welfare, ethics and aesthetics, as well as the institutional forms that serve to facilitate society's and the individual's pedagogic aims'.[14] At Kursk, the teachers had encountered a similar breadth in their five-year training, ranging from 'general culture' (philosophy, ethics, Russian history, economics, literature, art, anatomy and politics) through psychology, theory of upbringing (i.e. *vospitanie*), child development, pedagogical history, child law, 'defectology', to a wide range of subjects and an equally wide range of 'method' courses in those subjects, and finally options which included religion and folklore. The full list is too long to record here, but this selection serves to make the point: in the continental European tradition, pedagogy is both the *act* and the *idea* of teaching, and its knowledge base can be both broad and eclectic.

One important component of this knowledge base is the field known as 'didactics' (*didaktika* in Russia, *la didactique* in France, *die Didaktik* in Germany). While in continental European usage pedagogy is a broad intellectual domain which encompasses the study of education and a variety of forms of human enquiry and endeavour relevant to it, didactics is much more specifically concerned with methods of teaching, and specifically methods of teaching subjects. In Germany, the field subdivides into *allgemeine Didaktik* (general didactics) and *Fachdidaktik* (specialist or subject didactics) and this distinction to a degree holds in Russia. There, however, we found that *metodika* (methods) brought to bear elements of both didactics and wider pedagogical analysis on the question of how this or that particular subject should be taught, for Russian pedagogy traditionally has a strong psychological thrust and developmental and motivational issues are considered no less important for the teaching of, say, mathematics than are epistemic ones.

In France, the importance of didactics was made very evident to us, not just in providing a rationale for classroom decisions, but also because of its critical role in protecting the integrity of *les disciplines*. At the simplest level, we were told, didactics deals with the logical aspects of teaching while pedagogy covers the psychological aspects: on the one hand the disciplines, on the other hand children and learning. This recalls D. W. Hamlyn's discussion of the 'logical' and 'psychological' aspects of teaching in the context of early debates about the nature and purpose of educational studies in Britain.[15]

In France, as some years ago in England and the United States, one has a sense of the logical and the psychological in opposition here, and this problem is partly what Hamlyn tried to address. In English primary education, 'subjects' were at one stage anathema to many teachers, and induction into culturally shaped disciplines of enquiry and understanding was held to be fundamentally incompatible with the 'natural' course of children's development. Hence, in the popular slogan of the day (which is still occasionally heard) 'we teach children, not subjects'.[16] An alternative perspective on this dichotomy was revealed to us in France, where some of our Level 1 respondents suggested that universities' initial opposition to the idea of IUFMs – that is to say, to bringing primary teacher training into the university sector – was based partly on the suspicion that the disciplines would be submerged by a tidal wave of 'generalized pedagogy', especially once the 1989 *Loi Jospin* claimed to place the child rather than the subject at the heart of educational policy (two decades after the Plowden report sought to do the same in England).[17]

The French variant on the general/special didactics distinction refines the latter component. The field of didactics, we were told at one IUFM, divides into *didactiques des disciplines* and *transpositions didactiques*. This 'transposition' reflects a separation of *savoir savant* and *savoir enseigné*, or scholarly and taught knowledge, and deals with 'the way in which the subject knowledge to be taught … adapts, re-moulds and sometimes disfigures elements borrowed from the broader field of subject knowledge'.[18] This corresponds to the English contrast of 'subject' and 'subject application' and the American 'content' and 'pedagogical content' as propounded by Shulman. Pedagogical content knowledge embodies

> the aspects of content most germane to its teachability … the most useful forms of expression of those ideas, the most powerful analogies, illustrations, examples, explanations and demonstrations – in a word, the ways of representing and formulating the subject that make it comprehensible to others …[19]

Thus far, the French, English and American definitions of didactic transposition, subject application and pedagogical content knowledge more or less coincide, and gloss the hopeful maxim, which Jerome Bruner advanced in the early 1960s, that 'any subject can be taught effectively to any child at any stage of development'.[20] But Shulman adds to 'ways of representing and formulating the subject' the important qualification 'including the conceptions that students of different ages and backgrounds bring with them to learning'. Herein lies an important cultural divergence.

For the French academics' objection to IUFMs was precisely targeted at this kind of dilution – as they saw it – of disciplinary purity, while in the United States Shulman for his part was accommodating to a significant tide of academic and professional opinion which argued that children's personal knowledge and unique ways of making sense of the world must be respected. The rationale for this argument, however, varied. To some, especially within the early years movement, children's personal knowledge mattered for its own sake: to respect it was to respect the child, and for some teachers adult ways of knowing counted for little by comparison. The overriding value here was individualism. To others, the case had more to do with finding effective ways to scaffold between Vygotsky's 'natural' and 'cultural' lines of development and move the child via his or her own understandings to those embodied in the mature forms of understanding central to the culture. Bruner's sustained contribution to this complex area of debate over several decades has been his ability to show how not just the logical and psychological, but also the cultural can be reconciled in a viable theory of teaching.

In England, the equivalent figure is Alan Blyth. Blyth approached the question from a social and historical as much as a psychological standpoint and demonstrated the essential mutuality of 'development', 'experience' and 'curriculum'.[21] He defined curriculum as 'planned intervention in the interaction between development and experience' and subsequently applied this principle in an account of the transition from 'subjective' to 'objective' modes of understanding between early childhood and adolescence. However, where Bruner's 'spiral curriculum' kept subjective understanding and discipline-based knowledge in equilibrium from the earliest pedagogical interventions, Blyth's 'dendritic' model began with the unity of experience and consciousness and progressed through subjective knowledge to objective. He suggested that children 'grow into' disciplinary understanding.[22] Blyth's model is more sympathetic to the English developmental tradition in primary education than either Bruner's or Vygotsky's, and indeed he was in part searching for a version of curriculum to which English primary teachers, with their particular inherited professional consciousness, could accommodate.

Such debates seem to have bypassed our French teachers and, to some degree, the teacher trainers. One IUFM director suggested that the researchers at the Institut National de Recherche Pédagogique (INRP) had only lately discovered Piaget and Bruner and had hardly heard of Vygotsky, but that although it was busy pushing constructivist theories of teaching, the INRP in any case had limited influence on practice. The situation was not helped, Beattie suggests, by the fact that until the 1990s, French universities showed no interest in education as a discipline and the INRP had a monopoly of such educational research as was undertaken.[23] More significantly, while our Russian teachers referred – and deferred – to psychologists, those of their French counterparts who felt the need to legitimate their teaching in this way claimed inspiration from theorists of 'didactic transposition' rather than theorists of learning or human development. So the composition lesson at Coulanges (lesson 11.3, discourse extract 16.9) was based on Larivaille's schematic representation of how events could be transformed into narrative. This was a psychologically uncompromising framework that made no mention of the need to engage with the existing understandings of nine-year-old children. Not for these teachers, as yet anyway, the Anglo-American agonizings of the past four decades about how to bring child and subject into equilibrium. It was not that the French teachers counted the individual of lesser worth: more that cultural and disciplinary induction was unquestionably the most important goal. Brian Simon's question 'Why no pedagogy in England?' might with equal justice have been applied to France; to this the French would almost certainly have retorted, 'Perhaps – but a least we have *la didactique*'.

The only exceptions to this stance that we encountered were two teachers and an IUFM member who referred to the work of Célestin Freinet (1896–1966), the communist and internationalist theorist of education who resisted what he saw as the skewed and unsophisticated educational discourse of France and sought to introduce a pedagogy which was grounded in more than *les disciplines* alone, and above all in a more critical social consciousness. He proposed a balance of collective and individual activity, the one to ensure the child's socialization, the other to respond to his or her specific needs. In the latter case, children would have self-marked files and part of their programme would be individually negotiated. Several teachers whom we observed had introduced the latter system. […]

Although it is tempting to view Freinet as France's equivalent of the luminaries of the English primary progressive movement of the 1960s, the similarities are balanced or outweighed by contrast. Like them, Freinet challenged the dominance of discipline-based knowledge and urged a pedagogy that respected the individual; unlike them, he held to the importance of cultural socialization. Where the English progressives celebrated individualism, Freinet balanced individual and collective needs. He was, after all, not only left wing but also French. Freinet was based near Nice, and locally there was a *mouvement Freinet*, a small Freinet cadre in the IUFM and a few 'Freinet schools'. But in a centralized educational system, the chances that someone working at the southern fringes of the country will loosen the grip of so powerful an orthodoxy are slim.[24] Yet it seems probable that the local Freinet influence may be one reason why we observed more group work in Alpes Maritimes and Var than the QUEST team encountered in neighbouring Bouches du Rhône or distant Pas de Calais.[25]

The Indian situation was different again. There the espoused theory of teaching was strongly developmental, and Piaget featured fairly frequently in the teacher interviews. More common, however, were unattributed references, of a generically progressive kind, to 'discovery', 'activity' and 'enquiry' methods. Sometimes these were filled out by reference to one or more of the important learner-centred and community-based initiatives, some of them taking place outside the government system, which are fully reviewed by John Shotton: *Jan Vigyan Manch* in Bihar, *Charvaha Vidalaya* in Bihar, PROPEL in Maharashtra, *Shiksha Karmi* and *Lok Jumbish* in Rajasthan, and the total literacy campaigns in Rajasthan, Kerala, Haryana and Tamil Nadu.[26] These were not, however, methodological reforms so much as more fundamental attacks on the problem of rural illiteracy, low recruitment and poor retention. India has a formidable record of grass-roots initiatives in the 'non-formal' sector, and of experimental schools. Some of the ideas thereby generated have been mainstreamed into Government of India initiatives, such as the District Primary Education Programme and its successor *Sarva Shiskkha Abhiyan* (SSA). 'Pedagogical renewal' is an important component of both.

Three points on the emerging pedagogic discourse of Indian primary education must be made, however. First, it makes much of developmental/progressive imports of the kind noted above. Second, it is not yet clear how far an individualistic, enquiry-based ideology is compatible with either the deeply rooted collective orientation of Indian primary teaching or the unassailable fact of very large classes. Third, our fieldwork was conducted in schools outside the administrative districts in which DPEP has been introduced and is thus more representative of both national resource levels and national practice, at least as these remain until programmes like DPEP and SSA come closer to their objective of universalizing elementary education. The 1999 PROBE report also confirms the typicality of what we saw and heard in our fieldwork classrooms.[27]

Thus, in the Indian schools there was no mention of subject transformation or transposition. Rather, subject matter for teaching, like the subjects themselves, was 'given' and the challenge for the teacher in the context of large classes was to devise procedures, and make materials, which would render the concepts more accessible. If we note that teachers in England during the 1970s and the 1980s were advancing a similar rationale to these 1990s Indian teachers, yet that in the one setting children were working on separate tasks in groups while in the other they were working on identical tasks as a class, we have confirmation here, as in the other examples, of another kind of 'transposition', that of pedagogical theory itself. Bruner describes how the ideas advanced in his book *The Process of*

Education were turned to very different purposes, as they were domesticated to suit the prevailing political and educational ideologies of the various countries into whose languages the book was translated. In Italy, the book was used 'for clubbing Marxists and classicists alike'. In the Soviet Union, it was used to attack Stalinist education. In Japan, it was used to give intellectual legitimacy to technical subjects. In Israel, it was seen as a basis for maintaining standards among immigrants. In the United States, it was seen to attack rather than sustain a belief in childhood spontaneity.[28] Educational ideas do not just migrate; in speaking to different cultural histories and conditions, they also change.

Thus it is that we find the same names crossing national and cultural boundaries to appear in different political guises, for pedagogy, as noted at the start of this section, is discourse, not merely procedure. So, too, in respect of the task of *teaching* 'by method *x* to enable pupils to learn *y*', pedagogy comes into play once we see how in different cultures the various nodal points of this simple formulation – the pupil, the subject matter, the method – take on greater or lesser significance and stand in different relations to each other.

In the Central European tradition, pedagogy is the overarching concept and didactics is that branch of pedagogy which deals with what is to be taught and how. Comenius's *Great Didactic* (perhaps the earliest recognizably modern application of the term) deals with both, setting out a view of humankind, its relation to the divine, to eternity and to nature, the goals of education and the kinds of institutions – common 'mother schools', 'vernacular schools' and gymnasia – in which formal education should be pursued, together with principles of instruction. In respect of the latter, Comenius makes a clear distinction between what later became 'general' and 'special' or subject didactics, differentiating 'the universal requirements of teaching and learning' before expounding on key principles such as 'facility', 'thoroughness' and 'conciseness and rapidity' and setting out 'the methods of the sciences', 'the methods of languages' and other subjects.[29] Comenius justifies his central place in European pedagogy not just in respect of the continuing resonance of some of his institutions and instructional principles [...] but also to the extent that he mapped out the territory of pedagogy in ways many continue to find persuasive.

I have referred frequently to this 'central European' pedagogic tradition. It is rooted in the humanism of Erasmus, the empiricism of Bacon and the Protestantism of Luther. The line crystallizes with Comenius and passes by way of Pestalozzi, Herbart, Froebel and Montessori into modern educational thought. In placing French education close to this line it is important to stress that French education accommodated the didactic element much more readily than the pedagogic one. In this, religion is probably the important variable. Comenius was a member of one of the earliest Protestant churches, Unitas Fratrem or the Moravian Brethren. His concern with education was about much more than 'method' alone. His relatively democratic view of schooling, who should have access to it and how it should be organized, not to mention his resistance to the tyranny of Latin and his advocacy of the vernacular, were all at variance with pre-revolution education in Catholic France. Even now, Sharpe suggests, French education may be secular but it still has the structure and stamp, even the catechistic pedagogy, of ecclesiastical hierarchy, absolutism and social control.[30]

Pedagogy and curriculum

In English and American pedagogical discourse, curriculum issues are of central importance, although the Anglo-American concept of curriculum connotes a field which is rather different from 'didactics'. During the postwar period, curriculum studies expanded rapidly in American universities, spawning societies, journals, books and – especially after the 1957 Sputnik panic – federal grants.[31] The national spur was curriculum development and renewal, and academics grabbed the opportunities afforded by this bonanza with both hands. The scope of the term 'curriculum' widened in proportion to the growth in activity (for few wished to be left out and careers were there for the making), and by the 1960s 'instruction' and much else besides were gathered under the one umbrella term 'curriculum'. Indeed, few aspects of the educational enterprise were able to escape its clutches, for curriculum was defined as most of what went on in schools. Thus, a typical (and impressive) representative text of the early 1960s, Taba's *Curriculum Development: theory and practice*, is positively Germanic in its scope and aspirations. Its theoretical stance, however, is unambiguously American, especially in relation to social reconstruction and the nature of knowledge, and in common with other texts of the period it has a strong emphasis upon 'process'.[32]

Bruner's interventions in this debate were important. His idea of a 'spiral curriculum' which enabled a child to revisit the conceptual and structural foundations of a discipline at different levels as he/she progressed from 'enactive' to 'iconic' and 'symbolic' stages of development and representation seemed to resolve the logic/psychologic tension I referred to earlier, for

> a curriculum reflects not only the nature of knowledge itself but also the nature of the knower and of the knowledge-getting process … We teach a subject not to produce little living libraries … but rather to get a student to think mathematically … to consider matters as an historian does, to take part in the process of knowledge-getting. Knowing is a process, not a product.[33]

This Deweyan last assertion became the epistemic credo for a generation of teachers, teacher trainers and administrators on both sides of the Atlantic. For many, it still is, and the one dichotomy was happily absorbed into others. For example, prominently displayed on the classroom wall of one our Michigan schools, we found this notice:

> *Important issues to me –*
> Process orientation vs product orientation
> Teaching students vs teaching programs
> Teacher as facilitator vs teacher as manager
> Developing a set of strategies vs mastering a set of skills
> Celebrating approximation vs celebrating perfection
> Respecting individual growth vs fostering competition
> Capitalizing on student's strengths vs emphasizing student's weaknesses
> Promoting independence in learning vs dependence on the teacher.

Similar lists could be found in British texts and courses for primary teachers during the 1970s and the 1980s (the second item in the manifesto above is recognizably the Michigan version of 'we teach children, not subjects'), and the habit of setting up complex areas of educational debate in such adversarial terms remains the stock-in-trade of popular speakers at primary teachers' conferences.

Try replacing the 'versus' in the list above by 'and' and you create a refreshingly new and inclusive pedagogy. That is all it takes, but for many teachers and education ideologues, such inclusivity is inconceivable, for what is education without its barricades? This adversarialism lies behind some of the problems in American and English pedagogy to which we have already alluded.

In Britain, too, curriculum development and curriculum studies expanded, the one during the 1960s and the 1970s under the auspices of the Schools Council and the other in universities and colleges. In effect, then, the Anglo-American academic–professional nexus inflated 'curriculum' far beyond its original meaning. However, in the process, the new curriculum discourse became normative as well as to a degree scholarly; and the terms 'pedagogy' and 'didactic' acquired undeniably adverse overtones, suggesting nothing so strongly as the chalk-and-talk, fact-transmitting Gradgrinds of progressive folklore. In this context, although they may not have intended this, it strikes me as symptomatic of the English view of curriculum that in the Watkins and Mortimore definition of pedagogy ('any conscious activity by one person designed to enhance learning in another'), *what* is to be learned is not a variable.

There is, however, another reason for the prominence of curriculum themes in England and the United States. If we draw back from the all-inclusive definition to one which deals with *what* is to be taught and how (the field covered in central Europe by didactics), we find that one of the clearest differences within the *Five Cultures* data is the degree to which teachers in each country see curriculum in this sense as problematic. Broadly, in Russia, France and India, teachers took the prescribed curriculum as given and talked about how to implement it; those in Michigan and England were much more inclined to contest it. In Russia, the very notion of curriculum – conceptually, I think, rather than linguistically – provoked difficulties in some of the teacher interviews.

The reasons for this difference seem clear. Until 1988, England did not have a national curriculum, so instead of being pre-empted by national government, curriculum questions were open for debate. 'Minister', remarked 1940s education minister George Tomlinson, 'knows nowt about curriculum' (non-English readers will have to unpick the dialect which is essential to this well-worn and possibly apocryphal quotation). Although in 1960 another minister, David Eccles, mused darkly about entering the 'secret garden of curriculum', his successors showed little inclination to do so until the late 1970s. Even in 1986, just two years before it arrived, ministers insisted that the idea of national curriculum was unthinkable. So teachers were not only able to debate such matters for themselves; they were actively encouraged by government to do so. In the primary sector, the abolition of secondary school selection in effect made the curriculum open territory (at secondary level, there was less debate about the scope and balance of the curriculum as a whole, because this was to a greater degree shaped by the external pressures of public examinations and the requirements of university entrance and employment).

Therefore, when the National Curriculum was summarily imposed by the Thatcher government in 1987–8 in the teeth of professional opposition, not only was it widely condemned as an affront to professional autonomy and local democracy, but the government's behaviour also guaranteed that education professionals would continue to resist long after the proposals became law, especially as government's railroading tactics set the style for their subsequent handling of national curriculum matters.

Although the United States has not experienced this kind of curriculum takeover (nor, without a change in the American Constitution, is it likely to), we were made aware in Michigan of a growing pressure washing down through the system, from federal to state and from state to district, to secure greater curriculum uniformity in the interests of 'standards' and international competitiveness ('By the year 2000, United States students will be first in the world in mathematics and science achievement'[34]), following the publication of *A Nation at Risk* in 1983.[35] However, although by the year 2000 more and more state education departments had produced curriculum statements, these were far less prescriptive than the English national curriculum, and many states were content to promulgate 'frameworks' or 'guides' and leave the detail to be worked out by teachers. The professional subject associations frequently did that job.

All this, of course, relates to a narrower definition of 'curriculum' – curriculum as content, subject matter or outcomes – than the imperialist 'curriculum as everything the school does in pursuit of its goals' which emerged from American and English universities during the 1960s and the 1970s. But this only sharpens the difference between these two countries and the other three. In the central European tradition, the debate concerns not curriculum but didactics, the transposition of knowledge rather than its initial specification. In Russia, questioning either version has only recently become possible; and, in India, an underpowered and dispersed teaching force is not in a strong position to do more than voice concern about the 'burden' of curriculum on pupils, by which it is as likely to mean the weight of books in the child's satchel as conceptual overload. But we have also to consider the strong possibility that what we have in post-Soviet Russia, France and India is a classic illustration of the Gramscian hegemonic process – domination with consent, at least where the curriculum is concerned. In the United States, as has become clear at so many levels of our data, educational values are everywhere contested as a matter of habit and cultural circumstance as well as by constitutional right. In England, the memories of decentralization die slowly, and power-coercive policies are strongly resisted (for the time being, anyway: conceivably something approaching the French curriculum settlement may begin to prevail, if only as those in the field discover that the battle is lost).

Let us reconsider our map of pedagogy in the light of this. In the Anglo-American tradition, pedagogy – in so far as the word is used in professional contexts –is subsidiary to curriculum. Curriculum has both a broad sense (approaching the continental usage of 'pedagogy') and a narrow one (what must be taught) which is closer to continental 'didactics'; and pedagogy is defined no less narrowly as teaching method. In the Central European tradition, it is the other way round. Pedagogy frames everything else, including curriculum (in so far as *that* word is used) and didactics. So in professional discourse, pedagogy and curriculum are differentiated. As we look at our five countries, we see sharp variations in the counterpoint of pedagogy, curriculum and didactics, which intimate how the cultures perceive the central pedagogical relationship between the learner, the process of learning, and what is learned.

The case of academic discourse is different. Although, as I have noted, 'curriculum' has become a considerable edifice in England and the United States, there is a growing parallel literature on pedagogy more broadly defined, in which cultural critique is dominant and which tends to focus on pedagogy and pedagogic discourse as mechanisms of social control and cultural reproduction. Thus [...] 'poisonous pedagogy' enslaves, 'critical pedagogy' liberates.[36]

Is the question of definition of genuine importance, or are we just playing with words? I believe that these differences are indeed significant. First, the emphases within a culture's educational discourse say a great deal about what matters most and least to those engaged in that discourse: the whole curriculum and the whole child; efficient induction into an accepted version of culture, citizenship and knowledge; moral, personal and civic upbringing; cultural reproduction; cultural transformation; and so on. Second, one of the definitions actually works better. The inherent ambiguities of meaning surrounding 'curriculum' – is it everything the school does or merely what is prescribed to be taught, the formal curriculum

1	Specification	National or state curriculum	
2	Translation	School curriculum	Frame
3	Translation and/ or transposition	Class curriculum and timetable	
4		Lesson plan	
5	Transformation	Lesson	Form
6		Task	
7		Activity	Act
8		Interaction	
9		Task product	Outcome
10		Learning outcome	

Figure 1.1   Curriculum metamorphosis

or the not-so-hidden 'hidden' curriculum'? – cause communication on such matters to be more difficult than it deserves. And for teachers and administrators in countries with national curricula […] there is no longer any ambiguity about the term, for curriculum is what is prescribed. Further, once content is detached in this way, it encourages the narrow treatment of matters of teaching strategy and style. […]

My own preference, therefore, is to eschew the ambiguities of 'curriculum' and the resulting tendency to downgrade pedagogy, and use the latter term to encompass the entire field. The model of the narrower idea of 'teaching' remains as I have advanced it elsewhere in this chapter. […] 'Pedagogy' contains both teaching as defined there and its contingent discourses about the character of culture, the purposes of education, the nature of childhood and learning and the structure of knowledge. These discourses bear on, and are manifested in, the various aspects of teaching which I identified: space, pupil organization, time, routine, rule, ritual, task, activity, interaction, judgement – and, of course, curriculum (see Figure 1.2). This is close to Bernstein's judgement that 'pedagogic discourse … selectively relocates, refocuses, and relates other discourses to constitute its own order and orderings'.[37] Defining pedagogy rather than curriculum as the overarching term allows us to understand how it is not just curriculum, which, in Lawton's words, is a 'selection from culture',[38] but every other aspect of what goes on in schools and class-rooms as well. Moreover, because 'pedagogy' in both its broad and narrow senses retains an inescapable whiff of the classroom, we are constantly reminded that the real power of pedagogy resides in what happens between teachers and pupils and can avoid qualifica-tory distinctions like 'curriculum as prescribed'/'curriculum as transacted'. […]

Frame	Form	Act
Space		Task
Student organisation		Activity
Time	Lesson	
Curriculum		Interaction
Routine, rule and ritual		Judgement

Figure 1.2   A broad generic framework for the analysis of teaching

In fact, the curriculum is probably best viewed as a series of *translations, transpositions* and *transformations* from its initial status as published statutory requirements or non-statutory guidance. At the beginning of this process of metamorphosis is the national or state curriculum. At its end is the array of understandings in respect of each specified curriculum goal and domain that the pupil acquires as a result of his or her classroom activities and encounters. In between is a succession of shifts, sometimes bold, sometimes slight, as curriculum moves from specification to transaction and as teachers and pupils interpret, modify and add to the meanings that it embodies. Sometimes the change may be slight, as a school takes a required syllabus or programme of study and maps it onto the timetable. This we might call a *translation*. Then a school or teacher may adjust the nomenclature and move parts of one curriculum domain into another to effect a *transposition*, which then leads to a sequence of lesson plans. But the real change, the *transformation*, comes when the curriculum passes from document into action and is broken down into learning tasks and activities and expressed and negotiated as discourse. Figure 1.1 schematizes this process, and ties it into the families of 'frame', 'form' and 'act'. [...]

In this sense, therefore, curriculum is a 'framing' component of the act of teaching, [...] only before it is transformed into task, activity, interaction, discourse and outcome. From that point on, it becomes inseparable from each of these. In the classroom, curriculum *is* task, activity, interaction and discourse, and they are curriculum.

However faithful to government, state or school requirements a teacher remains, teaching is always an act of curriculum transformation. On the other hand, the degree of transformation varies, sometimes by a great deal. Teachers in Russia, India and France generally worked within the labels and syllabuses laid down for them, often using centrally produced textbooks. There, the journey from specification to the first stage of transformation was short and direct. In Michigan, it could be longer and more complex, as teachers took curriculum guides (which in any case did not have the force of law), extracted those components which they and their schools deemed important, moved them around, relabelled the resulting combinations, and set about teaching them. Some stuck closely to the official terminology; others introduced stipulative variants. Most were influenced by personal and local belief systems that made the transformation more radical than mere terminological adjustment. The degree to which teachers can interpose their own 'critical pedagogies' between the child and the transmission pedagogy of the state may be, I suggest, seriously underestimated by macro-level pedagogical theorists. [...]

In practice, the direct and indirect pressures of assessment, inspection and target-setting might seem to lead the teaching of literacy and numeracy towards translation rather than transformation, while the other subjects, especially history and geography (the core of traditional 'topic work'), remained free to emerge in the classrooms in somewhat different guises. Certainly, the UK government understood the power of external assessment and inspection to minimize transformation in those subjects in which it had the greatest political investment. But the pedagogical intensity of the final act of transformation is such that control can never be absolute. [...]

Pedagogy and culture: teaching

Prema Clarke has set out a number of 'cultural models of teacher thinking and teaching'. Working from the research literature, she conflates studies from Europe, North America and Australia into 'Western European models' and those from eastern and southern Asia, Africa and South America into 'non-Western models'. She uses six 'pedagogical categories' ('teacher presentation', 'instructional goals', 'attitudes towards the curriculum', 'communication of knowledge', 'teacher-student verbal interaction' and 'discipline'). This framework allows her to locate research studies which between them point to several of the differences which have been explored in this book: curriculum as given, teacher as authority, the importance of the group (non-Western); curriculum as negotiable, teacher as carer, the importance of the individual (North America); curriculum as given but methods as negotiable, teacher as controller, group/individual ambivalence (Europe).[39] However, the limitations of the research surveyed ensure that these perspectives remain mainly in the domain of teachers' espoused values rather than observed practice, and we know how far apart values and practice may be. The adoption of a single 'non-Western model' is surely unacceptable (Clarke's includes material from three continents under that heading), especially as within her 'Western' category she is prepared to differentiate Europe and North America.

Reynolds and Farrell do a similar job with Europe (drawing on material from Germany, Holland, Switzerland and Hungary) and the Pacific Rim, both of which they contrast with England.[40] In this, again, they itemize culturally specific tendencies: homogeneous teaching groups, textbooks, whole-class teaching, high expectations (Europe); emphasis on effort rather than ability, high parental aspirations, high pupil motivation, sharp task focus, whole class interactive instruction, textbooks, predictable school day, the class as a single unit (Pacific Rim).

Then there are the many comparative studies that treat cultures separately, rather than grouping them within categories such as 'Pacific Rim', 'European', 'Western-European' or 'non-Western'. [...] Thus, the Tobin study of pre-schooling in Japan, China and the United States identifies the powerful strand of individualism which runs through American culture, language and education, but also draws attention to its downside and a growing anxiety among Americans that 'in our celebration of individualism the threads that bind people to one another have been stretched too thin and ... the fabric of American society, already frayed at the edges, has begun to unravel'.[41] Bronfenbrenner had already made a similar point in 1970, on the basis of comparisons with the Soviet Union, adding that the American tendency to age-segregation separates children from adult models and further erodes social cohesiveness.[42] Using data from the same three countries, Stevenson and Stigler work at the recurrent divide between individualism/innate ability (United States) and collectivism/effort (eastern Asia), noting that the latter orientation is much more appropriate to the context of a crowded classroom. They also – and are rare in this regard for doing so – examine classroom discourse and note differences, such as the way Chinese and Japanese teachers use and build on pupils' answers while American teachers merely – if that is the right word – praise them.[43] Broadfoot and her colleagues make much of the Gemeinschaft/Gesellschaft distinction in comparing primary education in England and France, and link this with 'national orientations', such as charisma, achieved roles, particularism, individualism, diffuse interaction, affectivity and personalized discourse (England); and bureaucracy, role ascription, universalism, collectivism, focused interaction, affective neutrality and objectified discourse (France).[44]

In this study, I have dealt with five separate countries and have taken pains to identify not just national differences but also within-country differences, and one of the values of using lesson transcript extracts in combination with narrative lesson summaries [...] is that these within-country differences readily show themselves. I have also ventured a broader classification, however, of 'Anglo-American' and 'Central European' pedagogy which I believe is justified by history as well as the patterns revealed by the *Five Cultures* data. This is at variance with both of Clarke's groupings. Her 'Western European' category rightly picks up transatlantic divergence, but fails to identify divergence within Europe. Her 'non-Western' category, as I have said, needs refinement. Crucially, as far as India (which in included in the latter category) is concerned, the grouping disregards the colonial legacy, and the way that as a result Indian pedagogy is both European and Asian.

In loosely pairing English pedagogy with that of the United States rather than continental Europe, I have tried not to imply that the classrooms of the two countries represent a single pattern of teaching or a single cultural orientation. After a century of what some see as unremitting American cultural imperialism and a half-century of British prostration to American foreign policy interests, England and the United States remain resolutely different, educationally no less than culturally. Values are expressed in the classrooms of Michigan, and events take place there, which would never be expressed or take place in England, and vice versa. Americanisms like 'zero tolerance' and 'intervention in inverse proportion to success', adopted by the UK government and suggestive of convergence, should be seen as the opportunistic slogans that they are.

In particular, I argued that the negotiated pedagogy that seems to unite some of the classrooms of England and Michigan reflects values which are in fact both distinctive and divergent. In Michigan, we observed the uneasy working out of the tensions of individualism and democracy within the context of compulsory schooling. In England, there was no obvious democratic commitment within the classrooms, but rather a strong allegiance to a developmental view of the individual within a framework of unambiguous teacher authority. The challenges for this version of negotiated pedagogy were organizational rather than ideological.

Yet for all that, the balance of pedagogical commonalities and differences as between England, Michigan, France and Russia suggests that the Dover Strait is a more fundamental cultural barrier than the Atlantic and that when it comes to some of the defining practices and values of primary education, France appears to look east and England appears to look west.

However, even if we can sort out the family resemblances and locate them culturally and historically, how far does this allow us to define them as supranational cultural *models* of pedagogy? The claim seems to present three main problems.

First, commentators such as those cited are surely right to seek out the ideas which underpin the practice, and in doing so may well find themselves straying into social and political theory. This is not a problem; on the contrary, it reinforces the 'situatedness' of what goes on in schools and classrooms, and is in accordance with the broad definition of pedagogy and pedagogic discourse adopted here. However, most such accounts are stronger on the ideas than the practice, [...] for comparative educationists have until recently had disappointingly little truck with close and sustained observation of teaching and learning as they happen. Pedagogic practice may well be theory-soaked but pedagogic theory without practice is meaningless. Without observational research, it is impossible to test whether or to what degree a cited idea or value which may have considerable cultural currency really does impact on children and the learning in schools. And without the voices of participants, it will be hard, if not impossible, to separate from the tangle of ideas those which engage with practice and those that merely surround it, or to tease out craft knowledge from researcher interpretation and official propaganda. Thus, do French teachers *themselves* set out to be 'affectively neutral' or is that just how they appear to an observer used to the English rhetoric of 'caring' and child centredness, and to English teachers' generous use of terms of endearment? And who says that the curriculum in American schools is negotiable and that the teacher is a carer? Teachers? Children? Researchers? And which, if any, is right?

Second, this latter barrage of questions indicates that we probably need to take greater care to differentiate the prescriptive from the descriptive here, and the quasi-objective from the subjective and intersubjective. Otherwise we end up with something about whose purpose or claim to truth one can never be sure. Does a 'cultural model of pedagogy' say 'Pedagogy is ...' or 'Pedagogy ideally should be ...' or again, 'No, I work there and I'm telling you that pedagogy *really* is ...' ?

Third, a random collection of values or beliefs, even when practices are thrown in, does not make a model. Something more coherent is implied. [...] Note Leach's warning that descriptive models are best kept simple while prescriptive models are likely to be complex (1964). But if the act of teaching is the *sine qua non* of pedagogy, then a reasonably coherent account of teaching must be at the heart of any pedagogic model.

Pedagogy and culture: learning

Another way to approach the question of cultural models of pedagogy is to start with the process of learning rather than the act of instruction. Jerome Bruner, by his own account, has moved form a 'solo, intrapsychic' view of knowing and learning to one which engages with the relationship between learning and culture:

> Culturalism's task is a double one. On the 'macro' side, it looks at the culture as a system of values, rights, exchanges, obligations, opportunities, power. On the 'micro' side, it examines how the demands of a cultural system affect those who must operate within it ... it is much concerned with intersubjectivity – how humans come to know 'each other's minds'.[45]

This sounds familiar – it is the same task as G. H. Mead set himself [46] and during the 1970s it entered educational research in the UK via symbolic interactionism – except that Bruner advances upon culture by way of the individual psyche and continues to give to individual cognition much closer attention than do, by and large, sociologists and anthropologists. He has also been closely involved with the thinking and development of young children, and therefore has always had a great deal to say to those involved in early years and primary education. Bruner identifies four 'dominant models of learners' minds that have held sway in our times' as the basis for his quest to reposition educational psychology more firmly in the cultural domain:

1. seeing children as imitative learners
2. seeing children as learning from didactic exposure
3. seeing children as thinkers
4. seeing children as knowledgeable.[47]

The prefix 'seeing' is important: Bruner is characterizing the way in which, in educational contexts, children and their capacities have been defined by teachers, whatever those capacities really are. Age is an objective fact but childhood is a construct. The first model – seeing children as imitative learners – is the basis of apprenticeship, a system for 'leading the novice into the skilled ways of the expert'. Expertise requires practice, and implies not just prepositional or procedural knowledge but also talents, skills and abilities. The second – seeing children as learning from didactic exposure – informs the classic transmission model of teaching; it is heavily geared to the acquisition of facts, principles and rules, and presumes that children are not knowledgeable until they have demonstrated that they can recall and repeat the facts, principles and rules in question. The third – seeing children as thinkers – presupposes that children can and do think for themselves, that it is the task of the teacher to uncover and understand that thinking and through discussion and a 'pedagogy of mutuality' to help the child move from a private to a shared frame of reference. The main pedagogical tool is dialogic discourse. Finally, seeing children as knowledgeable starts with the premise that in any culture there is a 'given' of knowledge, that knowledge is not exclusively personal or intersubjective or relative, and that it is the teacher's task to 'help children grasp the distinction between personal knowledge ... and "what is taken to be known" by the culture'.[48]

Bruner adds that what distinguishes the 'given' cultural knowledge in the fourth model from the 'received' knowledge in the second is that children learn why such knowledge stands up to scrutiny. They engage with its history. This, then, is Karl Popper's 'World Three' – 'the world of the logical contents of books, libraries, computer memories and suchlike',[49] and it is not dead information but ideas which live because children are encouraged to pursue how they impact upon Popper's 'World Two' of subjective knowledge, 'the world of our conscious experiences'.[50]

We can now bring together our culturally located versions of primary teaching and Bruner's four models or views of learning and the learner. [...]

Let us consider each country in turn. In France, much of the teaching we observed appeared to be premised on the importance of children's encountering and engaging with the culture's stock of World 3 objective knowledge, but was in fact steered by the more limited objective of didactic exposure. As Bruner points out, there are good reasons why: for some kinds of knowledge, simple transmission is appropriate and necessary (we made a similar point earlier about rote and recitation teaching). However, we also observed lessons, for example, in comprehension, where teachers would take a cultural artefact such as a section of literary text and get children to work with it in a way that encouraged them to see it as meaningful in terms of their personal understandings. The other deviation from didactic exposure was in the direction of Bruner's dialogic or dialectical third model, when teachers sought to promote scaffolded understanding, although it is a matter of debate whether sequence 16.9, which I suggested was a good example of such teaching in the French context, goes as far as Bruner urges and finds 'in the intuitions of the child the roots of systematic knowledge'.[51] Indeed, Bruner's 'model 3' comes closest to scaffolding as he defines it elsewhere, but seems to give the natural line of development (as opposed to the cultural) rather greater weight than in his earlier writing.

Russia presents a somewhat similar case, initially at any rate. Teaching there had a strong emphasis upon the acquisition of facts, principles and rules, and some of this was narrowly and very instrumentally directed at memorization and recall. However, we saw how teachers' collective pedagogical theorizing emphasized the scaffolding function of interrogatory classroom discourse, and how, in practice, teachers implemented this by working publicly on the understandings of individual children until the scaffolding process was complete. Further, like France, Russia values rather than ossifies its World 3 cultural stock. However, the dividing line between a 'pedagogy of mutuality' and 'didactic exposure' was not the culture so much as, quite simply, the difference between good and run-of-the-mill teaching.

The Russian model at best generates far more cognitive dynamism than some Western observers are prepared to admit. At worst, as with whole-class direct instruction in France, India or anywhere else, it very easily regresses to rote and ritualized rather than principled knowledge.[52]

India, in its pedagogy as in so many other respects, is a culture of extremes. The teaching which we observed, which was within the mainstream of government primary education rather than innovations such as the District Primary Education Programme or *Lok Jumbish,* was dominated by fact transmission, propositional knowledge and ritualized understanding. [...] Yet we did observe teachers who, within the considerable constraints of small and overcrowded classrooms, were able to secure dialogue and scaffolded understanding. [...] However, the true alternative to rote in the Indian context was not this version of teaching but apprenticeship (Bruner's first model), as we witnessed it in a few music and dance lessons and in experimental settings like Delhi's Bal Bhawan. Now this form of pedagogy, and its assumptions about the learner and the learner–teacher relationship, have a central place in Indian culture and the quality and longevity of Indian artistic life testify to its effectiveness. Although it is predicated on teacher authority, it is not the same as the Brahmanic ashram education that Kumar claims has degenerated into modern-day rote learning,[53] for its form of initiation develops skills which can allow the novice eventually to disengage from, and perhaps surpass – rather than merely copy – the expert. We might note that a similar pedagogy may be witnessed in instrumental master classes in some Western conservatoires. The question we have to ask, then, is why Indian primary education generally makes so little use of the culture's other indigenous pedagogic tradition. In this matter, it is important to differentiate the 'simple theory of imitative learning', which Bruner insists does not suit an advanced society, from its more sophisticated counterpart, which – as we observed in India, and as one may observe it in music conservatoires– combines imitation with dialogue and knowledge transformation.

In Michigan, we saw no examples of apprenticeship, some of straightforward didacticism, and many which aspired to Bruner's third model. Some reflected, [...] however, the more common condition which never quite managed to square the circle of learning. The professional discourse of some of the teachers made much of respecting the child's ways of making sense of the world, but having encouraged them to make that sense, they too often left it at that. So we observed teachers, who out of respect for the child's autonomy and understanding, simply accepted from nine year olds brief fragments of writing on topics which required discussion but did not receive it and at a level which showed little advance on what had been done one year previously. The classroom poster referred to earlier in this chapter reveals the extent of the problem, for by setting up pedagogical values as mutually exclusive, you end up with a view of teaching which is in danger of going nowhere: 'process orientation ... teacher as facilitator ... developing strategies... celebrating approximation'. Yes, but what next? The other side of the coin, that which moves processes and approximations towards shared understanding, has been ruled out of court.

In England, again, we saw no examples of initiation into expertise as defined in Bruner's first model, except at the lowest level of imitation without engagement, skill or independent judgement such as can be all too often observed in ill-taught music or art lessons (in which depressing practice England was certainly not alone). Propositional knowledge predominated, although because teaching leaned away from collective dialogue and towards reading, writing and semi-private conversational talk, knowledge was there to be 'looked up' rather than 'listened to'.[54] This can be a characteristically English sleight of hand, for at first sight the group ambience, buzz of conversation and movement to and from the class library suggest nothing more strongly than pedagogy of both enquiry and mutuality. But again we have to ask what children *do* with what they look up and find out. If they simply write it down without examining either its substance or status, then this is mere canonical knowledge. Worse, because it lacks the cognitive challenge that goes with the discourse of well-conducted direct instruction, it may yield facts but not principles and rules. If we put this tendency with three others that teachers themselves may not espouse but to which they are vulnerable because they are prominent in English society and government, we have a serious problem. The tendencies are institutionalized anti-intellectualism, the reduction of history and culture to prepackaged 'heritage', and an overweening admiration for electronic information. In this scenario, classroom discourse may lack the structure, continuity and precision needed for real dialogue and handover, while World 3 knowledge remains inert.

The UK government's literacy and numeracy strategies may offer an alternative. Consciously emulating continental European practice, they seek to stiffen and collectivize classroom talk and – in the numeracy strategy at least – to encourage children to make public their private understandings in order that they can move towards a shared frame of reference. The *Five Cultures* data contain too few examples to allow a judgement on whether or not the strategies are proving successful in these respects, although at the time of writing, the evidence from research and inspection is in conflict and inspectors are more optimistic than researchers.[55] This is perhaps because inspectors concentrated on the numeracy and literacy targets which the government set itself for the year 2002, rather than on the strategies' broader pedagogic claims. [...]

Bruner's four models of learners' minds, derived from the 'vernacular' of 'folk' pedagogy,[56] therefore take us further along the road towards a coherent set of cultural models of pedagogy. But they also remind us how, when one confronts adult assumptions about how children think and learn, the range of possibilities is not so very great and some models have near-universal currency. Which is why, as a footnote to this section, it is interesting and symptomatic to find a recent English book on pedagogy using the Bruner account so selectively. Watkins and Mortimore refer only to Bruner's third and fourth versions (seeing children as thinkers, and seeing children as knowledgeable).[57] They do this for a good reason – to encourage teachers to abandon mere didacticism – but in doing so overstate, I think, the hierarchy implied by Bruner, seeing apprenticeship as 'primitive', transmission as 'traditional', and only the third and fourth models as appropriate to Western schooling in the twenty-first century. For their part, Gipps and MacGilchrist, writing about 'primary school learners', use the first three but not the fourth.[58] In justification, they cite Bruner's conclusion that 'achieving skill and accumulating knowledge are not enough' (his first and second model), and so presumably set up the third as the appropriate 'modern' pedagogy for primary schools. But again, have they over-stated the objections to skill apprenticeship and the acquisition of propositional knowledge? And why leave out the fourth model (through which pupils engage with Popper's 'World 3' of 'what is taken to be known by the culture') unless they are saying that for primary children this realm of knowledge is of no account?

If that is what they propose, then it confirms my earlier concern [...] about the loss of historical consciousness and the restricted treatment of culture in English primary education.[59] Equally serious, to focus the entire pedagogical enterprise upon Bruner's third model is to confine children to a limbo of intersubjectivity in precisely the way we encountered in some of the discourse extracts from England and Michigan [...] where children and teachers talk but do not communicate. This, in other words, is the Michigan poster problem of process without product, and approximation without perfection.

The virtue of Bruner's framework, I take it, is that it allows us to test the place in a modern pedagogy of four contrasting stances on learning and knowledge and to allow for the possibility that all may have some part to play. Its limitation, certainly in the use made of it by Gipps and MacGilchrist, is that it takes little account of *curriculum,* and the fact that different ways of knowing and understanding demand different ways of learning and teaching. Mathematical, linguistic, literary, historical, scientific, artistic, technological, economic, religious and civic understanding are not at all the same. Some demand much more than others by way of a grounding in skill and propositional knowledge, and all advance the faster on the basis of engagement with existing knowledge, understanding and insight. That, I know, is an unfashionable standpoint.

This, perhaps, replays or rather transposes an old, old theme in English and American educational thinking: the status of received and reflexive knowledge, and the contrast between reproductive and empowering views of education. In English and American progressivism, World 3 knowledge is dismissed as *ipso facto* 'inert', or at best as 'information' to be treated as authoritative and never challenged. In postmodernist critique, World 3 knowledge, as embodied in the 'technology and culture of the book', is so much 'high learning' which regulates, sorts and controls.[60] Both characterizations of knowledge do a disservice to children as well as to their culture; they also reflect an abiding failure to distinguish between the character of the knowledge in question and how it is, or might be, taught. If it is inert, that is because teachers make it so. Whether school knowledge imprisons or liberates depends in part on its cultural currency, but in part too on how it is taught and what the learner does with it.

Pedagogy and culture: control

[…] It makes no sense to advance a cultural model of learning or teaching, or a theory of pedagogy, which ignores the place of public education in societies where power, wealth and influence are unequally shared. The controlling function, as we have seen, is exercised at different levels. At national level (or state level in the United States), governments devise policies and structures, allocate budgets, determine goals, define curricula and institute mechanisms for assessing and policing what goes on at the system's lower levels. At regional and local levels, such systems may be replicated or, depending on the balance of control, they may simply be implemented. At school level, heads exercise varying degrees of influence or direct control over what goes on in classrooms; and at the end of the line, in classrooms, children are every day subjected to the pedagogic controls of teaching and curriculum. These controls extend into the furthest recesses of task, activity and interaction, and are mediated through routine, rule and ritual.

Comparative macro–micro analysis illuminates the way these stack up and cumulatively impact upon the child. If we confine ourselves to the level of the national or state system, the variable of centralization–decentralization seems persuasive. Certainly, it provides a way of differentiating systems such as the five which have featured here. But if we study a system at meso and micro levels as well as macro, we soon perceive the limitations of this mode of analysis, and, by extension, of simple reproductive models of public education. The intermediate levels may transmit; alternatively, they may mediate, selectively gate keep, reshape or replace what comes from above, even when governments introduce procedures to prevent or discourage them from doing so. Conversely, in a decentralized system, the power available at local level is open to challenge both from other local quarters and above.

Meanwhile, in the classroom, as was discovered several decades ago, 'open' or 'child-centred' pedagogy may no more free the child from external controls than does traditional didactic pedagogy.[61] Pedagogy is by its nature a shaping process, and freedom, say, in choice of task may be offset by control through differentiation and assessment. Above all, we have seen the power of talk to define not just communicative competence, rights and responsibilities, but what it is to know, to understand, to learn and to be a child.

If pedagogy is, in Bernstein's words, a 'cultural relay' governed by the rules of hierarchy, sequence, pacing, appropriateness and acceptability – the 'regulative' rules of structure and hierarchy and the 'discursive' rules of instruction – the workings of that relay are nevertheless complex and variable.[62] The mechanisms are universal: structure, curriculum, assessment, inspection, qualifications, school organization and teaching. At the top of the system is the regulatory power of government and ministry; at the bottom is the regulatory power of classroom discourse. At one end is a view of the social worth of a group: qualified or unqualified, rich or poor, male or female, white or black, employed or unemployed, brahman or dalit, young or old, urban or rural, metropolitan or provincial; at the other end is a view of the communicative competence of the individual. Bernstein's studies since the 1950s have emphasized the overriding force of social class, as is inevitable in an English context.[63] To these, now, in an era more sensitive to the cultural politics of difference, we add gender, age, income, religion and ethnicity, and, in India, caste. Yet our detailed encounters with Bernstein's 'discursive' level show clearly that even when these many and profound structural divisions and inequalities are factored in, we must avoid an overdetermined view of what education does to people.

Schools and classrooms are places where meanings are, depending on the mode of pedagogy adopted, transmitted, negotiated and/or created. The formal curriculum sets out the meanings which a government, administration or school expects teachers to transmit; and this version of curriculum presumes that the primary function of teaching is transmission, for no government is in the business of prescribing subversive curricula or critical pedagogy. These meanings are variously reinforced, confused or subverted as the curriculum goes through is various phases of translation, transposition and transformation on its way to its final transformation by the child (Figure 1.1).The greater the degree of external control, the shorter the line and the closer the congruence between curriculum as prescribed, curriculum as transacted and curriculum as experienced.

As far as the prescribed curriculum is concerned, we have learned to look well beyond the surface international similarities that are revealed by OECD data or the Benavot study.[64] It *does* matter whether children encounter information technology, the arts, science or citizenship alongside the universal 'basics' of literacy and numeracy, for these can enable them to gain access to and participate in different cultural domains. Equally, a badly skewed curriculum will deny access to, and ultimately belittle and weaken, the aspects of the culture which are underrepresented. In England, at the time to writing, the critical question in this regard is whether the government's electoral pledge of raising standards in basic literacy and numeracy has been at the expense of the arts and humanities, and of the kinds of understanding and skill which these domains are uniquely able to foster. Needless to say, when they observe the impact of this policy on the curriculum as transacted, few are reassured by the official rhetoric of 'breadth and balance'.

[...]

Note on chapter

This chapter is an extract from a large comparative study of the relationship between culture, education, policy and pedagogy in five countries (England, France, India, Russia, the United States) which was first published as *Culture and Pedagogy* in 2001 (Alexander, 2001). Since then, though in the view of others besides the author *Culture and Pedagogy* continues to stand the test of time, the author's own thinking has moved on. For a current discussion of some of the matters explored here, see Alexander (2008). This collection applies and extends the *Culture and Pedagogy* insights in a number of areas: the uses and abuses of international educational comparison; the politics of educational decision-making in England during the era of centralisation, 1987–2008; the improvement of learning and teaching, and the empowerment of the learner, through the reform of classroom talk; the nature of outstanding teaching; and the challenges for education policy, pedagogy and the curriculum of globalisation, geo-political instability and climate change – preoccupations now as urgent as they are contemporary. *Essays on Pedagogy* also takes forward the conceptualisation of pedagogy itself.

Notes

1. Watkins and Mortimore, 1999, p. 3.
2. Simon, 1981.
3. Simon, 1994.
4. Simon, 1983, p. 10 (my italics).
5. The considerable literature on this matter is reviewed by various contributors to the symposium edited by Alexander, Craft and Lynch in 1984. For a history of teacher training in England from the 1944 Education Act to the arrival of national accreditation in 1984, see the chapter by Alexander (pp. 103–60) in the same publication.
6. See, e.g., Lawlor, 1990, the many articles by Anthony O'Hear in the *Daily Telegraph* and the accusations of HMCI Woodhead in his annual RCA lectures (e.g. Woodhead, 1998) and elsewhere.
7. In his circular to primary schools announcing the launch of the 'three wise men' enquiry (DES, 1991).
8. Prime Minister John Major at the Conservative Party Conference, Oct. 1991.
9. Ball, 1990.
10. For example, Woodhead, 1998, and linked articles in the tabloid press which actually targeted supposed members of the progressive conspiracy under headlines such as 'The men failing our children, by school chief', 'Trio at heart of darkness' (I was one of those so named) and 'Luddites at the school gates' (Halpin, 1998; *Mail on Sunday*, 1999).
11. Millett, 1999.
12. DES, 1991.
13. Ibid.
14. Marton and Booth, quoted in Watkins and Mortimore, 1999, p. 2.

15. Hamlyn, 1970 ('The logical and psychological aspects of learning').
16. In Alexander, 1984, I provide a detailed critique of this line of argument, which at that time – before the arrival of the national curriculum – was accepted unconditionally by many English primary teachers, and indeed was actively fostered in their teacher training courses.
17. See Judge's account of this episode in Judge *et al.*, 1994, pp. 87–93.
18. The gloss is from Chévellard, 1991, cited by Moon, 1998.
19. Shulman, 1987.
20. Bruner, 1963, p. 33.
21. Blyth, 1984.
22. Blyth, 1990, especially pp. 11–16.
23. Beattie, 1998.
24. Ibid.
25. Broadfoot *et al.*, 2000.
26. Shotton, 1998, pp. 64–159.
27. PROBE, 1999, especially pp. 68–82.
28. Bruner, 1972, pp. 100–1.
29. The references here are to the fine 1896 Keatinge translation of *Didactica Magna* (Comenius, 1657).
30. Sharpe, 1997; Broadfoot *et al.*, 2000.
31. See Ravitch, 1983, ch. 7.
32. Taba, 1962.
33. Bruner, 1968, p. 72.
34. From the 1994 Educate America Act.
35. National Commission on Excellence in Education, 1983.
36. Macedo, 1999; McLaren, 1997.
37. Bernstein, 1990, p. 184.
38. Lawton, 1983.
39. Clarke, 1996.
40. Reynolds and Farrell, 1996, pp. 52–9.
41. Tobin, Wu and Davidson, 1989, ch. 5.
42. Bronfenbrenner, 1974.
43. Stevenson and Stigler, 1992.
44. Broadfoot *et al.*, 2000, chs 3, 6.
45. Bruner, 1996, pp. 11–12.
46. In *Mind, Self and Society* (Mead, 1934).
47. Bruner, 1996, pp. 53–63.
48. Ibid. I have reduced a complex argument to its essentials without, I trust, doing it harm.
49. Popper, 1972, p. 74.
50. Popper, 1972, p. 73.
51. Bruner, 1996, p. 57.
52. See Edwards and Mercer, 1987.
53. Kumar, 1991.
54. Bruner, 1996, p. 55.
55. Compare Galton *et al.*, 1999, and Mroz, Smith and Hardman, 1999, with OFSTED, 1998a, 1998b.
56. 'Folk pedagogy' is Bruner's usage. It is similar to David McNarmara's idea of 'vernacular pedagogy' (McNamara, 1994) or Brown and McIntyre's 1993 account of 'craft knowledge'.
57. Watkins and Mortimore, 1999, p. 7.
58. Gipps and MacGilchrist, 2000, pp. 50–2.
59. Hobsbawm, 1995, p. 3.
60. Giroux, 1999, p. 100.
61. Sharp and Green, 1975.
62. Bernstein, 1990, pp. 63–93.

63. This remains a powerful determinant of education and pedagogy, and of children's educational prospects.
64. OECD, 1998; Benavot *et al.*, 1991.

References

Alexander, R. J. (1984) *Primary Teaching*. London: Cassell.

Alexander, R. J. (2001) *Culture and Pedagogy: international comparisons in primary education*. Oxford: Blackwell.

Alexander, R. J. (2008) *Essays on Pedagogy*. London: Routledge.

Alexander, R. J., Craft, M. and Lynch, J. (eds) (1984) *Change in Teacher Education: context and provision since Robbins*. London: Holt, Rinehart and Winston (published by Praeger in New York as *Change in Teacher Education: context and provision in Great Britain*).

Ball, S. J. (1990) *Politics and Policy-making in Education*. London: Routledge.

Beattie, N. (1998) 'Freinet and the Anglo-Saxons', *Compare* 28: 1, 33–47.

Benavot, A., Cha, Y-K., Kamens, D., Meyer, J. W. and Wong, S-Y. (1991) 'Knowledge for the masses: world models and national curriula, 1920–1986', *American Sociological Review* 56.

Bernstein, B. (1990) *The Structuring of Pedagogic Discourse* (Class, Codes and Control, Volume 4). London: Routledge.

Blyth, W. A. L. (1984) *Development, Experience and the Curriculum in Primary Education*. London: Croom Helm.

Blyth, W. A. L. (1990) *Making the Grade for Primary Humanities*. Buckingham: Open University Press.

Broadfoot, P., Osborn, M., Planel, C. and Sharpe, K. (2000) *Promoting Quality in Learning: does England have the answer?* London: Cassell.

Bronfenbrenner, U. (1974) *Two Worlds of Childhood: US and USSR*. London: Penguin Books.

Brown, S. and McIntyre, D. (1993) *Making Sense of Teaching*. Buckingham: Open University Press.

Bruner, J. S. (1963) *The Process of Education*. New York: Random House.

Bruner, J. S. (1968) *Toward a Theory of Instruction*. New York: W. W. Norton.

Bruner, J. S. (1972) *The Relevance of Education*. London: George Allen and Unwin.

Bruner, J. S. (1996) *The Culture of Education*. Cambridge, MA: Harvard University Press.

Chévellard, Y. (1991) 'La transposition didactique: du savoir savant au savoir enseigné'. Paris: la Pensée Sauvage.

Clarke, P. (1996) 'Cultural models of teacher thinking and teaching'. Unpublished paper. Cambridge, MA: University of Harvard.

Comenius, J. A. [1657] tr. M. W. Keatinge (1896) *The Great Didactic*. London: A. & C. Black.

Department of Education and Science (1991) *Primary Education: statement by the Secretary of State for Education and Science*. London: DES.

Edwards, D. and Mercer, N. (1987) *Common Knowledge: the development of understanding in the classroom*. London: Routledge.

Galton, M., Hargreaves, L., Comber, C., Wall, D. and Pell, A. (1999) *Inside the Primary Classroom: 20 Years On*. London: Routledge.

Gipps, C. and MacGilchrist, B. (2000) 'Primary school learners', in P. Mortimore (ed.) *Pedagogy and its Impact on Learning*, pp. 45–67. London: Paul Chapman.

Giroux, H. A. (1999) 'Border youth, difference and postmodern education', in M. Castells, R. Flecha, P. Freire, H. A. Giroux, D. Macedo and P. Willis, *Critical Education in the New Education Age*, pp. 93–116. Lanham: Rowman & Littlefield.

Halpin, T. (1998) 'The men failing our children, by schools chief', *Daily Mail*, 25 February.

Hamlyn, D. W. (1970) 'The logical and psychological aspects of learning', in R. S. Peters (ed.) *The Concept of Education*, pp. 24–43. London: Routledge and Kegan Paul.

Hobsbawm, E. J. (1995) *Age of Extremes: the short twentieth century 1914–1991*. London: Abacus.

Judge, H., Lemosse, M., Paine, L. and Sedlak, M. (1994) *The University and the Teachers: France, the United States, England*. Oxford: Triangle Books.

Kumar, Krishna (1991) *Political Agenda of Education: a study of colonialist and nationalist ideas*. New Delhi: Sage.

Lawlor, S. (1990) *Teachers Mistaught*. London: Centre for Policy Studies.

Lawton, D. (1983) *Curriculum Studies and Educational Planning*. London: Hodder & Stoughton.

Leach, E. (1964) 'Models', *New Society*, 14 June.

Macedo, D. (1999) 'Our common culture: a poisonous pedagogy', in M. Castells, R. Flecha, P. Freire, H. A. Giroux and P. Willis (eds) *Critical Education in the New Information Age*, pp. 117–38. Lanham: Rowman & Littlefield.

Mail on Sunday (1999) 'Luddites at the school gates'. London: *Mail on Sunday*, 14 March.

McLaren, P. (1997) 'Multiculturalism and the postmodern critique: toward a pedagogy of resistance and transformation', in A. H. Halsey, H. Lauder, P. Brown and A. S. Wells (eds) *Education: culture, economy and society*, pp. 520–40. Oxford: Oxford University Press.

McNamara, D. R. (1994) *Classroom Pedagogy and Primary Practice*. London: Routledge.

Mead, G. H. (1934) *Mind, Self and Society*. Chicago: University of Chicago Press.

Millett, A. (1999) 'Why we need to raise our game', *The Independent*, 11 Feb.

Moon, B. (1998) *The English Exception: international perspectives on the initial education and training of teachers*. London: Universities Council for the Education of Teachers.

Mroz, M., Smith, F. and Hardman, F. (1999) 'The discourse of the literacy hour', *Cambridge Journal of Education* 30:3.

National Commission on Excellence in Education (1983) *A Nation at Risk: the imperative for educational reform*. Washington, DC: US Government Printing Office.

Office for Standards in Education (1998a) *The National Literacy Project: an HMI evaluation*. London: OFSTED.

Office for Standards in Education (1998b) *The National Numeracy Project: an HMI evaluation*. London: OFSTED.

Organization for Economic Co-operation and Development (1998) *Education at a Glance: OECD indicators 1998*. Paris: OECD.

Popper, K. (1972) *Objective Knowledge: an evolutionary approach*. Oxford: Oxford University Press.

PROBE (1999) *Public Report on Basic Education in India*. Delhi: Oxford University Press.

Ravitch, D. (1983) *The Troubled Crusade: American education 1945–80*. New York: Basic Books.

Reynolds, D. and Farrell, S. (1996) *Worlds Apart? A review of international surveys of educational achievement involving England*. London: HMSO.

Sharp, R. and Green, A. (1975) *Education and Social Control: a study in progressive primary education*. London: Routledge and Kegan Paul.

Sharpe, K. (1997) 'The Protestant ethic and the spirit of Catholicism: ideological and instructional constraints on system change in English and French primary schooling', *Comparative Education* 33:3, 329–48.

Shotton, J. (1998) *Learning and Freedom: policy, pedagogy and paradigms in Indian education and schooling*. New Delhi: Sage.

Shulman, L. (1987) 'Knowledge and teaching: foundations of the new reform', *Harvard Educational Review* 57:1, 1–22.

Simon, B. (1981) 'Why no pedagogy in England?', in B. Simon and W. Taylor (eds) *Education in the Eighties: the central issues*, pp. 124–45. London: Batsford.

Simon, B. (1983) 'The study of education as a university subject', *Studies in Higher Education* 8:1, 1–13.

Simon, B. (1994) *The State and Educational Change: essays in the history of education and pedagogy*. London: Lawrence & Wishart.

Stevenson, H. W. and Stigler, J. W. (1992) *The Learning Gap: why our schools are failing and what we can learn from Japanese and Chinese Education*. New York: Simon & Schuster.

Taba, H. (1962) *Curriculum Development: theory and practice*. New York: Harcourt, Brace and World.

Tobin, J. J., Wu, D. Y. and Davidson, D. H. (1989) *Preschool in Three Cultures: Japan, China and the United States*. New Haven, CT: Yale University Press.

Watkins, C. and Mortimore, P. (1999) 'Pedagogy: what do we know?', in P. Mortimore (ed.) *Pedagogy and its Impact on Learning*, pp. 1–19. London: Paul Chapman.

Woodhead, C. (1998) 'Blood on the tracks: lessons from the history of education reform' (RSA HMCI Annual Lecture, 1998). London: OFSTED.

2

Defining Pedagogy

Patricia Murphy

Introduction

Pedagogy is a term widely used in educational writing but all too often its meaning is assumed to be self-evident. An examination of how the term is used and the implicit assumptions about teaching and education that underlie its use is a valuable way of understanding how the education process is perceived. Many of the strategies that have been developed to redress inequity in schooling have targeted classroom practice and teaching as an important site of change. For this reason, attention has been paid to pedagogy, its meaning and relationship to curriculum. Feminist research has revealed how particular relations are reflected and reproduced in schooling at a number of levels. At the ideological level, ideologies of 'race', 'ethnicism' and 'gender' act to socialize students for their future roles. At the structural and organizational level of institutions, both in their overt and covert practices, messages are relayed to students about the relative power positions of different groups and individuals; and about the subjects and aspects of those subjects which are deemed appropriate for them to study. These subject divisions typically reflect the occupational structures in societies and the sources and selection of knowledge represented in curriculum subjects.

In different cultures at different points of time in history, the meaning and status of pedagogy have shifted. Simon (1981) describes the situation in Britain where the 'dominant educational institutions ... have had no concern with theory, its relation to practice, with pedagogy' (p. 11). The absence of critical accounts of pedagogy in Britain contrasts with other western and eastern European countries where pedagogy has a tradition of study. However, in spite of this tradition or because of it, the study of pedagogy is one of confusion, ambiguity and change (Best, 1988). In Best's view, the status and meaning of pedagogy have changed in recent times and have been 'devalued, deflected from its original meaning or even discredited'.

The failure to examine pedagogy limits the potential for effecting change through education. Simon quotes Fletcher's (1889) view that 'without something like scientific discussion on educational subjects, without pedagogy, we shall never obtain a body of organised opinion on education.' This viewpoint is echoed by Shulman (1987). He argues that to advance teacher reform it is essential to develop 'codified representations of the practical pedagogical wisdom of able teachers'. For Shulman, one of the major problems

From: 'Defining Pedagogy' by Patricia Murphy in *Equity in the Classroom: Towards Effective Pedagogy for Girls and Boys*, ed. by P.F. Murphy and C.V. Gipps © UNESCO 1996. Used by permission of UNESCO, with bibliographic references native to the original edition excised.

for understanding teaching is that 'the best creations of its practitioners are lost to both contemporary and future peers … teaching is conducted without an audience of peers. It is devoid of a history of practice' (1987, p. 12). For Shulman, accounts of practice must include the management of students in classrooms and the management of *ideas* within classroom discourse.

There has been recognition in recent years of the unique, interactive nature of pedagogy. This interactiveness makes it difficult to capture and represent professional expertise as practised in classrooms. Interventions that have been developed to enhance female participation in aspects of the education process or to challenge sexist ideology in schools and society provide detailed accounts of practice. They are, therefore, invaluable sources of illumination of a pedagogy that is seen more as an art than a science.

In this chapter, we consider some of the historical accounts of pedagogy and identify some of the key elements in its conception. We then turn to more current debates that extend this conception and draw upon developments in understanding about the nature of human learning and knowledge. Finally, we consider feminist research and review the characteristic of feminist pedagogy and how these relate to the general debates about pedagogy. […]

Changing perceptions of pedagogy

Simon, in his critique of pedagogy in the British context, highlights the important link between views of ability and learning and education. He describes how early attempts to integrate theoretical knowledge with the practice of education during the late nineteenth century in Britain were based on associationist psychological theories of learning. In these theories, learners are viewed as passive responders to external stimuli. The pedagogy emerging from elementary schools in the 1890s and secondary schools in the early 1900s reflected this. Walkerdine (1984) described the purpose behind the introduction of compulsory schooling in Britain as social and disciplinary, to inculcate in the populace good habits to redress the perceived consequences of bad habits, i.e., crime and poverty.

The next significant change in the form of pedagogy, Walkerdine associates with the emergence of the term 'class' in the discourse that developed when population statistics became available. This led to a shift in the organization of educational apparatuses from school rooms to classrooms, from mixed age groupings to same age 'class' groupings. Education for regulation and citizenship was now to be achieved not through coercion as previously believed, but through the development of rational powers of the mind, hence the content of what children were to study also changed. As Walkerdine points out, these changes in pedagogy emerged as a result of conflicts and struggle and were 'simultaneously discursive transformation and a transformation of apparatuses and practices'. The next development in approaches to pedagogy was influenced by the new emphasis on psychometrics in education.

Psychometric constructs such as mental age are premised on the concept of the norm, i.e., normal behaviour, normal achievement, the normal child. These constructs were appropriated by psychologists who believed that humans were possessed of a general innate ability that was distributed in the population normally (Spearman, 1927). Individuals' innate ability sets the ceiling on their achievements: it follows from this that teaching cannot alter children's *potential* to learn. Such a perspective fits well with those educators who hold a hereditarian view of intelligence (see Gould, 1981). As Walkerdine

(1984) put it, 'the development of the "child" as an object both of science in its own right and of the apparatuses of normalisation … provided the possibility for a science and a pedagogy based on a model of naturally occurring development which could be observed, normalised and regulated.'

The emergence of new theories of learning which challenged the notion of innate ability independent of environmental, social and educational influences reasserted in the education community the belief in the human capacity to learn. Child-centred theories of learning led to what is commonly and often misleadingly referred to as discovery approaches to pedagogy or non-directive pedagogy. In these theories of learning, the child is believed to possess certain qualities and potentials which can be realized, given the appropriate environment. The focus on individual potential in these theories introduced the notion and possibility of an individualized rather than a class-based pedagogy. The teacher's role was also recast. She was no longer the inculcator of rational powers of the mind, but the 'guide' who enabled individual growth. This theory of pedagogy drew heavily on interpretations of aspects of Piagetian theories including notions of stages of development and 'readiness' for learning. Central to the pedagogy was the belief that a child's development towards scientific rationality emerges spontaneously as she explores and 'plays' with the environment. However, a child can only learn from certain experiences if 'ready', i.e., at the appropriate stage of development.

Walkerdine (1984) has described the circumstances that led to Piagetian theories being taken up in the particular ways they have been in classrooms. She details inherent conflicts between Piaget's theories that aim to normalize children's behaviours and a pedagogy that is premised on the aim of liberating the individuality of the child. Of particular value is Walkerdine's analysis of the web of related practices and apparatuses (such as record cards, classroom layout, work-cards, teacher training) which together 'produce the possibility and effectivity of the child-centred pedagogy'. The continuing and important message from Walkerdine is that the apparatuses of the pedagogy are not merely applications, but a site of production in their own right. Feminist research has paid particular attention to the apparatuses of pedagogy and how they are implicated in producing and maintaining differentiation in schools. For example, assessment practices or forms of questioning may only enable certain students to reveal what they know and may act as barriers to others (Murphy, 1995). Less obvious are those practices and customs […] which make assumptions about gender differences, in particular, the way the physical school constructs a different 'place' for girls and boys by unduly restricting the use of space for girls. Gordon (1996) describes how this, in turn, becomes one of the influences that affects teachers' judgments and expectations of girls.

Developments in views about learning and teaching

Whilst Piagetian theories continue to be reinterpreted and applied to aspects of education, other influential theories have emerged in recent years, in particular other forms of constructivism and socio-cultural theories of learning. Common to all of these theories, however, including Piaget's, is the notion of the student as agent, the active constructor of meaning and knowledge. Although views vary about the nature of this agency, it is generally agreed that in order to teach one must first establish what students know, how they know it and how they feel about that aspect of their experience. The concept of agency has other implications for teaching and learning. If it is the student who constructs meaning out of the opportunities school offers, then, to progress, students need to gain an explicit understanding of what they know and how they come to know it, i.e., to develop *operative* knowledge that allows them to select from their knowledge appropriately in order to solve the problems and dilemmas they face in making sense. This operative knowledge (von Glasersfeld, 1989) has to be *taught* and requires teachers to develop strategies to make students' thinking explicit to them. The development of such metacognitive awareness relies crucially on language.

This focus on the role of language in learning coupled with a quite different perception of human ability distinguished social constructivist and socio-cultural theories of learning from certain Piagetian based and behaviourist perspectives. For example, on the conception of students' ability, Bruner (1986) considers that children develop an understanding of others' minds from a very early age. He considers the shared use of language to be the key which unlocks others' minds to us. Learning how to use language involves 'both learning the culture and learning how to express intention in congruence with the culture.' For Bruner, culture is the 'implicit semi-connected knowledge of the world, from which, through negotiation, people arrive at satisfactory ways of acting in a given context.' If we consider differential power relations in schools and the differing cultural experiences and values of teachers and students, we can begin to anticipate how such negotiation could, in certain contexts, break down or operate to the disadvantage of individuals and groups.

Bruner's thinking was influenced by the Russian psychologist Vygotsky (1978). Vygotskian perspectives have been increasingly applied to the process of education in recent years. Vygotsky similarly saw language as intimately involved in the process of learning and development. Through the use of language, children mediate their actions. As such, egocentric speech represents the transition between external and internal speech. Faced with difficulties, a child communicates with another adult or peer, and this socialized speech is subsequently internalized by the child. Seen in this way, language comes to form higher mental processes. It structures and directs thinking and concept formation, and is the product of social experience.

Vygotsky's view of development, and his concern with language and communication as central to learning, have major implications for teaching. In his view, students' potential for learning depends both on their existing knowledge and their capacity to learn. The potential for achievement can be realized through the help of a more informed adult or peer — a quite different conception to that of age-related staged development. Learning triggers developmental processes that only operate when the learner interacts and cooperates with people and the environment. In Bruner's words, the teacher 'serves the learner as a vicarious form of consciousness until such time as the learner is able to master his own actions' (Bruner, 1985, p. 24). The teacher's role is now much more demanding than that of a 'guide'. From this notion of the teacher's role, the term 'scaffolding' was coined (Wood, 1988). Scaffolding describes how teachers act to focus students' attention on 'relevant and timely aspects of the task and highlight things they need to take account of' (Wood, 1988, pp. 80–1). The teacher actively structures the support students need until they attain 'stand alone' competence. The ability to scaffold tasks suggests that teachers are aware of individual students' different needs. Indeed it is one of the reasons for the current focus on formative assessment practice. However, it is documented in research that many boys and girls approach learning activities in different ways. The 'scaffolds' that teachers provide for students would need to take into account the influence of students' different cognitive styles if they are to serve as supports for them.

Bruner talks of students establishing joint reference between each other on the basis of shared contexts and assumptions. However, meaning produced through this process of reference is always 'undetermined and ambiguous'. Von Glasersfeld applies this to teaching and argues that teachers construct models of students' notions and operations. The teacher's goal is to gain understanding of the students' understanding. The 'best' that can be achieved in this process is a model that remains 'viable within the range of available experience'. These notions of modelling and referencing place both teachers and students in a *dialectical relationship*. The theory of learning once again redefines the teacher's role and relationship to the student. Paulo Freire similarly viewed the process of learning as a dialectical movement (Freire, 1971). 'The act of knowing involves a dialectical movement that goes from action of reflection and from reflection upon action to a new action' (Freire, 1985). For Freire, the learning process implies the existence of two interrelated contexts. These he labels as 'authentic dialogue' between students and teachers, and the second the 'social reality' in which people exist. The teacher's role in Freire's perspective is to pose problems about 'codified existential situations in order to help learners arrive at a more critical view of their reality'. Whilst it is not possible to go into theories of learning and knowledge in any great depth here, it is important to raise a few other central ideas that have come to the fore in thinking about the learning process. These ideas have particular relevance to the equity debate and, to an extent, extend the notions already discussed.

One significant issue is the context dependency of learners' knowledge. Context in this debate is seen as the common knowledge of the speakers invoked by the discourse (Edwards and Mercer, 1987). Context is therefore an integral aspect of making sense along with learners' prior knowledge and understanding. Many of the differences in girls' and boys' responses to teaching and assessment activities indicate that the common knowledge invoked by the activities is not shared (Murphy, 1996). […] In similar circumstances, girls and boys perceive different problems because their view of what is relevant differs (Harding, 1996). These differences mean that the opportunities that students have to develop particular understandings will vary in spite of the apparent commonality in teaching provision. The teachers' selections and those reflected in textbooks can therefore support the learning of some students to the disadvantage of others. Traditionally, it has been the meanings that girls more than boys value that are marginalized in curriculum activities — English being an exception. For many teachers and students, these context effects are invisible and their impact on learning unanticipated. […]

Traditionally, knowledge has been viewed as an 'integral, self-sufficient substance, theoretically independent of the *situations* [my emphasis] in which it is learned and used' (Brown, Collins and Duguid, 1989). Situated cognition theorists challenge fundamentally the separation of what is learned from how it is learned and used. Knowledge in their view is not separable from the activity and situation in which it is produced. Rather, knowledge is like language: 'its constituent parts index the world and so are inextricably a product of the activity and situations in which they are produced' (Brown, Collins and Duguid, 1989). Conceptual tools are seen to reflect the cumulative wisdom of the culture and are a product of *negotiation*. According to Brown *et al.* 'activity, concept and culture are interdependent'.

For those educators concerned with equity in the classroom, the force of situated cognition is in the implications it raises for school knowledge systems. The social construction of knowledge is a product of negotiation. In order to understand key ideas in subjects, students need to understand, and have access to, this process of negotiation. This suggests a need to examine critically the status of subject knowledge claims and whose cumulative wisdom is reflected in teachers' practice and in the curriculum guidelines within which they work. This examination needs to include gender, ethnicity, race and socio-economic class to determine which individuals and groups the knowledge is accessible to, and/or valuable for. In this per-spective of learning, the teacher has the task of making cultural practices available to students for consideration. The implication of this is that reflection on the selection and sources of school knowledge should happen as part of the dialogue *between* teachers and students. Introducing examples of assessment practice for critical examination can help support this process by providing explicit examples of what is 'valued'. A further strategy involves teach-ers introducing controversial knowledge claims, e.g., hypothesized causal links between diet and cancer, as part of the subject curriculum. This provides opportunities for students to 'learn' about the nature of evidence while they examine the validity of such claims.

Kruse (1996) refers to a strategy where everybody in a teaching group is given the opportunity to express their opinion about a subject matter. [...] Burton (1996) argues similarly for a shift from 'knowledge control by authorities external to the student, to the development of a community of voices with whom authority and indeed authorship rest'. [...] From these theories of learning and of knowledge, there has emerged a different per-ception of the teacher–student relationship. This reflects both a different understanding of the significance of students' knowledge and ways of knowing and of the purpose of education, the latter now being seen as providing entry into different cultural practices and knowledges. In current theories, the teacher's role is much more complex: the teacher has to find ways of helping students 'find, create and negotiate their meanings' (Lerman, 1993). This involves providing activities which are meaningful and purposeful from the students' perspective and which allow them to apply and develop their understandings in explicit relation to others. The focus on meaning and purpose in learning and assessment is a central feature of many interventions advocated to support girls' learning. Authenticity in tasks ensures that the links between school learning and out-of-school practices are explicit. That this is a need perceived by girls more than boys is a matter for concern. The literature on situated cognition shows that the activities from which students' knowledge is derived are intimately linked to that knowledge. Hence, if learning is focused on abstracted school tasks and rituals, what students will acquire is ritualistic knowledge applicable only to those situations in which it is learned. Consequently, authenticity in tasks is a prerequisite for developing knowledge that can be applied in the culture. It is therefore essential for *all* students' learning.

In current theories of learning, the responsibility for learning rests with students and teach-ers. Students are expected to engage in dialogue with each other, and with teachers, and to val-idate their own understandings rather than merely accept transmitted views. Students need particular study skills to participate in this type of learning. Interventions to enhance girls' learning typically involve collaborative ways of working. Girls more than boys prefer to coop-erate and engage in dialogue with peers about their learning. Consequently, girls more than boys have the study skills that are needed for the type of pedagogy advocated. It is to be expected that many boys will need support to acquire these skills. A first step will be in estab-lishing with them the significance of skills that hitherto have been devalued. [...] As Kenway (1996) points out, the resistance of students to pedagogic intervention needs to be reflected on when evaluating their effectiveness and future direction.

We turn next to consider how debates about pedagogy are being considered in the wider education arena and what key elements in the conceptualization of pedagogy are emerging from this debate.

Redefining pedagogy

Didactics was a term introduced to bring coherence to the debate about pedagogy: it describes the study of the relationship between learners, teachers and educational subject knowledge. Didactics placed an emphasis on the uniqueness of school subjects and accorded them equal status with the *process* of presentation. Didactics is concerned with the processes of the person learning and the particular content to be learned (the knowledge and the know-how). However, the practical element of pedagogy, the putting into practice, was seen to be absent from such a description. Tochon and Munby (1993), in developing a wider definition of pedagogy, distinguish didactics from pedagogy in the following way:

> Pedagogy is concerned with our immediate image of the teaching situation. It is live processing developed in a practical and idiosyncratic situation. Didactic goals can be written down, but pedagogical experience cannot be easily theorised, owing to its unique interactive aspects. Though action research and reflection reveals the existence of basic principles underlying practical classroom experience, no matter what rules might be inferred, pedagogy still remains an adventure. (p. 207)

This move away from conceptions of pedagogy as the *science* of teaching, reflects a new epistemology of practice — an epistemology in which the notion of praxis is central. Praxis is a term used to describe the dialectical relationship between theory and practice in teaching — a form of reasoning informed by action. Schon (1987) describes this new epistemology of practice in the following way:

> ... one that would stand the question of professional knowledge on its head by taking as its point of departure the competence and artistry already embedded in skilful practice — especially the reflection-in-action ... that practitioners sometimes bring to situations of uncertainty, uniqueness and conflict.

The reconceptualizing of pedagogy as art is not a small matter. The way professional knowledge is perceived as ambiguous and incomplete, a 'tacit knowledge that is hard to put into words, at the core of the practice of every highly regarded professional' (Schon, 1987), has led to a crisis of confidence in the profession of education.

It is for these reasons that reformists such as Shulman are currently attempting to articulate the knowledge base of teachers. He defines *pedagogical content knowledge* as 'that special amalgam of content and pedagogy that is uniquely the province of professional understanding' (1987, p. 8). He argues, as others do, that it is the *wisdom of practice* that is the 'least codified source of teacher knowledge'. What is challenged by those educationists examining Shulman's concept of pedagogical content knowledge is that it presumes subject knowledge is absolute, uncontestable, unidimensional and static (Meredith, 1995). Others argue the need to see the transposition of content knowledge to school knowledge as a didactic rather than pedagogic process. The didactic process involves change, alteration and restructuring if the knowledge is to be teachable (Chevellard, 1991, quoted in Banks, Bourdillon, Leach, Manning, Moon and Swarbrick, 1995). Hence, a split between school knowledge and pedagogical school knowledge is envisioned to 'create a dynamic which leaves open to question curriculum constructs [such as subjects]' (Banks *et al.*, 1995, p. 8).

To reflect on this new epistemology of practice requires a discourse that Alexander refers to as 'dilemma-language' (Alexander, 1992). Dilemma-language is the articulation of 'doubts, qualification, dilemma, consciousness of nuance, alertness to the affective dimension … [which] can indicate true insight … [and] inner strength rather than mere professional machismo.' Such a discourse, according to Alexander, has not yet been legitimized because of the imbalance in power between practitioners and others in the educational hierarchy. The dilemmas teachers face also need to be examined in the political, social and cultural contexts in which teachers practise. Osborn and Broadfoot (1992) observed in their study of French and English primary teachers that:

> … for English teachers the critical issue … [is] how to resolve the practical problems inherent in delivering an individualised pedagogy in the context of a range of external pressures and large class sizes. For French teachers the dilemma is providing equal justice under law with the assumption of a common cultural base. … given growing differentiation in the social context and individual values. (p. 12)

The redefinition of pedagogy as an art follows from the view that pedagogy is about the *interactions between teachers, students and the learning environment and learning tasks —* our working definition given in the introduction. However, we have argued that pedagogy cannot be disembedded from the wider educational system. So, in order to address what is an effective pedagogy, we must be agreed on the goals of education. In the context of the equity debate, it is Freire's view that has been influential. In his liberatory pedagogy, Freire (1971) argues that education must help students develop an increasingly critical view of their reality. […] It is appropriate now to examine the feminist contribution to the debate about pedagogy. It was feminist research which first drew attention to inadequacies in pedagogy in relation to groups and individuals. Through feminist interventions and evaluations of these, we now have a much richer understanding of the nature of pedagogy.

Perspectives on feminist pedagogy

Feminist pedagogy grew out of concern about the absence of any discourses concerned with transformative and critical pedagogy in the debate about teaching and learning. Its aim is to create awareness of 'difference' and of the process by which social divisions such as race, sex and socio-economic class structure individual experiences and opportunities. Feminist pedagogy is based on an 'analysis of females' and males' multiple and different material realities and illuminates females' and males' multiple and different experiences' (Weiner, 1994, p. 130). To reveal the varying positions of students and teachers, pedagogy has to become a site of discourse.

A feminist pedagogy provides students with access to alternative discourses to help them understand how identities are shaped and meanings and truths constructed. [...] Davies (1989) describes the way children acquire the discursive practices of their society and learn to position themselves as male or female. As in all human actions, people are not passively shaped: each is active in taking up discourses through which he or she is shaped. For feminists, it is essential to reveal to students how meanings related to gender are produced and how these in turn influence the construction of femininity and masculinity. Gemma Moss (1992) describes her approach to reading which stresses the role that diverse social and cultural practices play in shaping how texts get read. For example, when looking at popular magazines, she suggests issues that can be considered with students, such as the appeal of technical language in boys' magazines and the common requirement for 'expertise' on the part of the male reader. The application of different discourses offers students opportunities to see how individuals can be reconstructed in discourse, as different discourses offer different subject (i.e., individual) positions and points of view. Introducing students to concepts of discourse provides them with the means to deconstruct and reconstruct 'texts' both representational and 'lived', whatever the topic of study.

Feminist pedagogy advocates making students theorists by encouraging them to interrogate and analyse their own experiences in order to gain a critical understanding of them. In a similar way, students can become theorists about subject knowledge as it is presented. This theorizing starts with students conceptualizing their own experiences and then, through action and dialogue on aspects of subjects, students gain new awareness and understanding, which, with the support of the teacher and peers, are analysed, organized and evaluated in relation to others' understandings. In this way, students and teachers can deconstruct the 'cultural wisdom' that shapes the curriculum and thus understand it.

Taking a critical stance to the curriculum and its processes not only empowers students, it provides them with a far more robust sense of the nature of knowledge and the status of subject knowledge claims. The knowledge they acquire is useful knowledge that can be applied outside of school. National surveys in the UK found that as students progressed through school, they acquired more and more fragments of knowledge but *not* the ability to apply them to make sense of new situations and to solve problems (DES, 1988a, 1988b). Teachers have to help make explicit to students theirs' and others' ways of making sense to enable them to achieve a critical stance. As we have already noted, there will be constraints on teachers' abilities to do this because of their own subjectivity and the various subjectivities of their students. Furthermore, such a pedagogy disrupts normative values that are deeply embedded in both teachers and students, hence resistance to examining alternatives is to be expected. [...] If movement towards such a pedagogy can be achieved, it opens up the potential for choice both in students' use of knowledge and in their desires to access alternative discourses and the 'truths' they produce in order to gain real insight into cultural knowledge.

A feminist pedagogy, as described here, reflects current theories about the nature of learning, of learners and of knowledge. This is evident in the practices it advocates and the relationships between teachers and students it aims to foster. Feminist research has provided a rich source of evidence about practice as interventions have been developed and revised as a result of experience. A major contribution to the general debate has been the exposition of the concepts of discourses. There is an emerging consensus about the socially constructed nature of knowledge and the need for students to understand this and to adopt a critical stance toward the curriculum. However, how this is to be achieved is less well articulated. Another major contribution of feminist practice has been the revelation and treatment of difference in classrooms. This has highlighted the necessity for continual reflection on practice by teachers. A further contribution has been the attention paid to the ramifications of such a pedagogy beyond the classroom door. It is essential to remember that the apparatuses of pedagogy are a site of production in their own right. We cannot therefore advocate a particular teacher–student relationship that ends abruptly at the classroom door. The relationships have to be seen to exist at all levels in a school. Students need to feel a sense of community in a school, a sense of a safe place — place not just in physical terms but in ideological terms as well. Furthermore, if we encourage students to adopt a critical stance to the curriculum, then the same approach would have to hold for their engagement in the derivation of school policies and rules. [...]

To put this into practice requires change in the organizations and apparatuses of schools. For example, if strong ongoing relationships between teachers and students are necessary for effective pedagogy, does the typical secondary school practice of many short timetabled sessions with different teachers allow for this? Research suggests that heterogeneous groupings where teaching takes careful account of individual knowledge and experience are the most appropriate for learning. How does this approach 'fit' in schools committed to tracking or streaming, working in the context of time-pressured lessons? Learning areas also need to be seen to support the ways of working advocated, in the arrangements and accessibility of furniture and resources, etc. These few questions only touch on the issues that need to be considered in schools to enable an effective pedagogy to develop. They do, however, indicate the direction that needs to be taken if we treat seriously the demands of such a pedagogy.

Summary

In this chapter, attention has been paid to the relationship between understandings about pedagogy and views about learning and the purpose of education. Current theorizing has radically altered the way the teacher–student relationship is perceived and *gives* status to personal experiences as a source of knowledge. Feminist pedagogy similarly reflects these characteristics and has extended them to recognize overtly the issue of difference. In developing practice that is based on, and illuminative of, difference, feminist pedagogy has extended understanding of what constitutes effective pedagogy. [...]

Whilst significant steps have been taken in identifying and articulating effective pedagogic strategies, we remain with an unresolved question and debate. We need to ask 'what is an educated person?' in a world that recognizes difference and how answers to this question help define a curriculum and pedagogy for equity. We need to continue to apply the principles of critical pedagogy enunciated here to reflect on subject knowledge in school in order to better understand what alternative forms exist and whose purposes they might serve. However, as has been pointed out, there is still a long way to go (Longino and Hammonds, 1990). Nor can we afford to develop pedagogic strategies that empower only some individuals within a group. We need to understand what is meaningful and relevant to working-class boys and girls, to ethnic minorities, for all groups who share an identity.

Any developments in pedagogic practice must rely on teacher involvement. A first step in ensuring involvement is for teachers in their training to be helped to understand the problem and how it impacts on students' learning and teachers' expectations, behaviours and attitudes. The pedagogy advocated within schools should be mirrored in the pedagogy of teacher education. Unfortunately, higher education institutions lag behind many schools in their commitment to, and understanding of, equity issues. Sue Lewis's description of the 'chilly learning environment' and the resistance to, and marginalization of, curriculum reform intervention programmes in higher education institutions testifies to this. This is a situation which needs to change if pedagogy in school is to become more effective for more students.

References

Alexander, R. (1992) 'The problem of good primary practice', in Alexander, R. (ed.) *Policy and Practice in the Primary Curriculum*, London, Routledge.

Banks, F., Bourdillon, H., Leach, J., Manning, P., Moon, B. and Swarbrick, A. (1995) 'Knowledge, school knowledge and pedagogy: Defining an agenda for teacher education', Paper presented at the first meeting of the European Educational Research Association, Bath, September.

Best, F. (1988) 'The metamorphoses of the term "pedagogy"', *Prospects*, XVIII(2), pp. 157–66.

Brown, J. S., Collins, A. and Duguid, P. (1989) 'Situated cognition and the culture of learning', *Educational Researcher*, 18(1), pp. 32–42.

Bruner, J. S. (1985) 'Vygotsky: A historical and conceptual perspective', in Wertsch, J. V. (ed.) *Culture, Communication and Cognition: Vygotskian Perspectives*, Cambridge, Cambridge University Press.

Bruner, J. S. (1986) *Actual Minds, Possible Worlds*, Cambridge Massachusetts, Harvard University Press.

Burton, L. (1996) 'A socially just pedagogy for the teaching of mathematics', in Murphy, P. and Gipps, C. (eds) *Equity in the Classroom: Towards Effective Pedagogy for Girls and Boys*, London, Falmer Press, Unesco Publishing.

Chevellard, Y. (1991) *La Transposition Didactique: Du Savoir Savant au Savoir Enseigné*, Paris, La Pensée Sauvage.

Davies, B. (1989) 'Education for sexism: A theoretical analysis of the sex/gender bias in education', *Educational Philosophy and Theory*, 21(1), pp. 1–19.

Department of Education and Science (1988a) *Science at Age 11 — A Review of APU Survey Findings*, London, HMSO.

Department of Education and Science (1988b) *Science at Age 15 — A Review of APU Survey Findings*, London, HMSO.

Edwards, D. and Mercer, N. (1987) *Common Knowledge: The Development of Understanding in the Classroom*, London, Methuen.

Fletcher, A. E. (ed.) (1889) *Cyclopedia of Education* (2nd edn), Swan Sonnenschein.

Freire, P. (1971) *Pedagogy of the Oppressed*, New York, Herden and Herden.

Freire, P. (1985) *The Politics of Education*, London, Macmillan.

Gordon, T. (1996) 'Citizenship, difference and marginality in schools: Spatial and embodied aspects of gender construction', in Murphy, P. and Gipps, C. (eds) *Equity in the Classroom: Towards Effective Pedagogy for Girls and Boys*, London, Falmer Press, Unesco Publishing.

Gould, S. J. (1981) *The Mismeasure of Man*, New York, W. W. Norton.

Harding, J. (1996) 'Girls' achievement in science and technology: Implications for pedagogy', in Murphy, P. and Gipps, C. (eds) *Equity in the Classroom: Towards Effective Pedagogy for Girls and Boys,* London, Falmer Press, Unesco Publishing.

Kenway, J. (1996) 'The emotional dimensions of feminist pedagogy in schools', in Murphy, P. and Gipps, C. (eds) *Equity in the Classroom: Towards Effective Pedagogy for Girls and Boys*, London, Falmer Press, Unesco Publishing.

Kruse, A. M. (1996) 'Single-sex settings: Pedagogies for girls and boys in Danish schools', in Murphy, P. and Gipps, C. (eds) *Equity in the Classroom: Towards Effective Pedagogy for Girls and Boys*, London, Falmer Press, Unesco Publishing.

Lerman, S. (1993) 'The Problem of Intersubjectivity in Mathematics Learning: Extension or Rejection of the Constructivist Paradigm', London South Bank University Technical Report, SBU-CISM.

Longino, H. E. and Hammonds, E. (1990) 'Conflicts and tensions in the feminist study of gender and science', in Hirsch, M. and Fox-Keller, E. (eds) *Conflicts in Feminism*, London, Routledge.

Meredith, A. (1995) 'Terry's learning: Some limitations of Shulman's pedagogical content knowledge', *Cambridge Journal of Education*, 25(2), pp. 175–87.

Moss, G. (1992) 'Rewriting reading', in Kimberley, K., Meek, M. and Miller, J. (eds) *New Readings: Contributions to an Understanding of Literacy*, London, A & C Black, pp. 183–93.

Murphy, P. (1995) 'Sources of inequity: Understanding students' responses to assessment', *Assessment in Education*, 2(3), pp. 249–70.

Murphy, P. (1996) 'Assessment practices and gender in science', in Parker, L. H., Rennie, L. J. and Fraser, B. J. (eds) *Gender, Science and Mathematics: Shortening the Shadow*, Dordrecht, Kluwer Academic Publishers, pp. 105–17.

Osborn, M. and Broadfoot, P. (1992) 'A lesson in progress? Primary classrooms observed in England and France', *Oxford Review of Education*, 18(1), pp. 3–15.

Schon, D. (1987) *Educating the Reflective Practitioner*, San Francisco, Jossey-Bass.

Shulman, L. S. (1987) 'Knowledge and teaching: Foundations of the new reform', *Harvard Educational Review*, 57(1), pp. 1–22.

Simon, B. (1981) 'Why no pedagogy in England?', in Simon, B. and Taylor, W. (eds) *Education in the Eighties*, London, Batsford Ltd.

Spearman, C. (1927) *The Nature of 'Intelligence' and the Principles of Cognition*, London, Macmillan.

Tochon, F. and Munby, H. (1993) 'Novice and expert teachers' time epistemology: A wave function from didactics to pedagogy', *Teacher and Teacher Education*, 9(2), pp. 205–18.

Von Glasersfeld, E. (1989) 'Learning as a constructive activity', in Murphy, P. and Moon, B. (eds) *Developments in Learning and Assessment*, London, Hodder and Stoughton.

Vygotsky, L. S. (1978) *Mind in Society: The Development of Higher Psychological Processes*, Cambridge, Massachusetts, Harvard University Press.

Walkerdine, V. (1984) 'Developmental psychology and the child-centred pedagogy', in Henriques, J., Holloway, W., Unwin, C., Venn, C. and Walderdine, V. (eds) *Changing the Subject: Psychology, Social Regulation and Subjectivity*, London, Methuen.

Weiner, G. (1994) *Feminisms in Education: An Introduction*, Buckingham, Open University Press.

Wood, D. (1988) *How Children Think and Learn*, Oxford, Blackwell.

3

Learning from Other People in the Workplace

Michael Eraut

[...]

Introduction

Our research project on Early Career Learning at Work was started with theoretical frame-works from previous projects, and sought to develop these frameworks as well as provide empirical data to compare with those from different workers and contexts. The funding was three times that for our project on mid-career learning in the Learning Society Programme (Eraut *et al.*, 2000), and this enabled us to both conduct a longitudinal study of the learning of early career professionals and to include observations of participants at work before interviewing them. Our initial sample comprised 40 newly qualified nurses and 38 gradu-ate engineers, but only 14 trainee chartered accountants; and our plan was to make four visits over a period of three years. The nurses were the most mobile and difficult to retain, and it was also difficult to find partner organisations in accountancy. Our retention rate was 50% in nursing and 72% overall.

Both projects shared the same three research questions:

1. What is being learned?
2. How is it being learned?
3. What factors affect the level and direction of learning efforts?

The first two questions raise difficult methodological problems for three main reasons:

- Professional knowledge has a large and important tacit dimension (Eraut, 2000).
- Implicit learning also plays a significant role because (1) people are often unaware that they are learning through the work they do, and (2) the word 'learning' weakens awareness of informal learning modes through its close association in respondents' minds with formal class-based teaching (Eraut, 2000).

From: *Oxford Review of Education,* 33 (4), 2007, pp. 403–422. Reprinted by permission of the pub-lisher (Taylor & Francis Ltd, http://www.informaworld.com).

- Much professional work deals with complex situations that require the use of complex knowledge that defies simple forms of representation. These problems do not challenge only researchers, they also have a huge influence on early career learning.

Another addition to this second project was the expansion of the third question to include factors affecting the use and extension of prior knowledge brought into employment from higher education and other life experiences. This has been a major issue in professional formation for a considerable time, but one that has received insufficient attention because of the failure to establish the ownership of the problem. While education and practice settings each have both theories and practices, they have very different cultures and very different discourses (Eraut, 2004). People who work in both contexts have to be bilingual, but this does not mean that they become good interpreters. Knowledge of how to use formal knowledge from higher education settings in practice contexts has a very strong tacit dimension; and this affects how it can be learned.

We anticipated that the use of observation would play an important role in tackling these issues. We found that its advantages included:

- Educating the observer/interviewer about the working context, and thus enriching subsequent data gathering.
- Enabling us to use workplace documents and activities as starting points for conversations about embedded knowledge and its acquisition that would otherwise have been impossible.
- Providing 'clues' to the use of knowledge that must have been previously learnt, thus making it easier to track down implicit learning.
- Allowing complexity to be appreciated, even if it was not fully explained to, nor fully understood by, the observer.
- Discouraging the painting of 'ideal pictures' by informants when they know reality has been observed.
- Opportunities to introduce some further triangulation by interviewing significant others (152 managers, team leaders and mentors) in the workplace of our main participants.

As predicted, we found observation also enabled us to start conversations in the discourse of *description*, which could then be extended to events that we had not witnessed, rather than the discourse of *justification*, based on what Argyris and Schön (1974) called 'espoused theories'. However, contrary to the claims of Nonaka and Takeuchi (1995) and the advocates of reflective learning, the elicitation of tacit knowledge remained very difficult and appeared to require a more interactive approach to data collection. This increased the need for reflexivity and respondent verification in order to minimise any unintended influence on our participants' responses. A full account of our methodology can be found in Steadman *et al.* (2005).

Towards an epistemology of practice

In addition to this further development of our methodological approach to researching learning at work, we had a set of theoretical resources that provided a basis for the further development of our theoretical position. These were important because (1) they transcended the specific influences of profession and career stage, and (2) they established connections between what was being learned, how it was being learned and the critical factors situated in our wide array of learning contexts.

My epistemology treats socio-cultural and individual theories of learning as complementary rather than competing (Eraut, 2007). The cultural perspective on knowledge focuses on knowledge creation as a social process, whose outcomes may take the form of *codified/reified knowledge* and/or *shared meanings and understandings* that have not been codified or translated into mediating artifacts. Universities are primarily concerned with *codified knowledge* published in books and journals. Each publication of status has editors and referees controlling *acceptance*, using criteria that include recognition of previous work, originality and credible evidence and argument. Journals of a more scientific nature use the criterion of *truth* according to the norms of the community from which the publication draws its readership.

Other *cultural knowledge*, which has not been codified, also plays a key role in most work-based practices. There is considerable debate about the extent to which such knowledge can be made explicit or represented in any textual form; and the evidence gathered so far suggests that its amenability to codification has been greatly exaggerated (Eraut, 2000). What does appear to be generally acknowledged is that much uncodified cultural knowledge is acquired informally through participation in social activities; and much is often so 'taken for granted' that people are unaware of its influence on their behaviour. This phenomenon is much broader in scope than the implicit learning normally associated with the concept of socialisation. In addition to the cultural practices and discourses of different professions and specialities, one has to consider the cultural knowledge that permeates the beliefs and behaviours of their co-workers, their clients and the general public.

The individual perspective is captured by my definition of *personal knowledge* as 'what individual persons bring to situations that enables them to think, interact and perform'. This incorporates both people's capabilities—what they can do—and the understandings that inform them. The distinctive feature of this definition is its focus on the *use* of personal knowledge, rather than its *truth*. This allows one to investigate the effects of personal knowledge without necessarily being able to represent that knowledge in codified form, thus incorporating aspects of personal expertise, practical wisdom and tacit knowledge that have not yet been made explicit. Thus it includes not only personalised codified knowledge (see below) but also everyday knowledge of people and situations, know-how in the form of skills and practices, memories of cases and episodic events. It could also include various aspects of self-knowledge, attitudes and emotions.

Two sources of evidence are available for describing personal knowledge, communications from the person concerned and observations of professional performance. A wide range of discourses may be used in such descriptions, but none of them are very satisfactory. This makes it important for an epistemology of practice to tackle the challenging problem of the nature of performance; and I use the term *'performance'* in a broad sense that includes those thoughts and actions, which take place within a chosen performance period, or which focus primarily upon preparing for, or reflecting on, that period. After several attempts I decided to build my analysis of performance around three dimensions. The first comprises four distinct but interconnected elements of almost any form of practice:

1. *Assessing clients and/or situations* (sometimes briefly, sometimes involving a long process of investigation) and continuing to monitor them;
2. *Deciding what, if any, action to take,* both immediately and over a longer period (either individually or as a leader or member of a team);

3. *Pursuing an agreed course of action,* modifying, consulting and reassessing as and when necessary;
4. *Metacognitive monitoring* of oneself, people needing attention and the general progress of the case, problem, project or situation.

Although analytically distinct, they are normally combined into an integrated perform-ance, which does not necessarily follow a simple sequence of assessment, decision and then action. [...]

These four elements of practice take different forms according to the speed and context and the type of technical and personal expertise being deployed. Table 3.1 incorporates my second dimension, time, and focuses on how the time variable affects the mode of cognition of the professionals concerned. The model divides the time-continuum into three columns, whose headings seek to describe the mode of cognition used by the performer. Hence, their timescales may differ according to the way the performer works. For example, in one context *rapid/intuitive* might refer to a minute, while in another context it might include periods of up to ten minutes or even half an hour. The critical feature is that the performer has limited time to deliberate or think in any depth.

The *instant/reflex* column describes routinised behaviour that, at most, is semicon-scious. The *rapid/intuitive* column indicates greater awareness of what one is doing, and is often characterised by rapid decision making within a period of continuous, semi-routinised action. Typically, it involves recognition of situations by comparison with similar situations previously encountered; then responding to them with already learned proce-dures (Klein, 1989; Eraut *et al.,* 1995). The time available affects the degree of mismatch that is tolerated, because rejection of familiar actions based on prior experience leads to deliberative, problem-solving and hence to a more time-consuming approach. The *deliberative/analytic* column is characterised by explicit thinking by individuals or groups, possibly accompanied by consultation with others. It often involves the conscious use of different types of prior knowledge, and their application to new situations. These areas of knowl-edge may be used in accustomed ways, sometimes with adaptation, or combined in novel ways that require a significant period of problem solving.

This leads us to Boshuizen's excellent (2003) summary of the changes in representation that accompany the development of expertise in doctors. Her interpretation of her own and other people's research is that successive modes of representation are developed as a per-son's expertise increases, and that the key advantages conferred by later modes of repre-sentation are their lower demand on the expert's cognitive capacity, more rapid access to usable information and a reduced need for deliberation. The building block for this devel-opment is the accumulation of individual cases; and the aggregation of those cases into increasingly large chunks of recognition is a largely unconscious process. In general, early career professional learning is characterised by the accumulation of a massive amount of experience, not all of which is consciously processed; and their representations of their acquired knowledge change as their learning progresses.

My third dimension, the context, is too complex to be included in the table, but its strong influence on professional formation is of great practical importance. Our project found the contextual influence on cognition was particularly strong for newly qualified nurses, and Jacklin *et al.* (2006) found similar problems affecting teachers. Both took on very chal-lenging roles in their first week and struggled to survive in extremely crowded and demanding environments. Their survival depended on them being able to reduce their

Table 3.1   Interactions between time, mode of cognition and the nature of practice

Type of Process	Mode of Cognition		
	Instant/Reflex	Rapid/Intuitive	Deliberative/Analytic
Assessment of the situation	Pattern recognition	Rapid interpretation	Prolonged diagnosis Review with discussions and/or analysis
Decision-making, single or serial	Instant response	Intuitive	Deliberative with some analysis or discussion
Overt actions or sequences of actions	Routinised action	Routines punctuated by rapid decisions	Planned actions with periodic progress reviews
Metacognition	Situational awareness	Implicit monitoring Short, reactive reflections	Conscious monitoring of thought and activity Reflection for learning

cognitive load by prioritisation and routinisation during their first year of employment. In addition to reducing their cognitive load, such routinisation frees up more thinking time for interacting with clients. However, our research experience with mid-career nurses and teachers indicates that what start as explicit routines often become tacit routines after several years of experience. This can make it difficult for them to explain their skills to novices, although working with novices may help them to make their routines explicit when needed for coaching or self-evaluation.

The development of a new typology of learning processes and activities

Much of the debate about the significance of our research into mid-career learning centred around our conclusion that the majority of the learning was informal learning within the workplace itself, and this was mostly triggered by (1) consultation and collaboration within the working group, (2) consultation outside the working group and (3) the challenge of the work itself (Eraut *et al.*, 2000). We anticipated that formal learning or formally supported learning would be more significant for early career professionals, and that a binary distinction between informal and formal learning might be a useful start. However, we found that this distinction was difficult to sustain when most new recruits were clearly recognised as 'learners', as in formal settings, but more likely to be given advice and feedback informally by those around them than by those designated as their mentors.

Hence we took a hint from Activity Theory and decided to classify learning processes according to whether their *principal object* was working or learning. Processes in the left column of Table 3.2 were judged to be working processes, from which learning was a by-product, while those in the right column are clearly recognisable as learning processes. Another problem arose when we became dissatisfied with including processes, which were clearly bounded and relatively time consuming, in the same list as very generic and often quite short activities, such as asking questions, observing or reflecting. These activities

Table 3.2   A typology of early career learning

Work Processes with learning as a by-product	Learning Activities located within work or learning processes	Learning Processes at or near the workplace
Participation in group processes	Asking questions	Being supervised
Working alongside others	Getting information	Being coached
Consultation	Locating resource people	Being mentored
Tackling challenging tasks and roles	Listening and observing	Shadowing
Problem solving	Reflecting	Visiting other sites
Trying things out	Learning from mistakes	Conferences
Consolidating, extending and refining skills	Giving and receiving feedback	Short courses
Working with clients	Use of mediating artifacts	Working for a qualification
		Independent study

could occur many times in a single process, and were found within almost every type of process, often several at a time. When we moved these 'activities' into a different category, the central column in Table 3.2, we obtained the much tidier typology that we finally used. We also included the use of mediating artifacts in the central column because, although some artifacts were used mainly during learning processes, more artifacts used for working were also used for learning.

Work processes with learning as a by-product

These processes accounted for a very high proportion of the reported learning of people we interviewed during our mid-career and early career projects. Their success depends both on their prevalence and on the quality of relationships in the workplace. Hence, the amount of learning reported varied significantly with person and context.

1. *Participation in group processes* covers team-working towards a common outcome, and groups set up for a special purpose such as audit, development or review of policy and/or practice, and responding to external changes. Such opportunities were important for some engineers and nurses, but most common among accountants. Closer inspection, however, suggested that, while accountants derived important emotional support from working in teams on client premises to tight deadlines, most of their specific learning could be better described as learning through working alongside others.
2. *Working alongside others* allows people to observe and listen to others at work and to participate in activities; and hence to learn some new practices and new perspectives, to become aware of different kinds of knowledge and expertise, and to gain some sense of other people's tacit knowledge. This mode of learning, which included a lot of observation as well as discussion, was extremely important for both accountants and nurses. For example, an observant accountant with little experience suddenly

realised how she could be a more proactive member of her audit team; and this triggered a shift in her professional identity:

> I saw [a colleague] finish something and he had a look through the file … [to] see what has been done, and he'd say 'Well this has not been done and I did this last week so do you want me to go and ask the client now?' I thought I can do that, I can say 'I did that last job [before], do you want me to go and do it?' and it's just so much better than saying I have got nothing to do. I think that was when it changed, because I started thinking I can do things for myself; and I am not just an employee, I am supposed to be part of a team … before that I was a bit of a tag along, they were the team and I was someone who was learning. Since then I have tried to make sure that I am part of it, rather than just an outsider that is trying to learn.

3. *Consultations* within or outside the working group, or even outside the organisation, are used to co-ordinate activities or to get advice. For early career professionals, the distinction between a consultation and 'being supervised' is not always clear. For example, a third-year trainee accountant in charge of an audit on a client's premises might proactively consult their manager in head office about some issue that had arisen, or receive phone calls from their manager of a clearly supervisory nature. First-year trainees also felt able to initiate consultations and were encouraged to do so. For example, one trainee who was asked to reconcile income accounts said:

> The term they use here is 'material', and material is what is most important … I'm starting to get an idea now that a lot of the problems they have… with their clients is basically shuffling money about … and it's hard to decide … does it really matter? I mean they would change it and … some of them yes it does matter, some of them it doesn't matter and I'm still not quite sure how to … find out what ones are appropriate … what information you find out is actually important and what is just … information that you find.

He dealt with his uncertainty by putting a note in the file to remind him to ask his manager.

4. *Tackling challenging tasks and roles* requires on-the job learning and, if well-supported and successful, leads to increased motivation and confidence. One nurse was promoted to an E grade about 18 months after qualifying. She had discussed promotion with her ward manager in her last appraisal, and she remembered saying then that she felt ready for it because the D grade role had become less of a challenge:

> You feel like you can't grow any more in your role and I think that I needed to expand in order to extend my skills …

Her new role entailed responsibility for the whole ward on some shifts; and she saw this as a way of developing her managerial knowledge and skills:

> There is a lot going on in this ward, particularly overnight, you're left in charge and it's organising transfers, discharges, making sure who's going home, who's going for certain procedures … and supervising some of the junior staff and students.

Another example was an engineer who was suddenly asked to give a presentation for his company on gas distribution, because no senior people were available:

I said, 'Well I don't know anything about gas distribution'. They said 'You've got a week to learn, haven't you?' I actually got two days to learn, so I went on the internet, phoned up everybody I knew and asked all the silly questions. You look like a fool but you try and remember as much as you can ... I went to the meeting, we got the job and the rest as they say is history; but then that's where the hard work begins, that's where you have to read all the reports and the reports are always written from the point of view of somebody who understands [it all].

This incident led to him becoming a gas engineering specialist, hence his reference to history.

5. *Problem solving,* individually or in groups, necessarily entails learning; otherwise there would be no problem. Such problems were not just technical, they could also involve interpersonal negotiation:

    You speak to three clients within one organization who are all responsible for one end product but their individual responsibilities are open to question. So liaising three groups to ensure that each of the three groups agree with what you're thinking was something that I had never learned before ... and that was a problem. I didn't appreciate how difficult it is to identify an error ... it's just making sure you've got everybody's agreement because obviously there is a timetable ... [I'm] supposed to see that it happens, but I suppose ... you're more of a catalyst than a driver in that you may encourage things to happen ... but ... if you weren't there, it wouldn't have happened.

6. *Trying things out* is often the preferred approach of engineers, and was also used by nurses for improving non-clinical aspects of their job such as time management and communication:

    I think it's just trial and error ... you get used to how many children you know you can take per day or per week ... and then some weeks you get it right ... and then the next week you might have an emergency referral or something or one of your terminal children needs more packages and you might end up working quite a few extra hours, so it doesn't always work out ... I try and think ahead more now, which I didn't when I first started.

7. *Consolidating, extending and refining skills* is particularly important in early career work, when it is sometimes supported by episodes of supervision, coaching or feedback. Two first-year accountants emphasised the cumulative nature of this process:

    Every audit you go on you will have picked up things cumulatively from all the other audits you've been on. So if you come across that section again you might think 'last time I had to dig out that as well as that', and cross reference that back. So if you just took two snap shots, one of when you start and one of now, your work would be completely different. But rather than being one specific incident ... it's more cumulative ... especially as the jobs are pretty short.

A first-year nurse described her growing confidence in monitoring drug doses through picking things up at handover, observing other nurses and questioning the doctors:

    I think it's something that I've just learned and that's even been pretty recently over the last ... month or so, just kind of looking at peoples' drugs and realising

> why they're on them and questioning with the doctors whether they still need to be on them or whether the doses need to be upped or downed or things like that. That is something that … I've observed in other nurses … the basics are starting to really click now and I'm just thinking 'Well, why does this person need to be on this drug', for instance … yeah, I think just practice and … questioning the doctors and being told the rationale as well, and I think that rationale is beginning to stick now for why certain patients are on certain drugs and what the correct doses should be.

8. *Working with clients* also entails learning (1) about the client, (2) from any novel aspects of each client's problem or request and (3) from any new ideas that arise from the encounter. Nurses clearly learn from their daily experience of working with patients, and learning about their patients directly or indirectly is a constant feature of their work, which prompts routine responses, problem solving or consultation. In many wards, novices progress from looking after less ill patients to those at greater risk; and handling certain types of patient requires further formal training as well as more experience. Some graduate engineers never met a client, others had occasional meetings to plan or discuss ongoing work, which usually helped them to understand further facets of their projects. Most trainee accountants spent half their time on client premises, so learning from clients was a central part of their work. Like some nurses, they began with clients with less complex concerns and progressed to more complex clients. Their cumulative understanding of how clients did their business was an important part of their growing capability, as illustrated by the comments of a first-year trainee:

> When I started, [knowing] what was going on was the hardest thing, whereas … now I understand what's going on pretty much all the time … You have to understand the client's business … for example the one I went [to] today, timber agents, I can't say I've ever been anywhere near a timber agents until Tuesday morning when I went out there. So it's understanding what they do … because they all know their business backwards and you're expected to go in there and … pick up on it straight away, and that's sometimes the hardest bit I find … I think … the more businesses you go to, the more different things you see, actually the more you can take those different bits into new jobs with you. Every time you go into a new job it doesn't look quite as strange as it did the job before … you get more understanding and that … leads to a bit more confidence in what you're doing and questions you're asking.

There can also be a strong emotional dimension, which most professionals have to learn to handle. People expect this with nurses, but even accountants have to consider emotional responses when they communicate bad news:

> It is quite difficult because they're not very happy with you picking up problems.

Recognised learning processes

The right column of Table 3.2 lists nine processes whose prime object is learning. These are listed in terms of their proximity to the workplace. Thus, supervision, coaching and mentoring are at or very near the learner's normal workplace; shadowing and visiting other sites are usually in other people's workplaces; conferences, short courses and working for qualifications are usually not in workplace settings; and independent study can be followed almost anywhere that is quiet.

1. *Direct supervision by line managers* was rarely observed. Although all our participants had line managers, they rarely provided day-to-day supervision. In the first two years, this was provided by the person 'in charge' of the relevant working group. By the third year, our accountants and nurses often occupied this role themselves, but this was rare for the engineers.

2. *Designated mentors* were provided by all our partner employers for the first year. However, most support was provided by *'helpful others'*, who were not designated mentors, examplifying what Nielsen and Kvale (1997) call *'distributed apprenticeship'*. This worked so well in accountancy that mentors were rarely mentioned, whereas in nursing some official mentors were a lifeline for their novices, while others were allocated elsewhere or unwilling to take the role seriously. Engineers often had two mentors, one for normal company support and one for guidance on becoming a Chartered Engineer. Both were appointed for three years, but very few took their roles seriously. When our participants received mentoring in the third year, it was usually focused more on developing responsibility and tended to be provided by those managers who saw it as an investment.

> You see the senior engineers, the people like David, and you watch how they manage a project and, if your mentor's good, he will start feeding in bits and pieces; when you're comfortable with it, he'll give you a little bit more; when you're comfortable with that, he'll then give you a little bit more. With time you're doing pretty much everything he was doing and ... he's happy because that's one less responsibility for him ... he's invested the time in training you, your capability is now better and he can concentrate on other issues.

3. *Coaching* was quite common in the early months of our nursing and accountancy participants, but there was little sign of formally designated coaches. It occurred quite naturally on audit visits, when third-year trainees 'in charge' on a client site made time to coach newcomers on tasks that they were about to be assigned.

> I only just knew what a debtor was when I went to them [the seniors], and they sat down and just talked through the test and ... how they'd do it, and you went off [and] got all the information ... tried it out yourself and then, any problems [take to the senior] ... I almost had to be talked through the first few things when I was doing it ... once you've done it once ... even though each company does things a bit differently, you don't need nearly as much help ... the second time you do it.

In nursing, there were examples of spontaneous coaching being offered within the ward, but it usually needed a manager to find somebody to take on the duties of the would-be coach. As a result, the coaching was often more rushed than it should have been. Many of the technical skills taught by on-the-job coaching could have been taught on day courses and often such courses were available. But staff shortages frequently prevented novices from attending such courses or receiving important coaching when it was needed.

4. *Shadowing* and *visits to other sites* were usually formal extensions to the observation opportunities available through learners' normal work. For engineers, however, site visits were very important for building up a wider understanding of projects and the roles of other professional groups, as the following quotation from an engineer shows:

> Today I'm looking at one particular project preparing for a meeting on Thursday where we're going to need to discuss the different options for the provision of the storage tank; so I need to explore perhaps the different locations of different company set-ups. I will need to have a chat with other mechanical and electrical engineers and to discuss the pump sizes and see what's going to be the most efficient way … You can't isolate little bits … it's a complete story, it's as one. You can't just say well okay I'm going to go and size a pump … it depends on how you lay out the site whether you need any pumps at all … So you have to look at it as a sort of more global problem, which is why it's going to be discussed on Thursday … We could make a decision as to what kind of storage tanks are available, whether they will put the pumps within the tank or whether we're going to have the pumps further down the site.

We found that almost all civil and mechanical engineers got practical experience through site visits or secondments, but these opportunities were only available for four out of the 14 electrical engineers, leaving a major gap in their learning, which was much resented.

5. *Conference* attendance was unusual for our early career professionals, and *short courses* were the main kind of formal Continuing Professional Development. Our partner engineering companies and hospitals provided extensive short course programmes, but getting time off to attend them was often difficult for the nurses.

6. *Working for a qualification* was compulsory for the trainee accountants, who needed to get their initial professional qualification; and spent several months at private 'colleges' contracted by their employers to provide the associated training. With one or two exceptions, and sometimes an initial delay in recognising its relevance, this college work was appreciated and gave them more confidence when talking to clients:

> It's a combination really, it's not so much college as the knowledge you get from college, and that you understand the issues you're talking about more, that helps your confidence. It's a lot easier to talk about stuff you understand.

The graduate engineers were recruited to accredited training schemes intended to support their wish to become Chartered Engineers; but they soon encountered work contexts in which Chartered Engineers were scarce and the value of the qualification was not recognised. A small number of nurses started to take part-time degree courses a year or two after qualification and were supported in this by their employers.

7. *Independent study* may be supported by the provision of knowledge resources and/or agreed plans, such as lists of competences, learning projects or personal development plans. Formal training and knowledge resources such as manuals, reference books, documentation, protocols and an intranet were generally available to

all workers, the engineers in particular using the intranet as their prime source of current information. When considering the role of materials, it is important to distinguish between (1) materials such as audit files or protocols that are part of the work process and (2) manuals or guides to the work. Apart from essential textbooks for the trainee accountants, manuals and guides received limited use. Learners generally found it quicker and more effective to get information directly from more knowledgeable colleagues.

Learning activities located within the processes described above

The nine learning activities in the central column of Table 3.2 were embedded within most of the work processes and learning processes described above, but were also found in short opportunistic episodes. The key issues for learning are the frequency and quality of their use.

1. *Asking questions* and *getting information* are important, proactive activities; and good questions and knowledge searches are appreciated in positive learning contexts. Trainee accountants were expected to ask questions and criticised for not doing so, and this was usually eased by the presence of trainees only a few months ahead of them, who still remembered what it was like to be a novice:

   > I generally just ask lots of questions … because I'm conscious that I don't want to waste too much time trying to work it out myself.
   >   Every client is slightly different … So often by asking them how they do things their own way you can find out how it's normally done and that helps you get a better understanding of what's going on.

   The accountants and engineers were selected for their proactive attitudes, and most graduate engineers were encouraged by an 'ask anyone culture'. However, student nurses did not receive that kind of encouragement on many wards. Finding a good question depends on prior knowledge that newly qualified nurses may lack, but think they ought to know. They fear that asking a bad question may harm their reputation, so they are often reluctant to ask questions unless they have a good trusting relationship with those being asked. Even if you do have good questions, there are many situations where knowing when and how to ask them, or when to stop asking them, requires special social skills.

2. *Locating resource people* is also a proactive activity that requires confidence and social understanding. Some early career professionals were very proactive in seeking out and developing relationships with a wider network of knowledge resource people, while others gave it little attention, often because they did not appreciate its potential value. Finding the right people was particularly important for many accountants working on client premises, and engineers seeking particular types of specialist expertise:

> You need to speak to the right people and you need to figure out who the right people are. (Accountant)
>
> Well, you go to T, for a section of the work ... but he is not possibly the most helpful of people ... he sometimes doesn't understand what you're asking or doesn't give you a very full answer ... If I've got a problem, I really feel is important, I'd go to J or P. It's not that T is less approachable, it's just that I find J's input to my situation is more constructive, more helpful. (Engineer)

3. *Listening and observing* activities are very dependent on what the observer/listener is able to grasp and comprehend; and comprehension depends on awareness of the significance of what has been said and/or done. Such awareness and understanding are developed through discussion and *reflection.*

4. *Learning from mistakes* is possible in most working contexts, both from one's own mistakes and those of others; but opportunities for this activity are frequently missed. As one engineer observed:

> A lot of the time it depends on the individual and whether they learn from their mistakes on the job ... Everyone makes mistakes ... it's just whether or not we can sit down on a forum and say 'yes, I screwed up on that project, you know, but these are the lessons'. You don't make these mistakes again because I know them ... If you make another set of mistakes you get up and let me know what they were, so I'm aware ... We all learn off each other, this is at graduate level.

5. *Giving and receiving feedback* are both important, often vital, for most learning processes. We found that learners needed short-term, task-specific, feedback as well as longer-term, more strategic, feedback on general progress. Interestingly, good short-term feedback on performance was often accompanied by an almost total absence of strategic feedback, giving even the most confident workers an unnecessary sense of uncertainty and lowering their commitment to their current employers (Eraut, 2006).

6. *Mediating artifacts* like audit files, design specifications, circuit diagrams or handover notes plays a very important role in structuring work and sharing information. They mediated group learning about clients or projects in progress. Some artifacts in daily use served to carry information in a standard way that novices soon learned to understand. In both nursing and engineering, these included measurements, diagrams and photographs. For example, patient records covered temperature, fluid intake and output, drugs administration, biochemical data and various types of image. These referred both to the immediate past and to plans for the immediate future, and salient features considered important were prioritised for the incoming shift at every handover. Understanding the thinking behind the handover rituals was essential learning for newly qualified nurses.

A mechanical engineer was observed discussing virtual design 'drawings' on the screen over the telephone with colleagues, contractors and clients on an almost daily basis; and she also sent digital photographs and measurements to initiate a discussion about a sagging bar. A water mains planning engineer and her colleagues all used her meterage progress reports to decide whether to clean out a mains pipe, re-line it with plastic piping, or replace it—all with different associated cost and time implications.

Accountants learned how to interpret audit files and the 'tests' they were given for sampling their clients' data. They learned to give some priority to significant changes in accounts over time; and they needed considerable tact to find out how their clients' business processes were represented in their accounts, when their clients' accountants regarded this as self-evident.

Then at a higher level of complexity, engineers used design specifications and software packages; and nurses used the MEWS protocol for deciding when a patient needed urgent attention and patient pathway protocols for patients with particular conditions. Accountants used software packages for organising their auditing processes. The really expensive ones were used as a guide for the auditors through their tasks, as a framework for assigning subtasks, as a repository of accumulated judgements, as an archive of explanatory material, and as a record for the following year. The distinctiveness of these higher level artifacts was their incorporation of a considerable amount of professional knowledge, and they could be used, albeit under supervision, before all that knowledge had been acquired.

The factors affecting workplace learning

One prominent finding of our earlier research on mid-career learning was the overwhelming importance of *confidence*. Much learning at work occurs through doing things and being proactive in seeking learning opportunities; and this requires confidence. Moreover, we noted that confidence arose from successfully meeting *challenges* in one's work, while the confidence to take on such challenges depended on the extent to which learners felt *supported* in that endeavour by colleagues, either while doing the job or as back-up when working independently. Thus, there is a triangular relationship between challenge, support and confidence (Eraut *et al.*, 2000). The contextual significance of the word *'confidence'*, which was used by our respondents without further elaboration, depended on which aspects of this triangular relationship were most significant for particular people at particular points in their careers. The first meaning was context-specific, and related to their capability to execute a particular task or successfully perform a role. The second meaning related more to *relationships* than to the work itself. Did they feel confident about the *support* and *trust* of their working colleagues? This could range from being mutually supportive to giving only negative feedback. For early career professionals, this latter aspect of confidence was more prominent.

Figure 3.1 shows how our early career project, where observations over a three-year period added greatly to our understanding of contexts, was able to expand this triangular relationship to include new features. We added *feedback* to support and the *value of the work* to the challenge, because both had a major influence on *motivation* and *commitment*. Feedback was especially important during the first few months of a new job, when it was often best provided by the person on the spot. This happened within the 'distributed apprenticeship' approach we found in accountancy, and in other organisations where local workplaces had developed a positive learning culture of mutual support. In the longer term, more normative feedback on progress and meeting organisational expectations also became important.

Equally important for developing confidence after the first few months was the right level of *challenge*. Newly qualified nurses were *over-challenged* physically, mentally and

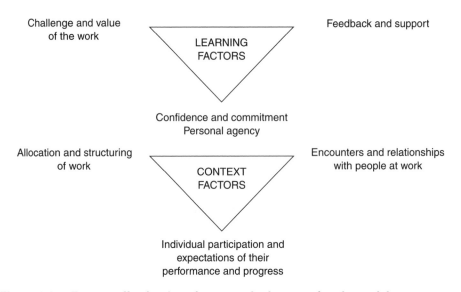

Figure 3.1   Factors affecting learning at work: the two triangle model

emotionally by their sudden increase in responsibility and the unceasing pressure of work in most ward environments. While some engineers progressed through a series of challenging assignments with remarkable rapidity, most of them were *under-challenged* and many of them were seriously under-challenged. Nearly all the accountants, however, were appropriately challenged for the majority of their traineeship. The *value of their work* carried many nurses through their unnecessarily pressured start, and this was strengthened in some contexts by their *social inclusion* in supportive teams. We also noted the importance of *personal agency* in sustaining their motivation after their early period of settling into their new environment; and this was significantly influenced by their *sense of choice* over work activities and a *sense of progress* in their purpose.

Figure 3.1 also presents a second triangle, which mirrors the first triangle but focuses on the *Contextual Factors* that influence the *Learning Factors.* The first of these factors, the *allocation and structuring of work,* was central to our participants' progress, because it affected (1) the difficulty or challenge of the work, (2) the extent to which it was individual or collaborative, and (3) the opportunities for meeting, observing and working alongside people who had more or different expertise, and for forming *relationships* that might provide *feedback and support.* For novice professionals to make good progress, a significant proportion of their work needed to be sufficiently new to challenge them without being so daunting as to reduce their confidence. Their workload needed to be at a level that allowed them to respond to new challenges reflectively, rather than develop coping mechanisms that might later prove ineffective. Thus, managers and/or senior colleagues had to balance the immediate demands of the job against the needs of the trainees to broaden their experience. This usually worked well in our two accountancy organisations; but in engineering the appropriateness of the allocated work differed hugely according to the company and the speciality. Very few graduate engineers in electronics or computer science had sufficiently challenging work and nobody appeared to take any responsibility for addressing this problem. In nursing, the quality of learning was mainly influenced by the ward manager and her senior nurses; some of the best and worst learning environments we observed were in the same departments of the same hospitals.

Once common problem across all our partner organisations was appraisal, where participants' concerns about meeting both their own and their employers' *expectations* of their *performance* and *progress* arose from inadequate *feedback* of a normative kind; and this weakened their *motivation* and *commitment* to their organisation (Eraut, 2006). Eraut *et al.* (2005b) provide a more substantial account of these factors and their interactions. We suspect that this problem may arise from (1) a lack of attention to the preparation and timing of appraisals, or (2) the appraiser not having sufficient information to provide normative feedback, or (3) a lack of any trust between the two parties.

We found that decisions affecting the structuring and allocation of work could be determined by any combination of the following factors:

1. The nature of the work, the way in which the organisation handled it and the discretion given to local managers in decisions of this kind. In all three of our professions, local managers had significant opportunities to facilitate learning through their allocation of work and support of novice workers.
2. The quantity and urgency of the work in hand at the time. This was a major issue in hospitals where work overload almost overwhelmed novice nurses, while at the same time reducing the amount of support they could get from more experienced colleagues; and was sometimes important in engineering, if a company was undergoing a fallow period that limited the supply of challenging assignments.
3. Periodic decisions made by managers in which learning needs might or might not have been considered. This was relevant when allocating novices to audit teams, nursing shifts or medium-term engineering tasks.
4. Decisions made by more experienced colleagues with delegated authority, who were currently working with the novice, and were probably best able to judge the appropriate level of challenge if they thought it was important.

Whether these decisions benefited the learning of the novice professional depended on the disposition, imagination, competence (in making these kinds of decisions) and available thinking time of those who made them.

Conclusions and their implications for enhancing workplace learning

This project has confirmed that the majority of workers' learning occurs in the workplace itself. Formal learning contributes most when it is both relevant and well-timed, but still needs further workplace learning before it can be used to best effect. Our data suggest that there is considerable scope for enhancing workplace learning in a wide range of contexts. Hence, the current neglect of workplace learning by national policies and by most public and private organisations needs to be remedied. Our key findings, summarised below, support, enhance and exemplify in greater detail and depth the results of our previous projects (Eraut *et al.,* 2000).

1. *Support and feedback*

   These are critically important for learning, retention and commitment. Feedback is most effective within the context of good working relationships. Much feedback is best provided by people on the spot, such as members of audit teams and in other contexts where the local workplace has developed a positive learning culture of mutual support. More normative feedback on progress, strengths and weaknesses, and meeting organisational expectations is also needed. The emotional dimension of working life requires ongoing attention, which goes well beyond supportive relationships to include a sense of being a valued professional whose progress meets expectations and who continues to construct a professional identity that is personally and socially valued.

2. *Enhancing workplace learning*

   The quantity and quality of learning can be enhanced by increasing opportunities for consulting with and working alongside others in teams or temporary groups. Both being over-challenged, like some of the nurses in the first few months, and being under-challenged, like several engineers, is detrimental to learning and bad for morale. Both issues can be tackled by giving greater attention to the allocation and structuring of appropriate work.

3. *The manager's role*

   Managers have a major influence on workplace learning and culture that extends far beyond their job descriptions. Their role is to develop a culture of mutual support and learning, not to provide all the support themselves. They need to share this role with experienced workers, and this implies some form of distributed leadership. This role should be given much greater priority in management development programmes, incorporated into qualifications for managers and supervisors, and included in the appraisal of all managers.

4. *The knowledge required*

   Novices, mentors and managers all need:

- To have greater awareness of the range of ways through which people can learn in the workplace (Table 3.2)
- To be able to discuss learning needs in the context of a record of progress in relevant aspects of performance. This is described in greater detail in Eraut *et al.*, 2005a and Eraut, 2007
- To recognise and attend to the *factors which enhance or hinder individual or group learning* (Figure 3.1) (Eraut *et al.*, 2005b). [...]

References

Argyris, C. & Schön, D. A. (1974) *Theory into practice: increasing professional effectiveness* (San Francisco, Jossey Bass).

Boshuizen, H. P. A. (2003) Expertise development: how to bridge the gap between school and work, Inaugural address (Heerlen, Open Universiteit Nederland).

Eraut, M. (2000) Non-formal learning and tacit knowledge in professional work, *British Journal of Educational Psychology,* 70, 113–136.

Eraut, M. (2004) Transfer of knowledge between education and workplace setting, in: H. Rainbird, A. Fuller & H. Munro (Eds) *Workplace learning in context* (London, Routledge), 201–221.

Eraut, M. (2006) Formative assessment in the workplace, symposium paper, *AERA Annual Conference,* San Francisco.

Eraut, M. (2007) Early career learning at work and its implications for universities, in: N. Entwistle & P. Tomlinson (Eds) *Student learning and university teaching, British Journal of Psychology, Monograph Series* II, 4, 113–133.

Eraut, M., Alderton, J., Boylan, A. & Wraight, A. (1995) *Learning to use scientific knowledge in education and practice settings* (London, English National Board for Nursing, Midwifery and Health visiting).

Eraut, M., Alderton, J., Cole, G. & Senker, P. (2000) Development of knowledge and skills at work, in; F. Coffield (Ed.) *Differing visions of a learning society,* Vol. 1 (Bristol, The Policy Press), 231–262.

Eraut, M., Maillardet, F., Miller, C., Steadman, S., Ali, A., Blackman, C. & Furner, J. (2005a) What is learned in the workplace and how? Typologies and results from a cross-professional longitudinal study, paper presented at the *EARLI Biannual Conference,* Nicosia.

Eraut, M., Maillardert, F., Miller, C., Steadman, S., Ali, A., Blackman, C. & Furner, J. (2005b) An analytical tool for characterizing and comparing professional workplace learning environments, paper presented at the *BERA Annual Conference,* Pontypridd.

Jacklin, A., Griffiths, V. & Robinson, C. (2006) *Beginning primary teaching: moving beyond survival* (Maidenhead, Open University Press).

Klein, G. A. (1989) Recognition-primed decisions, in: W. B. Rouse (Ed.) *Advances in man-machine systems research* (Greenwich, CT, JAI Press), 47–92.

Nielsen, K. & Kvale, S. (1997) Current issues of apprenticeship, *Nordisk Pedagogik,* 17(3), 130–139.

Nonaka, I. & Takeuchi, H. (1995) The *knowledge creating company* (Oxford, Oxford University Press).

Steadman, S., Eraut, M., Maillardet, F., Miller, C., Ali, A., Blackman, C. & Furner, J. (2005) Methodological challenges in studying workplace learning: strengths and limitations of the adopted approach, paper presented at the *EARLI Biannual Conference,* Nicosia.

4

Observing Sociocultural Activity on Three Planes: Participatory Appropriation, Guided Participation, and Apprenticeship

Barbara Rogoff

This chapter proposes a sociocultural approach that involves observation of development in three planes of analysis corresponding to personal, interpersonal, and community processes. I refer to developmental processes corresponding with these three planes of analysis as apprenticeship, guided participation, and participatory appropriation, in turn. These are inseparable, mutually constituting planes comprising activities that can become the focus of analysis at different times, but with the others necessarily remaining in the background of the analysis. I argue that children take part in the activities of their community, engaging with other children and with adults in routine and tacit as well as explicit collaboration (both in each others' presence and in otherwise socially structured activities), and in the process of participation become prepared for later participation in related events.

Developmental research has commonly limited attention to either the individual or the environment – for example, examining how adults teach children or how children construct reality, with an emphasis on either separate individuals or independent environmental elements as the basic units of analysis. Even when both the individual and the environment are considered, they are often regarded as separate entities rather than being mutually defined and interdependent in ways that preclude their separation as units or elements (Dewey & Bentley, 1949; Pepper, 1942; Rogoff, 1982, 1992).

Vygotsky's emphasis on the interrelated roles of the individual and the social world in microgenetic, ontogenetic, sociocultural, and phylogenetic development (Scribner, 1985; Wertsch, 1985) includes the individual and the environment together in successively broader time frames. Likewise, Vygotsky's interest in the mutuality of the individual and the sociocultural environment is apparent in his concern with finding a unit of analysis that preserves the essence of the events of interest rather than separating an event into elements that no longer function as does the whole (e.g., studying water molecules rather than hydrogen and oxygen to understand the behavior of water; Cole, 1985; Leont'ev, 1981; Wertsch, 1985; Zinchenko, 1985).

The use of 'activity' or 'event' as the unit of analysis – with active and dynamic contributions from individuals, their social partners, and historical traditions and materials and their transformations – allows a reformulation of the relation between the individual

From: Wertsch, J.V., Del Rio, P., Alvarez, A. (eds.) *Sociocultural Studies of Mind* (Cambridge: Cambridge University Press, 1995). © Cambridge University Press 1995, reproduced with permission.

and the social and cultural environments in which each is inherently involved in the others' definition. None exists separately.

Nonetheless, the parts making up a whole activity or event can be considered separately as foreground without losing track of their inherent interdependence in the whole. Their structure can be described without assuming that the structure of each is independent of that of the others. Foregrounding one plane of focus still involves that participation of the backgrounded planes of focus.

By analogy, the organs in an organism work together with an inherent interdependence, but if we are interested in foregrounding the functioning of the heart or the skin, we can describe their structure and functioning, remembering that by themselves the organs would not have such structure or functioning. (See Rogoff, 1992, for further discussion of this issue.) Similarly, we may consider a single person thinking or the functioning of a whole community in the foreground without assuming that they are actually separate elements. 'The study of mind, of culture, and of language (in all its diversity) are internally related: that is, it will be *impossible* to render any one of these domains intelligible without essential reference to the others' (Bakhurst, 1988, p. 39, discussing Ilyenkov and activity theory).

Vygotsky's and Dewey's theories focus on children participating with other people in a social order with a seamless involvement of individuals in sociocultural activity. For Vygotsky (1978, 1987), children's cognitive development had to be understood as taking place through their interaction with other members of the society who are more conversant with the society's intellectual practices and tools (especially language) for mediating intellectual activity. Dewey (1916) provided a similar account:

> Every individual has grown up, and always must grow up, in a social medium. His responses grow intelligent, or gain meaning, simply because he lives and acts in a medium of accepted meanings and values. (p. 344)

> The social environment … is truly educative in its effects in the degree in which an individuals shares or participates in some conjoint activity. By doing his share in the associated activity, the individual appropriates the purpose which actuates it, becomes familiar with its methods and subject matters, acquires needed skill, and is saturated with its emotional spirit. (p. 26)

Without an understanding of such mutually constituting processes, a sociocultural approach is at times assimilated to other approaches that examine only part of the package. For example, it is incomplete to focus only on the relationship of individual development and social interaction without concern for the cultural activity in which personal and interpersonal actions take place. And it is incomplete to assume that development occurs in one plane and not in others (e.g., that children develop but that their partners or their cultural communities do not) or that influence can be ascribed in one direction or another or that relative contributions can be counted (e.g., parent to child, child to parent, culture to individual).

In this chapter, I discuss apprenticeship, guided participation, and participatory appropriation (Rogoff, 1990, 1993), which I regard as inseparable concepts reflecting different planes of focus in sociocultural activity – community/institutional, interpersonal, and personal. I conceive of planes of focus not as separate or as hierarchical, but as simply involving different grains of focus with the whole sociocultural activity. To understand each requires the involvement of the others. Distinguishing them serves the function of clarifying the plane of focus that may be chosen for one or another discussion of processes in the whole activity, holding the other planes of focus in the background but not separated.

The metaphor of *apprenticeship* provides a model in the plane of community activity, involving active individuals participating with others in culturally organized activity that has as part of its purpose the development of mature participation in the activity by the less experienced people. This metaphor extends the idea of craft apprenticeship to include participation in any other culturally organized activity, such as other kinds of work, schooling, and family relations.[1] The idea of apprenticeship necessarily focuses attention on the specific nature of the activity involved, as well as on its relation to the practices and institutions of the community in which it occurs – economic, political, spiritual, and material.

The concept of *guided participation* refers to the processes and systems of involvement between people as they communicate and coordinate efforts while participating in culturally valued activity. This includes not only the face-to-face interaction, which has been the subject of much research, but also the side-by-side joint participation that is frequent in everyday life and the more distal arrangements of people's activities that do not require copresence (e.g., choices of where and with whom and with what materials and activities a person is involved). The 'guidance' referred to in guided participation involves the direction offered by cultural and social values, as well as social partners;[2] the 'participation' in guided participation refers to observation, as well as hands-on involvement in an activity.

The concept of *participatory appropriation* refers to how individuals change through their involvement in one or another activity, in the process becoming prepared for subsequent involvement in related activities. With guided participation as the interpersonal process through which people are involved in sociocultural activity, participatory appropriation is the personal process by which, through engagement in an activity, individuals change and handle a later situation in ways prepared by their own participation in the previous situation. This is a process of becoming, rather than acquisition, as I argue later.

The remainder of this chapter explores the concepts of apprenticeship, guided participation, and especially, participatory appropriation in greater detail. I illustrate them with observations of the processes involved in planning routes, keeping track of sales and deliveries, and calculating charges as Girl Scouts of America sell and deliver Girl Scout cookies. This activity was chosen for investigation because it allows us as researchers to examine personal, interpersonal, and community processes that we ourselves have not devised.

Apprenticeship

A metaphor that has appealed to many scholars who focus on the mutual embeddedness of the individual and the sociocultural world is that of apprenticeship. In apprenticeship, newcomers to a community of practice advance their skill and understanding through participation with others in culturally organized activities (Bruner, 1983; Dewey, 1916; Goody, 1989; John-Steiner, 1985; Lave & Wenger, 1991; Rogoff, 1990). The metaphor focuses attention on the active roles of newcomers and others in arranging activities and support for developing participation, as well as on the cultural/institutional practices and goals of the activities to which they contribute.

The apprenticeship metaphor has at times been used to focus on expert–novice dyads; however, apprenticeship involves more than dyads. Apprenticeship relates a small group in a community with a specialization of roles oriented toward the accomplishment of goals that relate the group to others outside the group. The small group may involve peers who serve as resources and challenges for each other in exploring an activity, along with experts (who, like peers, are still developing skill and understanding in the process of engaging in activities with others of varying experience). Apprenticeship as a concept goes far beyond expert–novice dyads; it focuses on a system of interpersonal involvements and arrangements in which people engage in culturally organized activity in which apprentices become more responsible participants.

Research that focuses on the community plane using the metaphor of apprenticeship examines the institutional structure and cultural technologies of intellectual activity (say, in school or work). For example, it encourages the recognition that endeavors involve purposes (defined in community or institutional terms), cultural constraints, resources, values relating to what means are appropriate for reaching goals (such as improvisation versus planning all moves before beginning to act), and cultural tools such as maps, pencils, and linguistic and mathematical systems.

I describe Girl Scout cookie sales and delivery in the three sections of this chapter dealing with apprenticeship, guided participation, and participatory appropriation to highlight the point that these different planes of analysis are mutually constituting and cannot stand alone in the analysis of the activity. In this section, description of this activity as apprenticeship – focusing on the community and institutional aspects of the activity – would be impossible without reference to the personal and interpersonal aspects of the endeavor. Likewise, to understand the personal or interpersonal processes that become the focus of later sections, it is essential to understand the historical/institutional contexts of this activity, which define the practices in which scouts and their companions engage and at the same time are transformed by successive generations of scouts. Individual scouts are active in learning and managing the activity, along with their companions, as they participate in and extend community, institutional practices that began more than seven decades before.

For readers who are familiar with the activity of Girl Scout cookie sales and delivery, information in this plane of analysis may be so taken for granted that it seems unnecessary to state. However, that is in the nature of cultural understanding: it is essential, yet so taken for granted that special efforts are needed to draw attention to important features of the obvious (Smedslund, 1984).

Our team (Rogoff, Baker-Sennett, Lacasa, & Goldsmith, 1995) chose to study cookie sales because we wanted to go outside the usual institutions of research such as those of schooling and laboratories, which of course also involve interpersonal and institutional contexts, but which are more difficult to study because researchers are more likely to take them for granted. Systems in which one is completely immersed are difficult even to detect. Analysis of the sociocultural nature of social and individual activity is difficult for researchers embedded in educational situations or research traditions that are often seen as the way things must be rather than just one way that things happen to be.

Comparisons across cultures are often useful in drawing the attention of insiders of a community to unnoticed assumptions and practices. Fortunately, the readership of this chapter – an international community of scholars – requires making the cultural/institutional plane explicit, for the practices involved in Girl Scout cookie sales are local to the United States. Historical changes in the practices of this activity provide another tool for becoming more aware of the cultural/community plane of analysis as present generations of scouts and cookie companies continue to contribute to the ongoing, developing cultural process constituting the practices of the apprenticeship. So, what follows in this section is an account of the institutional/cultural plane of the activity, which I am viewing as apprenticeship.

Cookie sales are a major annual fund-raising effort of the Girl Scouts of America, a voluntary organization dedicated to girls' moral education, the development of home, academic, and outdoor skills, and career preparation. The scouts meet on a weekly basis in units called troops, which involve about a dozen scouts and one or two women as leaders. The funds from cookie sales are used to support the troops' activities, regional administration, and girls' participation in day campus and summer camps run by the organization.

The scouts compose the sales force, trained and supervised by the organization, that goes door-to-door selling to family and friends (or getting their parents to sell cookies at work). Most scouts participate in the sales and take their economic role very seriously; their parents must sign a form agreeing to be responsible for the large sums of money involved. Originally, the cookies were both baked and sold by the scout troops; now the scouts have older sisters or mothers who themselves sold Girl Scout cookies when they were scouts; older customers are often eager to buy cookies as they remember their own efforts to sell Girl Scout cookies.

Our study involved working with two troops of 10- and 11-year-old scouts in Salt Lake City, Utah. In one troop, we became 'cookie chairs' and underwent the training to serve as the troop's organizers of the sale (a role usually filled by a mother of a girl in the troop, which one of us was). In the other troop, we observed the process. The girls became our collaborators and suggested that we give them tape recorders to carry around to record their sales and deliveries, which we did.[3]

The collective activity of planning cookie sales and delivery occurs with the constraints and resources provided by the traditions and practices of the Girl Scout organization and associated baking companies, which set deadlines and provide organizational supports to the girls in their efforts to keep track of sales, cookies, and money, as well as to manage their time and resources. The scouts (currently) take orders on a glossy order form provided by the cookie company and deliver cookies a month later, according to dates set by the regional administration. The cookie order form is color coded in a way that facilitates keeping track of the different kinds of cookie. (For example, customers order Thin Mints by indicating the number of boxes desired in the green column; the number of Trefoils is indicated in the yellow column. The boxes and cases of cookies and other materials maintain this color coding.) The order form is laid out to facilitate the calculation of amounts of money, the presentation of information to customers, and keeping track of deliveries.

To illustrate focusing on the apprenticeship or community plane of analysis, this section has described Girl Scout cookie sales in terms of the institutional organization and evolution of community practices. These, of course, could not be described without reference to the contributions and development of individual girls and their companions in the shared endeavor. Understanding the processes that become the focus at each plane of analysis – individual, interpersonal, and community/institutional – relies on understanding the processes in the background as well as those in the foreground of analysis.

Guided participation

'Guided participation' is the term that I have applied to the interpersonal plane of socio-cultural analysis. It stresses the mutual involvement of individuals and their social partners, communicating and coordinating their involvement as they participate in socioculturally structured collective activity (Rogoff, 1990; Rogoff & Gardner, 1984).

The concept of guided participation is not an operational definition that one might use to identify some and not other interactions or arrangements. Rather, it is meant to focus attention on the system of interpersonal engagements and arrangements that are involved in participation in activities (by promoting some sorts of involvement and restricting others), which is managed collaboratively by individuals and their social partners in face-to-face or other interaction, as well as in the adjustment of arrangements for each others' and their own activities.

The concept does not define when a particular situation is or is not guided participation, but rather provides a *perspective* on how to look at interpersonal engagements and arrangements as they fit in sociocultural processes, to understand learning and development. Variations and similarities in the *nature* of guidance and of participation may be investigated (such as in adults' and children's responsibilities in different cultural communities; Rogoff, Mistry, Göncü, & Mosier, 1993), but the concept of guided participation itself is offered as a way of looking at all interpersonal interactions and arrangements.

The interpersonal plane of analysis represented by guided participation is made up of the events of everyday life as individuals engage with others and with materials and arrangements collaboratively managed by themselves and others. It includes direct interaction with others as well as engaging in or avoiding the activities assigned, made possible, or constrained by others, whether or not they are in each other's presence or even know of each other's existence. Guided participation may be tacit or explicit, face-to-face or distal, involved in shared endeavors with specific familiar people or distant unknown individuals or groups – peers as well as experts, neighbors as well as distant heroes, siblings as well as ancestors. It includes deliberate attempts to instruct and incidental comments or actions that are overheard or seen as well as involvement with particular materials and experiences that are available, which indicate the direction in which people are encouraged to go or discouraged from going.

Participation requires engagement in some aspect of the meaning of shared endeavors, but not necessarily in symmetrical or even joint action. A person who is actively observing and following the decisions made by another is participating whether or not he or she contributes directly to the decisions as they are made. A child who is working alone on a report is participating in a cultural activity with guidance involving interactions with the teacher, classmates, family members, librarian and authors, and the publishing industry, which help the child set the assignment and determine the materials and approach to be used.

Guided participation is thus an interpersonal process in which people manage their own and others' roles, and structure situations (whether by facilitating or limiting access) in which they observe and participate in cultural activities. These collective endeavors in turn constitute and transform cultural practices with each successive generation.

Processes of communication and coordination of efforts are central to the notion of guided participation. New members of a community are active in their attempts to make sense of activities and may be primarily responsible for putting themselves in a position to participate. Communication and coordination with other members of the community stretch the understanding of all participants, as they seek a common ground of understanding in order to proceed with the activities at hand. The search for a common ground, as well as to extend it, involves adjustments and the growth of understanding. As Dewey (1916) put it, people 'live in a community in virtue of the things which they have in common; and communication is the way in which they come to possess things in common' (p. 5).

Communication and coordination occur in the course of participation in shared endeavors, as people attempt to accomplish something. Their activity is directed, not random or without purpose; understanding the purposes involved in shared endeavors is an essential aspect of the analysis of guided participation. As people direct their activity toward implicit, explicit, or emerging goals, they may not be able to articulate their goals. Their goals may not be particularly task-oriented (e.g., their aim may be to pass time enjoyably or to avoid an unpleasant task) or held entirely in common with others (e.g., some may resist the direction of others). However, people's involvements are motivated by some purpose (though it may often be sketchy), and their actions are deliberate (not accidental or reflexive), often in an opportunistic, improvisational fashion (see Baker-Sennett, Matusov, & Rogoff, 1992, 1993).

The perspective of guided participation, which builds on basic notions of Vygotsky's theory, emphasizes routine, tacit communication and arrangements between children and their companions. However, the concept of guided participation is intended to encompass scenarios of cognitive development that are less central in the Vygotskian account – especially the arrangements and interactions of children in cultural communities that do not aim for school-based discourse and concepts (Rogoff, Mistry et al., 1993), and the arrangements and interactions of middle-class children in their routine involvement in everyday cognitive activities at home and in their neighborhoods. It also draws attention to the active nature of children's own efforts to participate and observe the skilled activities of their community.

In the study of Girl Scouts selling and delivering cookies, analysis of guided participation involves attention to the arrangements between people, including the availability of particular resources and constraints (e.g., order forms, transportation, deadlines, children's and customers' daily schedules), as well as their close and complex interpersonal involvements. The cookies are usually sold and delivered with a partner – another scout, a sibling, or a parent. Child partners were more common during the sales phase (and some girls noted that younger partners were better because 'cute' makes for more sales). Adult partners were common during the delivery phase, when money needed to be collected and bulky merchandise delivered. Usually the management of the money was handled by a parent in collaboration with the scout; often the scouts recruited parents to drive them around with the cookies to make their deliveries, but they sometimes worked with siblings who helped carry boxes or loaned a toy wagon. The balance of responsibility between adults and children in keeping track of money and deliveries often changed over the course of the weeks of delivery.

The means of handling the problems of sales and delivery involved using various strategies developed in the process, as well as those borrowed from others and from long-standing cultural traditions. In organizing the individual orders, the girls often bundled the boxes for each order together using a technique that in some cases we could track as being borrowed from scouts with more experience or from mothers (e.g., putting a rubber band around the boxes and labeling the bundle with a Post-it adhesive note with the customer's address and the amount due). In calculating amounts due, the girls had available to them many sources of support: the number system used in their community and school, the calculation box on the order form provided by the organization, discussions with their mothers as they performed calculations for many customers, and talk-aloud calculations by customers at the time of the sale (when they filled out the order form) that demonstrated how calculations on a unit price of $2.50 could be handled – for example, by thinking of a box costing a fourth of $10, rather than by multiplying out each digit.

Guided participation included some arrangements and interactions that were meant to instruct (e.g., training organized by the national organization), and some that were simply available (e.g., in the format of the order form) or did not have the intent of instruction or assistance (e.g., in the conversations with customers or arguments among partners regarding how to proceed). The girls as well as their social partners were active in borrowing and developing one or another approach and making use of the resources available, as well as in negotiating a balance of responsibility for shared efforts. Their efforts were purposeful, with the general goals of selling cookies, delivering them as promised, not losing any money, and earning incentives (prizes and reduced rates for summer camp) offered by the organization for high sales.

An account of the Girl Scouts' activity illustrates the interpersonal plane of shared involvement and arrangements within cultural activity and at the same time requires reference to the other two planes of analysis. Understanding guided participation in Girl Scout cookie sales and delivery requires understanding the cultural/institutional plane and the individual plane of analysis. The girls and their companions participated in and contributed to the intellectual and economic institutions and traditions of their nation and the scout organization (such as numerical systems, accounting, the exchange of money and goods), with associated cultural values (such as efficiency, the persuasion of others within societal bounds of propriety, competition for achievement, and the responsible completion of agreed-upon tasks). The next section focuses on the individual plane of analysis of sociocultural activity, using the concept of participatory appropriation, to examine how individuals change through their participation in cultural activities.

Participatory appropriation

I use the term 'participatory appropriation' (or simply 'appropriation') to refer to the process by which individuals transform their understanding of and responsibility for activities through their own participation. This notion is a companion concept to those of apprenticeship and guided participation. The basic idea of appropriation is that, through participation, people change and in the process become prepared to engage in subsequent similar activities. By engaging in an activity, participating in its meaning, people necessarily make ongoing contributions (whether in concrete actions or in stretching to understand the actions and ideas of others). Hence, participation is itself the process of appropriation.

I have used the terms 'appropriation' and 'participatory appropriation'[4] to contrast to the term 'internalization' in discussing how children gain from their involvement in sociocultural activity (Rogoff, 1990). Rather than viewing the process as one of internalization in which something static is taken across a boundary from the external to the internal, I see children's active participation itself as being the process by which they gain facility in an activity. As Wertsch and Stone (1979, p. 21) put it, 'The process *is* the product'. Or in Dewey's words:

The living creature is a part of the world, sharing its vicissitudes and fortunes, and making itself secure in its precarious dependence only as it intellectually identifies itself with the changes about it, and, forecasting the future consequences of what is going on, shapes its own activities accordingly. If the living, experiencing being is an intimate participant in the activities of the world to which it belongs, then knowledge is a mode of participation, valuable in the degree in which it is effective. It cannot be the idle view of an unconcerned spectator. (1916, p. 393)

The participatory appropriation view of how development and learning occur involves a perspective in which children and their social partners are interdependent, their roles are active and dynamically changing, and the specific processes by which they communicate and share in decision making are the substance of cognitive development.

My contrast with the term 'internalization' concerns the usage that it often receives in information processing and learning accounts, where it implies a separation between the person and the social context, as well as assumptions of static entities involved in the 'acquisition' of concepts, memories, knowledge, skills, and so on. The dynamic approach of participatory appropriation does not define cognition as a collection of stored possessions (such as thoughts, representations, memories, plans), but rather treats thinking, representing, remembering, and planning as active processes that cannot be reduced to the possession of stored objects (see Baker-Sennett, Matusov, & Rogoff, 1992; Gibson, 1979; Leont'ev, 1981; Rogoff, 1990.) Instead of studying individuals' possession or acquisition of a capacity or a bit of knowledge, the focus is on the active changes involved in an unfolding event or activity in which people participate. Events and activities are inherently dynamic, rather than being static conditions to which time is added as a separate element. Change and development, rather than static characteristics or elements, are assumed to be basic (see Pepper, 1942).

Some scholars use the term 'internalization' in ways resembling how I use the term 'participatory appropriation'. Translations of Vygotsky often refer to internalization, but his concept may be similar to my notion of appropriation, at least in emphasizing the inherent transformation involved in the process.[5] Berger and Luckmann (1966) also provide a related account using the term 'internalization.' Forman (1989) summarized their approach:

> Berger and Luckmann argued that there are three components to the social construction of reality: externalization, objectivation, and internalization. All three components are necessary to their theory and together they explain how social institutions, technologies and knowledge are created, maintained, legitimated, and transmitted through social interaction. They proposed that knowledge begins as natural by-product of the externalization of human activity. As people try to interact over time with each other, an implicit mutual understanding develops between them. Soon, however, this tacit knowledge becomes objectified in explicit concepts and rules to which language and other sign systems can refer. The final step in the process occurs when this knowledge needs to be internalized by people who were not part of its creation. (p. 57)

I first noticed the word 'appropriation' in Bakhtin's (1981) writing, as I was searching for a way to express the difference between my views and the version of internalization involving importing objects across boundaries from the external to the internal. Bakhtin argued that the words people use belong partially to others, as they appropriate words from others and adapt them to their own purposes.

However, it is important to clarify some ambiguities in the use of the term 'appropriation.' It seems to have three uses: one use is simply the same as internalization – something external is imported. The second use goes beyond this but in my view is still a version of the concept of internalization – something external is imported and transformed to fit the purposes of the new 'owner'. An example of this use is Harre's (1983) explicit reference to appropriation as a process that precedes transformation. Newman, Griffin, and Cole (1989) also seem to refer to the internalization of something external in referring to the appropriation of cultural resources and tools (such as systems of language) through involvement in culturally organized activities in which the tool plays a role.

The third use of the term 'appropriation' is my concept of participatory appropriation, in which the boundary itself is questioned, since a person who is participating in an activity is a part of that activity, not separate from it. The idea that the social world is external to the individual becomes misleading from this approach. Rather, a person participating in an activity is involved in appropriation through his or her own participation. Appropriation occurs in the process of participation, as the individual changes through involvement in the situation at hand, and this participation contributes both to the direction of the evolving event and to the individual's preparation for involvement in other similar events. In my view, appropriation *is* a process of transformation, not a precondition for transformation. Thus, I use the term 'appropriation' to refer to the change resulting from a person's *own participation* in an activity, not to his or her internalization of some external event or technique.

Participation involves creative efforts to understand and contribute to social activity, which by its very nature involves bridging between several ways of understanding a situation. Communication and shared efforts always involve adjustments between participants (with varying degrees of asymmetry) to stretch their common understanding to fit with new perspectives in the shared endeavor. Such stretching to fit several views and to accomplish something together *is* development and occurs in the process of participation. Participants' individual changes in role and understanding extend to their efforts and involvements on similar occasions in the future.

The purpose of my emphasis on participatory appropriation rather than internalization is to distinguish between two theoretical perspectives: the appropriation perspective views development as a dynamic, active, mutual process involved in peoples' participation in cultural activities; the internalization perspective views development in terms of a static, bounded 'acquisition' or 'transmission' of pieces of knowledge (either by internal construction or by the internalization of external pieces of knowledge; see Figure 4.1). These are, I believe, quite different theoretical views.

An important difference between the participatory appropriation and the internalization perspectives concerns assumptions about time. In the internalization perspective, time is segmented into past, present, and future. These are treated as separate and yield problems of how to account for relations across time that are often handled by assuming that the individual stores memories of the past that are somehow retrieved and used in the present, and that the individual makes plans in the present and (if they are stored effectively) executes them in the future. The links between these separate time segments are bridged in mysterious ways to bring information or skills stored at one point in time to use in another. It involves a storage model of mind, with static elements held in the brain, and needs a homunculus or difficult-to-specify executive process to bring the elements stored at one epoch to implement in a later epoch (see Baker-Sennett, Matusov, & Rogoff, 1992). This is the same mysterious executive process that is required in the internalization perspective to acquire, accumulate, and store external pieces of knowledge or skill in the brain.

In the participatory appropriation perspective, time is an inherent aspect of events and is not divided into separate units of past, present, and future.[6] Any event in the present is an extension of previous events and is directed toward goals that have not yet been accomplished. As such, the present extends through the past and future and cannot be separated from them. Pepper gave a supporting example: the meaning of a word in a sentence (i.e., the present) brings with it the previous meanings of that word in other sentences and of other words already expressed in that sentence (the past in the present), and is also directed toward the overall idea to which the word contributes that is not yet fully expressed (the future in the present).

When a person acts on the basis of previous experience, his or her past is present. It is not merely a stored memory called up in the present; the person's previous participation contributes to the event at hand by having prepared it. The present event is different from what it would have been if previous events had not occurred; this does not require a storage model of past events.

Analogies can be drawn from physical and organizational change. The size, shape, and strength of a child's leg is a function of the growth and use that are continually occurring; the child's leg changes, but we do not need to refer to the leg accumulating units of growth or of exercise. The past is not *stored* in the leg; the leg has developed to be as it is currently. Likewise, the current situation of a company is a function of previous activities, but we do not need to account for changes in company direction or policy in terms of accumulated units of some kind. It is more useful simply to talk about the activities involved in the changes over time.

In this view, there is no need to segment past, present, or future or to conceive of development in terms of the acquisition or transmission of stored units. Development is a dynamic process, with change throughout rather than the accumulation of new items or the transformation of existing items.

In this view, participatory appropriation is an aspect of ongoing events. A person who participates in events changes in ways that make a difference in subsequent events. Participatory appropriation is ongoing development as people participate in events and thus handle subsequent events in ways based on their involvement in previous events. This contrasts with the internalization perspective in which one would look for exposure to external knowledge or skill, followed by internalization with or without transformation by the individual, followed by evidence of such internalization as the person retrieves the acquired knowledge or skill independently (see Rogoff, Radziszewska, & Masiello, 1993).

In some efforts to understand the internalization of social events, time is used as a tool, but still with the assumptions of a separation between internal and external, of time as independent of events, of boundaries between past, present, and future, and of development as the acquisition of static pieces of information or skill. Sequential analyses of social interaction, for instance, may examine change over time by breaking an event into smaller units (of either time or moves made by one person or the other) but often define the contribution of each partner separately in order to look at the impact of one upon the other. For example, a study may examine maternal assistance and child learning by choosing categories of maternal behavior (questions, directives, praise) and categories of child behavior (errors, correct response, off-task behavior) and examining the contingencies between them. Such a sequential strategy is consistent with the internalization perspective, in which time is separate from events, the external and internal events are arbitrarily separated, and development is seen as accumulation (see Figure 4.1).

The participatory appropriation perspective focuses instead on events as dynamically changing, with people participating with others in coherent events (where one could examine

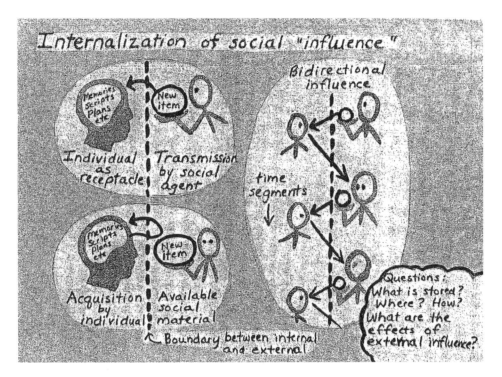

Figure 4.1   Internalization of social 'influences'

each person's contributions as they relate to each other, but not define them separately), and development is seen as transformation. Inherent to the participatory appropriation view is the mutual constitution of personal, interpersonal, and cultural processes, with development involving all planes of focus in sociocultural activity (see Figure 4.2).

The internalization view is based on as assumption that the individual is the primary unit of analysis, with static interpersonal and cultural influences added onto 'basic' individual processes. In the internalization model, the individual is either a passive recipient of external social or cultural influence – a receptacle for the accumulation of knowledge and skill – or an active seeker of passive external social and cultural knowledge and skill. In the participatory appropriation perspective, personal, interpersonal, and cultural processes all constitute each other as they transform sociocultural activity.

The transformations involved in participatory appropriation are developmental in the sense that they are changes in particular directions. The direction of development varies locally (in accord with cultural values, interpersonal needs, and specific circumstances); it does not require the specification of universal or ideal end points of development.

The questions to investigate are different if we move from internalization approaches and instead view cognitive development as participatory appropriation through guided participation in a system of apprenticeship. Questions of where memories are stored or how information is taken from external events or how children accumulate knowledge or implement plans all become less relevant ways to study development from this sociocultural approach.[7]

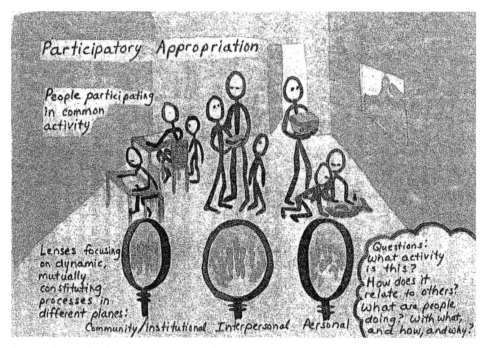

Figure 4.2   Participatory appropriation

Instead, we begin to examine in closer focus the actual processes by which children participate with other people in cultural activity and the ways they transform their participation. The investigation of people's actual involvement in activities becomes the basis of our understanding of development rather than simply the surface details that we try to get past. The central question becomes how people participate in sociocultural activity and how their participation changes from being relatively peripheral (see Lave & Wenger, 1991), observing and carrying out secondary roles, to sometimes being responsible for managing such activities.

Viewing development as participatory appropriation recasts the classic question concerning the transfer of knowledge. How an individual approaches two situations has to do with how he or she construes the relations between their purposes or meanings. Hence, the process is inherently creative, with people actively seeking meaning and relating situations to each other.

This creative process, of course, is itself a sociocultural activity. People, by themselves and with companions, puzzle out how to manage a new situation on the basis of their own and their shared history, to reach their own and their shared goals, through subtle and explicit communication indicating the 'kind' of a situation in which they are involved. All such communication is at one and the same time particular and general, as reference is made to the here and now in ways that draw on concepts one has met before (Dewey, 1916). For example, to refer to an object with a label (e.g., 'This is a chapter') links the present object with a general class of objects of sociocultural import. The ways that objects and events are classified in language and in action are sociocultural generalizations within which we all function and that we extend when we figure out how to handle a thing or event that is somewhat novel to us.

From my perspective, orienting our inquiry by focusing on how people participate in sociocultural activity and how they change their participation demystifies the processes of learning and development. Rather than searching for the nature of internalization as a conduit from external bits of knowledge or skill to an internal repository, we look directly at the efforts of individuals, their companions, and the institutions they constitute and build upon to see development as grounded in the specifics and commonalities of those efforts, opportunities, constraints, and changes.

In the study of Girl Scout cookie sales and delivery, we were able to observe changes in how the girls participated in a number of aspects of the activity.[8] In the calculation of charges to customers, we could track in many cases how the girls took on greater responsibility over the course of the delivery, with their mothers often initially managing the calculations and supervising the girls in keeping track of customers who had paid; in the course of participating in a system that was often set up by the mothers, the girls took on greater responsibility for handling these complicated and important aspects of the activity.

We could also track how the girls, over the course of the activity, became more familiar with the layout of the routes connecting their customers and often managed their parents' driving as the parents helped the girls deliver. We observed (actually, eavesdropped on) the girls learning to manage the complex planning involved in developing spatial routes, with sufficient flexibility to be efficient within the interpersonal and material resources and constraints of the situation.

We could observe how the girls sometimes participated with customers, following the structure provided by the scout organization in the format of the order sheet, which provided the girls with talk-aloud calculations that revealed arithmetic strategies. We followed the process by which the girls made use of and extended cultural tools (writing, calculating, using Post-it notes to remember, developing a common language to refer to places to be visited) that tied their efforts in this activity to practices in other institutions of their culture.

These observations all revealed cognitive developmental processes that occurred as the girls participated in this sociocultural activity. Through the girl's participation, they developed in ways that we could see leading to changed later participation. Their participatory appropriation was an ongoing feature of their guided participation in the apprenticeship system through which we can view the personal, interpersonal, and cultural processes of this activity.

Although it is beyond the scope of this chapter to discuss methodological considerations, the sociocultural approach that I have presented involves shifting such considerations associated with the changes in the conceptual base. The approach does not prescribe the use of specific methodological tools but does emphasize the relation of particular tools to the theoretical purposes to which they are put. An analysis of shifts in the interpretation of data given such a sociocultural approach is available in Rogoff, Radziszewska, and Masiello (1993). The tools that I have used for studying patterns of sociocultural activities emphasize close analysis of events through ethnographic methods, abstraction of generalities based on this analysis, extensive use of graphing of information and the application of quantitative methods to check and communicate the patterns discerned through the ethnographic and graphic analyses (see Rogoff, Mistry et al., 1993, for discussion and examples of these methods).

In sum, I have presented a sociocultural approach that is based on a consideration of personal, interpersonal, and community planes of focus in the analysis of the developmental process involved in the participation of individuals with others in cultural practices. The approach emphasizes seeking patterns in the organization of sociocultural activities, focusing variously on personal, interpersonal, or community aspects of the activities, with the other aspects in the background but taken into account. Research resulting from this approach emphasizes observing both similarities and differences across varying sociocultural activities, as well as tracking the relations among aspects of events viewed in different planes of analysis. Such a sociocultural analysis requires considering how individuals, groups, and communities transform as they together constitute and are constituted by sociocultural activity.

Notes

1. The metaphor appears to me to be equally applicable to culturally organized activities that can be regarded as desirable or undesirable. Although my own research focuses on learning to participate in activities valued in the communities studied, I think that the conceptual framework can be well applied to learning to participate in activities censured in the communities studied (such as interpersonal violence and addictive behavior, which raise concern).
2. Such direction/guidance does not simply include facilitation of involvement in certain activities; it also includes restriction or very indirect channeling of the activities in which people participate, for example, the exclusion of children from some adult activities or the message that they are allowed to participate only in certain ways. Guidance is thus a direct or indirect structuring of people's possibilities for participation that promotes some particular direction of development.
3. They also suggested that we disguise ourselves as bushes and follow them around, which we did not.
4. These two terms mean the same thing in my account. I add the word 'participatory' to emphasize that in my use of the term, appropriation is necessarily through a person's *own* involvement, not an incorporation of something external. This is a point of difference with others who also use the term 'appropriation', as I discuss in this section.
5. However, Vygotsky's characterization of internalization as proceeding from the interpersonal to the intrapersonal involves a separation in time of social and individual aspects of the activity, which is at odds with my idea of participatory appropriation, in which a person's participation is at one and the same time a social and an individual process.
6. My discussion of time is greatly influenced by Gibson's theory and Pepper's account of a contextual world hypothesis. I am endebted to Beth Shapiro and Christine Mosier for discussion of these issues.
7. The metaphor of stored mental representation and the characterization of plans, memories, concepts, etc. as objects of inquiry may still be useful in some scholarly endeavors. I am not arguing for necessarily dropping the metaphor but for recognizing it *as a metaphor*, perhaps useful for communication between scholars, but not to be automatically assumed to characterize the functioning of the people whom we study. It seems more parsimonious to drop it for some research.
8. We focus here on the development of the girls through their participation in this activity; similar analyses could be done of the development of the troop leaders, family members, customers, and researchers through their participation in the activity.

References

Baker-Sennett, J., Matusov, E., & Rogoff, B. (1992). Sociocultural processes of creative planning in children's playcrafting. In P. Light & G. Butterworth (Eds.), *Context and cognition: Ways of learning and knowing* (pp. 93–114). Hertfordshire, UK: Harvester-Wheatsheaf.

Baker-Sennett, J., Matusov, E., & Rogoff, B. (1993). Planning as developmental process. In H. Reese (Ed.), *Advances in child development* (Vol. 24, pp. 253–281). San Diego: Academic.

Bakhtin, M. M. (1981). *The dialogical imagination* (M. Holquist, Ed.). Austin: University of Texas Press.

Bakhurst, D. (1988). Activity, consciousness and communication. *Newsletter of the Laboratory for Comparative Human Cognition, 10,* 31–39.

Berger, P. L., & Luckmann, T. (1966). *The social construction of reality.* New York: Doubleday.

Bruner, J. S. (1983). *Child's talk: Learning to use language.* New York: Norton.

Cole, M. (1985). The zone of proximal development: Where culture and cognition create each other. In J. V. Wertsch (Ed.), *Culture, communication, and cognition: Vygotskian perspectives* (pp. 146–161). Cambridge University Press.

Dewey, J. (1916). *Democracy and education: An introduction to the philosophy of education.* New York: Macmillan.

Dewey, J., & Bentley, A. F. (1949). *Knowing and the known.* Boston: Beacon.

Forman, E. A. (1989). The role of peer interaction in the social construction of mathematical knowledge. *International Journal of Educational Research, 13,* 55–70.

Gibson, J. J. (1979). *The ecological approach to visual perception.* Boston: Houghton Mifflin.

Goody, E. N. (1989). Learning, apprenticeship and the division of labor. In M. W. Coy (Ed.), *Apprenticeship: From theory to method and back again* (pp. 233–256). Albany: State University of New York Press.

Harre, R. (1983). *Personal being.* Oxford: Basil Blackwell.

John-Steiner, V. (1985). *Notebooks of the mind: Explorations of thinking.* Albuquerque: University of New Mexico Press.

Lave, J., & Wenger, E. (1991). *Situated learning: Legitimate peripheral participation.* Cambridge University Press.

Leont'ev, A. N. (1981). The problem of activity in psychology. In J. V. Wertsch (Ed.), *The concept of activity in Soviet psychology* (pp. 37–71). Armonk, NY: Sharpe.

Newman, D., Griffin, P., & Cole, M. (1989). *The construction zone: Working for cognitive change in school.* Cambridge University Press.

Pepper, S. C. (1942). *World hypotheses: A study in evidence.* Berkeley: University of California Press.

Rogoff, B. (1982). Integrating context and cognitive development. In M. E. Lamb & A. L. Brown (Eds.), *Advances in developmental psychology* (Vol. 2, pp. 125–170). Hillsdale, NJ: Erlbaum.

Rogoff, B. (1990). *Apprenticeship in thinking: Cognitive development in social context.* New York: Oxford University Press.

Rogoff, B. (1992). Three ways to relate person and culture: Thoughts sparked by Valsiner's review of *Apprenticeship in Thinking. Human Development 35,* 316–320.

Rogoff, B. (1993). Children's guided participation and participatory appropriation in sociocultural activity. In R. Wozniak & K. Fischer (Eds.), *Development in context: Acting and thinking in specific environments* (pp. 121–153). Hillsdale, NJ: Erlbaum.

Rogoff, B., Baker-Sennett, J., Lacasa, P., & Goldsmith, D. (1995). Development through participation in sociocultural activity. In J. Goodnow, P. Miller, & F. Kessel (Eds.), *Cultural practices as contexts for development.* San Francisco: Jossey-Bass.

Rogoff, B., & Gardner, W. P. (1984). Adult guidance of cognitive development. In B. Rogoff & J. Lave (Eds.), *Everyday cognition: Its development in social context* (pp. 95–116). Cambridge, MA: Harvard University Press.

Rogoff, B., Mistry, J. J., Göncü, A., & Mosier, C. (1993). Guided participation in cultural activity by toddlers and caregivers. *Monographs of the Society for Research in Child Development, 58* (7, Serial No. 236).

Rogoff, B., Radziszewska, B., & Masiello, T. (1993). The analysis of developmental processes in sociocultural activity. In L. Martin, K. Nelson, & E. Tobach (Eds.), *Cultural psychology and activity theory*. Cambridge University Press.

Scribner, S. (1985). Vygotsky's uses of history. In J. V. Wertsch (Ed.), *Culture, communication, and cognition: Vygotskian perspectives* (pp. 119–145). Cambridge University Press.

Smedslund, J. (1984). The invisible obvious: Culture in psychology. In K. M. J. Lagerspetz & P. Niemi (Eds.), *Psychology in the 1990s* (pp. 443–452). Amsterdam: Elsevier.

Vygotsky, L. S. (1978). *Mind in society: The development of higher psychological processes.* Cambridge, MA: Harvard University Press.

Vygotsky, L. S. (1987). *Thinking and speech.* In R. W. Rieber & A. S. Carton (Eds.), *The collected works of L. S. Vygotsky* (N. Minick, Trans.) (pp. 37–285). New York: Plenum.

Wertsch, J. V. (1985). *Vygotsky and the social formation of mind.* Cambridge, MA: Harvard University Press.

Wertsch, J. V., & Stone, C. A. (1979, February). A social interactional analysis of learning disabilities remediation. Paper presented at the International Conference of the Association for Children with Learning Disabilities, San Francisco.

Zinchenko, V. P. (1985). Vygotsky's ideas about units for the analysis of main. In J. V. Wertsch (Ed.), *Culture, communication, and cognition: Vygotskian perspectives* (pp. 94–118). Cambridge University Press.

5

The In-between: Exposing Everyday Learning at Work

Nicky Solomon, David Boud and Donna Rooney

[…]

The social and physical environment of the workplace has a profound influence on work itself, the relationships between workers and their work and the personal lives of workers. How we learn to do our job and how we deal with the challenges we face in doing so are framed within this context. Part of this context is the social and physical spaces we occupy, the times we spend in them and the ways in which they shape our experience. This chapter is concerned with the ways in which ideas of space are helpful in thinking about workplace learning. Indeed, the term *workplace* learning itself draws our attention to its place or space. In other words, *workplace* learning has particular kinds of meanings and practices because of its location and because that location is not an *educational institution*. Similarly, understandings of *on-the-job* learning are connected to the place of that kind of learning and, in particular, that this place is not *off-the-job*.

Our interest reflects the significance of 'space' in contemporary social and cultural theory, as well as the increasing use of space metaphors in understanding the changing place of education, knowledge and learning in the contemporary moment. Unlike formal training or professional development, there is relatively little research on everyday learning and the ways in which the informal world of the workplace might be mobilized by workers or enhanced by employers. Similarly, while learning and space have intimate associations (Jamieson *et al.*, 2000), it is formal learning environments that attract most attention (Edwards and Clarke, 2002). Much has been written about how space and time are integral to understanding social relations (Nespor, 1994) and in turn understanding learning in workplaces (O'Toole, 2001; Clarke *et al.*, 2002; Edwards and Clarke, 2002). Furthermore, there are studies that draw parallels between space and identity (Groat, 1995), and those that deal with physical space and deterministic architecture (Kornberger and Clegg, 2003). While these studies are valuable in looking at specific meanings of space or learning or work, they have not accounted for the multiplicity of ways in which workers mobilize spaces for everyday learning. This chapter draws on broader understandings of space, identity and learning, and suggests that an analysis of everyday learning in spatial terms can usefully open up spaces and opportunities for investigating and problematizing workplace learning.

Such an analysis could also be undertaken in terms of time. For the sake of clarity of exposition, we restrict ourselves to space here. In many respects, many of the remarks that follow could equally be couched in terms of time rather than place, or more accurately space/time.

From: *International Journal of Lifelong Education,* 25 (1), 2006, pp. 3–13. Reprinted by permission of the publisher (Taylor & Francis Ltd, http://www.informaworld.com).

Background to the study

The study reported here was undertaken as part of a research project funded by the Australian Research Council that examined learning in work groups: 'Uncovering learning at work'. It followed from earlier outcomes from that project that focused on networking (Boud and Middleton, 2003) and the naming of learning at work (Boud and Solomon, 2003). Four work groups within a large organization were studied in detail over a three-year period. The employer is a public sector body involved in vocational education and training and two of the four work groups were groups of teachers. Observations were made of the groups, interviews conducted and meetings held with the overall goal of examining and describing informal learning in the workplace and considering the implications of this in light of enhancing learning in the workplace. A particular feature of the research was the multiple layers of collaboration designed to engage participants with the project (Solomon *et al.*, 2001). [...] While learning more about learning *spaces* was not among our initial aims, space has emerged as a common theme in the data.

Concern about space and learning arose in our investigation of the experiences of members of work groups relating to learning at work. In interviewing participants, and in holding meetings with groups in their place of work, we found many references in transcripts to space and the ways in which it had significance for them. Given that the workplaces were part of an educational institution, there were many predictable references to classrooms and offices as sites of learning. However, these were accompanied by an entirely unanticipated set of references to learning spaces that were not usually considered to be either learning or working spaces. These included meal breaks in staff rooms, coffee taken at local cafés and sharing transport with colleagues to and from work. These kinds of learning spaces may be described as 'work spaces' or 'socializing spaces' – but perhaps more appropriately they can be understood as hybrid spaces, that is, at one and the same time work and socializing spaces where the participants are both working and not working. This focus on social relationships in workplaces resonates with the cultural turn (du Gay, 1996) and a contemporary foregrounding of social relationships and 'talk' in workplaces (Rhodes and Scheeres, 2004).

Throughout the interviews and meetings, participants continually referred to (things that we name as) 'space' in their discussions about their jobs in general. At first, these discussions were almost overlooked because of their 'normalness'. Indeed, initially there appeared to be a sense of banality about the 'spaces' we later identified as significant sites of everyday learning in our project. In a sense, this is misleading because the very banality highlighted their importance. Space is central because of its ubiquity. Space is perhaps important because it does *not* appear central. It is part of the context of learning that has been gaining greater recognition in considerations of learning from very many perspectives (e.g. Lave and Wenger, 1991; Duranti and Goodwin, 1992, Rainbird *et al.*, 2004).

The meaning of space

In the literature, some authors use the notion of 'space', some use 'place' and some use both space and place. While not wanting to elide differences in usage as part of other discussions, we are using them synonymously here. We are not referring only to literal physical spaces or places – although to some extent the physical spaces we encountered in the workplaces have prompted our interest in ideas around space. Our attention was also engaged by the materiality of physical spaces and their relationship with people.

Our spatial focus in part draws on writings associated with actor-network theory (Callon, 1986; Latour, 1986). It appeals because of its emphasis on space-time relations, networking, human and non-human relations and an understanding of power as association and effect rather than one of cause. The work of Nespor (1994) is particularly illuminating. While the concern of his work differs to ours as it examines university courses and the ways students are inducted into disciplines or professions, his work usefully brings us to an understanding of how local practices and relationships are enmeshed in more expansive disciplinary and professional networks. This means that while our focus is on local spaces, we also need to understand these spaces as not discrete or disconnected ones, but rather as ones that are linked to broader social relations and networks of power. Also, of relevance here, is that Nespor in examining the 'making of' physics and management students explored the disciplining work of the physical buildings of the programmes. He considered the physical spaces the students congregated in, where they played, where they studied, where they worked, the amount of time they spent in the building and how they filled 'their waking hours' (1994: 30).

As indicated above, we are drawn to the notion of 'hybrid space' to name learning spaces at work that are considered to be and not to be working spaces. This naming of new learning spaces as hybrid spaces connects with the work of a number of cultural studies writers (such as Said, 1978; Bhabha, 1990, 1994; Sarup, 1996; Rizvi, 1997) who are concerned with identifying a third space that exposes the inadequacies of traditional binary oppositions and accompanying norms:

> … for me the importance of hybridity is not to be able to trace original moments from which the third emerges, rather hybridity to me is the third space which enables other positions to emerge. This third space displaces the histories that constitute it, and sets up new structures of authority, new political initiatives … The process of cultural hybridity gives rise to something different, something new and unrecognisable, a new area of negotiation of meaning and representation. (Bhabha, 1990: 211)

While Bhabha's interest in a third space is in terms of challenging conventional boundaries around East and West, we find that 'third space' is also a useful metaphor for investigating the complexities of the somewhat non-transparent new identities, processes and relationships being produced at work in the contemporary workplace.

Indeed, new ways of working, learning and being in the contemporary workplace are consistent themes in organizational studies and educational literature (e.g. Drucker, 1993; Handy, 1994; Gee et al., 1996; Rose, 1996; Marsick and Watkins, 1999). These writings draw attention to the complexities of organizations today and the way 'the organization has to become both a learning and a teaching organization' (Drucker, 1993: 2). In other words, these organizations as new spaces themselves are characterized by being both work and learning spaces where the boundary between the two is considerably blurred. In fact, our project is generated by the very existence of this hybrid space, a space that enables/ generates new ways of being, working and learning. Within this differently bounded space we, as a research team, in working collaboratively within a workplace in this particular moment of time are participating in a cross institutional network. And this network is constituted by participants aligned in terms of a particular set of shared interests. Moreover, our presence in this research site and our refusal to take on a conventional researcher and researched relationship, our border crossing identities and practices, are both cause and effect of the ambiguities and ambivalences around the boundaries of research and learning spaces (Stronach and Maclure, 1997).

The interest in workplaces making more use of informal learning, while not necessarily translating it into formal learning, emerges within a 'new work order' (Gee *et al.*, 1996) which in itself is a site of resistance to conventional understandings, norms and binaries around, for example, an individual employee and their organization. In this context, the concept of a hybrid space is a useful one in our investigations on uncovering learning at work, a task that could be readily understood as an investigation of the informal, rather than the formal.

As appealing as this third space is, it is also important not to over-romanticize it, imagining it to be unbounded, unregulated or undisciplined. As Nespor (1994) reminds us, local practices (or spaces) are not disconnected from broader social networks of power. Hybrid spaces are not neutral spaces but are sites of contested and at times less visible disciplinary practices. So the third space under our current gaze is a space where the hierarchies within the (post) bureaucratic institution, the hierarchy implicit in any research relationship between academics and other professionals, as well as the internal complex politics of each of the workgroups, cannot be neutralized or discounted. In other words, within this hybrid space there is no erasure of the previous identities of the workers or ourselves as they are practised in our various institutional positions. There are always traces and these traces may present themselves in multiple – and at times contradictory – practices and languages (Scheeres, 2003).

Spaces within: some vignettes

The discussion that follows draws on examples chosen from the individual interviews and feedback sessions with the workgroups. While they are only a sampling of the rich data that emerged around the thematic of space, these offerings serve to demonstrate the complexity of ways that space was talked about by the workers and the researchers in the transcripts.

We tried to understand the features of these hybrid learning spaces by examining:

- overlap periods (such as refreshment breaks) where workers are not 'entirely' workers
- actual spaces in workplaces that are typically labelled as productive or non-productive, such as workrooms or tearooms
- talking spaces were people have conversations within or between work times (e.g. in a car driving home from work).

These were not individual spaces where people engaged in solitary contemplation, but places where people gathered at various times. Relationships between people were continually being negotiated in these spaces. Arguably, there appears to be some lessening of the 'normal' workplace hierarchy – a kind of home territory that is not so much safe, but safer than formal meetings. In these spaces, the direction of 'talk' was not under the scrutiny of employers and some features of status temporally suspended. Topics of talk varied, people joked and it was not necessary to 'talk shop'.

In our examination of these places, we were exploring them as spaces where what is said or not said is not as governed by institutional judgement, accountabilities and hierarchical positions as in other work spaces. However, in doing so we were also aware that our company influenced the dynamics within these spaces. We, the researchers, although attempting to be understood as co-participants in the project, were inevitably positioning ourselves and positioned by the employees in particular ways. As we and others have written (e.g. Scheeres and Solomon, 2000; Solomon *et al.*, 2001), collaborative research projects are filled with complexities and tensions. They are not neutral spaces, but rather often sites of contestation.

The complexities around this hybrid space therefore cannot be underestimated. On the one hand, we were seeking to 'uncover learning', that is, everyday or informal learning (or learning that just happens), while on the other hand the act of uncovering requires an intervention, an intrusion, a judgement, and a formalizing or a codifying in order to identify, articulate and manage it. While we were working in that space in a workplace that is also in the learning industry, at the same time we were strangers (or even space invaders), and as academics our business was similar but also different.

Nevertheless, examining the hybrid or 'in-between' as useful sites of everyday learning was appealing, and its appeal is demonstrated in the following comment from a trade teacher:

On my way here this morning I had a look at a job that the owner's not happy with. It's a townhouse in a block of four where the tiles are all cracking. There's no obvious reason for it. I've never seen it before in a cottage situation. And I was going to toss it around with these guys at lunchtime and see what they thought.

This comment demonstrates many 'in-between' spaces. First, the geographical space between work and the participant's home. And there is also the temporal lunchtime, 'in-between' sanctioned working hours. In both these spaces there is potentiality for learning. The teacher learned something new about the behaviour of tiles in cottages, and it is reasonable to imagine that during 'tossing it around with the guys at lunchtime' he also learned something new. The important point is that neither of these 'between' spaces (travelling to work and lunchtimes) is generally considered a site of learning despite significant work-related learning occurring. A further example from this same group of trade teachers can be seen in the following comment when talking about their shared lunchroom:

Well, it's like we had someone talking to us from industry at lunchtime – it was pretty much an informal thing just over the lunchroom we had a guy out from industry and he was talking to us about different changes, quite often we have stuff like that where someone from industry comes out and talks to us and we find out new ways of doing things.

Again, the lunchroom can be thought of as in-between *on-the-job* and *off-the-job*. And again, there is learning occurring. Indeed, it is learning that can significantly contribute to the productivity and effectiveness of this organization.

It was these comments, and many more like them, that prompted us to examine further the nature of these spaces. In the spirit of the collaboration, we returned to the work groups with our findings and it was here that the complexities of our research work came to the fore. The challenges in some groups of our naming of certain spaces as learning spaces triggered a number of questions that we needed to ask ourselves: whose space was it to name in this way? Theirs? Ours? All of ours? Was it a new space? A different one? Indeed, by considering these questions we could not help but consider the ways in which we, as researchers, have been troubled by, and further trouble, the complex collaborative researching of this workplace.

Ambivalent sites: the trade teachers' tearoom

The tensions around understanding and naming the hybrid spaces as learning spaces were particularly prominent with one of the work groups involved in the study. It was the group of male trade teachers. This group had always presented itself in resistant ways, particularly when talking about learning through work and about being or not being learners. The ambivalence around this kind of talk is evident in the following quote:

> Researcher: How do you learn from each other as a team of teachers – do you learn from each other?
> Trade teacher: Well, we don't … OK, we do to an extent. Every lunchtime we're always sitting around the table and something will come up and we'll look at it there.

Another example came after one of the teachers had offered the anecdote cited earlier in this chapter, drawing attention to the usefulness of talk around the lunch table. When one of the researchers attempted to name the tearoom space as an informal learning space, another teacher clearly resisted this suggestion:

> Researcher: … you know how we were talking about informal learning spaces and how the lunchroom is a good example of that. And there's a lot of everyday talk that goes on there and a lot of learning as well.
> Trade teacher: I don't think we think about that as learning. I don't walk about there thinking I learned something today. To me it's not a learning environment. The classroom's a learning from me, to the student. The lunchroom sitting around here, it's not a learning environment at all. Even though I've learnt something.
> Researcher: … it seems to me a lot of learning takes place…
> Trade teacher: I'm sure there is learning there all the time but I don't look at it as learning, if you know what I mean.

It appeared that the teacher regarded the naming of the lunchroom as a learning space as transgressive. He could admit that learning occurred, but to formally acknowledge it as a learning space was to intrude into a protected environment.

At another encounter with this group of teachers, when the research team first entered the space, a short exchange occurred between colleagues before the tape recorder was switched on. The story was about the two teachers and their trip home together in a car. The teachers, who lived an hour or so away and consequently carpooled, talked about a conversation that they had had about some challenges they were experiencing in their classroom. The teachers talked about how they exchanged experiences and ideas around these challenges and reported details of how they had debriefed together about the teaching demands of a difficult class. Curiously though, later in the 'formal' part of the feedback session, both teachers were adamant that they did not learn from each other.

It seems that the issue is not whether or not these teachers are learning while working or where this learning is taking place. Indeed, there are many examples that suggest they are learning and they learn from each other in many different places. But rather the issue is how this learning is spoken about and who is initiating the talk. For example, while on the one hand, the researchers were sitting comfortably in the tearoom and chatting rather than interviewing, on the other hand, this comfort was not an untroubled one. Were we or were we not space invaders? Indeed, when one teacher remarked 'I think you're reading too much into this', questions around our presence became very legitimate ones.

Non-ambivalent site: work-based programme teaching group

However, our naming of in-between spaces as learning spaces was not met with the same resistance by all work groups. During feedback sessions with a group of teachers responsible for delivering workplace training, we talked about points arising from the first round of interviews. They were invited to take up or challenge our points. The interviews had sparked interest for us in 'what' is learned and from 'whom', and we asked if they saw themselves learning from each other. One teacher began a lengthy conversation about their tearoom chats:

… we sit around the tearoom a lot and every time we have a cup of tea we sit around I think the value without realising it is that we're analysing and reflecting and improving and discussing and its one of the things that keep you going.

A colleague added:

We make a cup of tea and solve the problem.

There was general consensus among this group that tearoom chats provided spaces where it was 'safe' to say things that couldn't be said in other situations. This group, and several others, told us that tearoom chat went in many directions. There was an intermingling of work and non-work topics. It was a space where problems and ideas were 'brought in', exemplified by one worker telling us about *3am thoughts* and how he took them to the tearoom the following day: 'Guess what I thought of last night?', he would ask.

These extracts suggest that this group was not resistant to our introduction of our language nor to our physical presence and intrusion in their space. This is likely to be the case for a number of reasons. While they, like the trade teachers, had been teachers for many years, their current teaching programme was a new one. It has a short history for them and the institution, and it is a programme that itself is crossing boundaries. Indeed, throughout the project this group often voiced their frustrations with the pressures of working at the cutting edge of the educational institution's prevailing commercial business whilst being limited by the workings of a large bureaucracy. They talked about the difficulties of working in (and for) both public and private sector organizations. Their professional and personal spaces were already complicated hybrid ones.

Some members of another work group, as part of a discussion about workplace learning, referred critically to a staff development day, where staff from different units met to examine particular issues. In this organization, it is typically arranged on a state-wide basis by a disciplinary grouping or staff development centre. After criticism of the value of such meetings at a time when there is so much work of one's own to do, one of them remarked:

> It's usually run as a meeting where they give us information, and we've got the oppor-tunity to ask questions. But one of the biggest values of it is that during the breaks, we network furiously. And it's amazing what you can pick up in terms of new ideas, or what's been tried and hasn't worked, when you've been thinking about trying the same thing. And you can modify it or adjust it because you've learnt from their expe-rience just listening to them.

While comments were made about the lack of opportunities in the formal sessions to do what one wanted, the occasion was more valued for what was not on the programme, that is, it permitted contact with others with similar roles and discussing common issues. The informal spaces between sessions were valued for the learning opportunities they provided even when the legitimate programme was not accorded much attention.

Discussing the in-between

Although our interpretation of 'spaces' was contested by some groups, and taking account of an awareness of our status as 'space invaders', we consider that naming these spaces as hybrid or 'in-between' offer some fruitful findings that have relevance beyond the study itself. For example, when considering the binaries that are so commonly accepted in workplaces: on-the-job/off-the-job, formal/informal, worker/social being, worker/learner, working/playing, productive/non-productive, the equality common privileging of the first of these pairs has to be unsettled. They no longer appear useful for thinking about learning in the workplace. It is in the in-between space that interesting things happen. As illustrated in some of the quotes above, the important point is the 'in-between' spaces (such as travelling to work and lunchtimes) are generally considered sites of learning despite significant work-related learning occurring.

In appearance, the physical spaces we have noticed can be described as transitional. For example, they are both work and socializing spaces. In the tearoom, for example, while the furniture is 'homely', the space is not entirely 'homey either'. Similarly, the identities involved are transitional. When they enter these spaces, they are neither entirely workers nor social beings, but located in between. Their activities are viewed as either working or socializing. They are not productive in the sense that they are performing the roles of normal work, yet the presence of significant learning means that they are not unproductive either.

Throughout study, we observed numerous ways in which participants resisted moves to formalize the informal. This ranged from denial that they were learning anything from each other (in the car trip), to exploiting the formal staff development day for their own ends, to avoiding the label of learner and rejecting our own prescriptions from the world of formal education. Occasions of reflection were overwhelmingly informal, but they could be seen as taking place close to the intersections of what Habermas (1986) refers to as the lifeworld and the system sphere of work and learning. Nonetheless, there was strong resistance to seeing reflection as part of the system world. Part of the original design of the research project was a stage in which some of the practices identified through the study would be developed as formal interventions to 'improve' learning at work. This idea was abandoned at an early point once it became clear that the richness of learning we identified could be compromised by attempting to move it into the system world of the organization. Welton (1995) has argued for the importance of adult educators protecting the lifeworld from such intrusions. It would seem that some of our participants had intuitively done the same as they perceived our interventions as system world intrusions – through naming learning and naming spaces as learning spaces – into their lifeworld.

Awareness of the inappropriateness and limitations of binaries in conceptualizing learning is illustrated well in other studies. The polarization of formal and informal learning in particular has been thoroughly criticized in a recent study by Colley, Hodkinson and Malcolm. Their analysis of a large range of accounts in the literature indicates that the use of the apparently discrete categories of 'formal', 'informal' and 'non-formal' is to misunderstand the nature of learning. They suggest that it is more accurate to conceive 'formality' and 'informality' as attributes present in all circumstances of learning (Colley *et al.*, 2003). Similarly, our study points to the need to view learning spaces at work as simultaneously work and social and to see features of both in all settings.

Attempts to formalise learning spaces can inhibit the positive benefits of them, but the absence of formalization may not necessarily foster it either. However, there is always a risk in formalizing the informal, and our formal intrusions (through 'doing research') in some way influence the informal interaction. The effect of formalization came up time and time again. When looking at learning at work, using a spatial lens and thereby looking at spaces that are not normally considered to be learning spaces, but more like hybrid spaces, conventional binaries no longer seem appropriate. This seems to be particularly the case with the formal/informal binary. There we were looking at the informal, but in doing so, we were, wittingly or perhaps unwittingly, formalizing it. It seems that by naming every-day learning as informal learning, this kind of learning can only be understood in relation to what it is not, that is formal learning. It is the binary that we seek to override, because we believe that it is the in-betweenness of the space that provides productive potential and once we start codifying or overcoding it, this potential can be lost.

References

Bhabha, H. K. (ed.) (1990) *Nation and Narration* (London: Routledge).

Bhabha, H. K. (1994) *The Location of Culture* (London: Routledge).

Boud, D. and Middleton, H. (2003) Learning from others at work: Communities of practice and informal learning. *Journal of Workplace Learning*, 15(5), 194–202.

Boud, D. and Solomon, N. (2003) I don't think I am a learner: Acts of naming learners at work. *Journal of Workplace Learning*, 15(7/8), 326–331.

Callon, M. (1986) Some elements of a sociology of translation. In J. Law (eds) *Power, Action and Belief* (London: Routledge & Kegan Paul), pp. 196–233.

Clarke, J., Harrison, R., Reeve, F. and Edwards, R. (2002) Assembling spaces: The question of 'place' in further education. *Discourse*, 23(3), 285–297.

Colley, H., Hodkinson, P. and Malcolm, J. (2003) *Informality and Formality in Learning* (London: Learning and Skills Research Centre).

Drucker, P. F. (1993) *Concept of the Corporation* (New Brunswick, NJ: Transaction Publishers).

Du Gay, P. (1996) *Consumption and Identity at Work* (London: Sage).

Duranti, A. and Goodwin, C. (eds) (1992) *Rethinking Context: Language as an interactive phenomenon* (Cambridge: Cambridge University Press).

Edwards, R. and Clarke, J. (2002) Flexible learning, spatiality and identity. *Studies in Continuing Education*, 24(2), 153–166.

Gee, J., Hull, G. and Lankshear, C. (1996) *The New Work Order: Behind the language of the new capitalism* (Sydney: Allen & Unwin).

Groat, L. (1995) Introduction: Place, aesthetic evaluation and home. In L. Groat (ed.) *Giving places meaning* (San Diego, CA: Academic Press), pp. 1–26.

Habermas, J. (1986) *The Theory of Communicative Action. Volumes One and Two.* (trans. T. McCarthy) (London: Polity Press).

Handy, G. (1994) *The Empty Raincoat: Making sense of the future* (London: Hutchinson Arrow).

Jamieson, P., Fisher, K. Gilding, T., Taylor, P. and Trevitt, G. (2000) Place and space in the design of new learning environments. *Higher Education Research and Development*, 19(2), 221–237.

Kornberger, M. and Clegg, S. (2003) The architecture of complexity. *Culture and Organization*, 9(2), 75–91.

Latour, B. (1986) The powers of association. In J. Law (ed.) *Power, Action & Belief: A new sociology of knowledge* (London: Routledge & Kegan Paul), pp. 264–280.

Lave, J. and Wenger, E. (1991) *Situated Learning: Legitimate peripheral participation* (Cambridge: Cambridge University Press).

Marsick, V. and Watkins, K. (1999) *Facilitating Learning Organizations: Making learning count* (Aldershot: Gower).

Nespor, J. (1994) *Knowledge in Motion: Space, time and curriculum in undergraduate physics and management* (London: The Falmer Press.).

O'Toole, K. M. P. (2001) Learning through the physical environment in the workplace. *International Education Journal*, 2(1), 10–19.

Rainbird, H., Fuller, A. and Monroe, A. (eds) (2004) *Workplace Learning in Context* (London: Routledge).

Rhodes, G. and Scheeres, H. (2004) Developing people in organizations: Working (on) identity. *Studies in Continuing Education*, 26(2), 175–193.

Rizvi, F. (1997) Beyond the East-West divide: Education and the dynamics of Australia-Asia relations. *The Australian Educational Researcher*, 24(1), 13–26.

Rose, N. (1996) *Inventing Our Selves: Psychology, power, and personhood* (Cambridge: Cambridge University Press).

Said, E. W. (1978) *Orientalism* (London: Routledge & Kegan Paul).

Sarup, M. (1996) *Identity, Culture and the Postmodern Worlds* (Edinburgh: Edinburgh University Press).

Scheeres, H. (2003) Learning to talk: From manual work to discourse work as self-regulating practice. *Journal of Workplace Learning*, 15(7/8), 332–338.

Scheeres, H. and Solomon, N. (2000) Research partnerships at work: New identities for new times. In: J. Garrick and C. Rhodes (eds) *Research and Knowledge at Work: Perspectives, case studies and innovative strategies* (London: Routledge), pp. 178–199.

Solomon, N., Boud, D., Leontios, M. and Staron, M. (2001) Tale of two institutions: Exploring collaboration in research partnerships. *Studies in the Education of Adults*, 33(2), 135–142.

Stronach, I. and Maclure, M. (1997) *Educational Research Undone: The postmodern embrace* (Buckingham: Open University Press).

Welton, M. (ed.) (1995) *In Defense of the Lifeworld: Critical perspectives on adult learning* (Albany, NY: State University of New York Press).

Section 2

Cultural Bridging

6

Leaving Middle Childhood and Moving into Teenhood: Small Stories Revealing Identity and Agency

Kathy Hall

Introduction

This chapter is about the processes by which people transform selves, exemplified by the processes through which one boy, Daniel, takes himself into adolescence. Subscribing to a sociocultural perspective, and helped by the theoretical notions of mediated action, figured worlds and positionality, the chapter shows how identity and agency are fundamental to an understanding of the processes of becoming, doing and participating in the social word of teenhood. Accepting that the notion of a coherent, integrated or stable self is elusive, I suggest that coherence is won momentarily through agentive investment in a discursively afforded, salient identity. Further, I will attempt to illustrate how, because identities and discourses are multiple and can be in tension, a person is forced to choose from those available, hence the space for agency and for the authoring of a self.

I will explain and develop my argument by describing and analysing some settings and practices of children as they co-author and co-authorize their identities. I will focus in particular on how Daniel effortfully maintains himself as a popular, teenage, heterosexual male, how this identity is jointly constructed, how it is granted, but never guaranteed, how it is mediated by class, and how it is at once empowering and constraining for himself and others.

Methodological and theoretical background

The chapter is based on a project, supported by a grant from the British Academy, about middle childhood in rural Ireland. It set out to explore children's perspectives on their social world and particularly their use of space and time, especially outside of school. Mindful of Bakhtin's insight that we know the world through the representations we make of it, the study set out to try to gain an understanding of how children represent their world.

A yet more specific focus of the work and the one to be pursued here is the way children build identities for themselves through networking with others in joint activities.

Middle childhood can be considered to span ages 8–13 years. Ethnographic methods were used to understand the life worlds of children in four different families. This involved *shadowing* the children in these families as they went about the everyday business of work, leisure, play and school. Observational, interview, focus group and diary approaches were used to collect data. A key method of considerable value in understanding how the participants shape themselves and others proved to be adult-guided group conversations. Here, the participants talked with an interested adult about what it meant, from their perspectives, to be growing up in a particular place and time. Underlying the conversational approach is the notion that the primary function of language is rhetorical and not merely referential and representational (Murray, 1989; Shotter, 1989). What is of interest is what goes on between people – how one takes into account one's relations with others. The emphasis on group conversation recognizes that the person is constructed through talk – one constructs oneself and others linguistically. This emphasis also recognizes that identities are performed and lived in the everyday (Lave, 2008), rather than simply narrated.

The conversations themselves varied in length from a few minutes to over an hour and some involved little intervention from the adult in terms of queries and questions. Many, but not all, were audio-recorded. My intention in this chapter is to select from the database excerpts and episodes that exemplify how identities are locally and discursively accomplished in everyday interactive social practice, and how children in middle childhood grow themselves into teenhood. These episodes or 'small stories', as opposed to life histories or life events (Bamberg, 2006), reveal how selves are emerging and fashioned – the accounts that are offered by the participants can be read as stories that are borrowed to do identity work. I have collected such small stories with the same people but at different times over a three-year period.

The study is premised on a view of identity or self as fragmentary, multiple, contradictory and always relational, and open to construction and reconstruction in different contexts (Bruner, 1986, 1990; Holland et al., 1998), and on a view of mind as inherently social and mediated (Penuel and Wertsch, 1995; Wertsch, 1991; Wertsch et al., 1995). Identities are made available and chosen through participation in activity and a person's agency lies in the choices made, the decision to choose one identity or position over another. In this sense, identities can be thought of as resources that can be employed in the construal of a self. Theoretically, three key interrelated concepts, which support the framing and analysis of the work, need to be briefly explained. These are mediated action, figured world and positionality.

Drawing on the work of Vygotsky, Bakhtin and others, James Wertsch talks about *mediated action* which is a term designed to bridge the gap between the person and the social world or socio-historical context in which the person lives. Mediated action is about how a person's (an agent's) actions and interactions are accomplished by the use of *mediational means* or *cultural tools*. Mediational means are shaping resources for acting or performing the self, examples being language/words/forms of discourse, ideology and artifacts. What mediational means people appropriate and how they appropriate them are of significance in understanding identity formation. What is fundamental is that they are acquired in participation and interaction with others and therefore they are always distributed.

Holland et al. (1998: 49) explain the notion of figured world by inviting readers to imagine the world of academia: '[wh]hat if there were a world called academia, where books were so significant that people would sit for hours on end, away from friends and family, writing them?'. They go on to say: '[p]eople have the propensity to be drawn to, recruited for, and formed in these worlds, and to become active in and passionate about them'. Figured worlds are historical and social phenomena into which individuals enter or are recruited and which are then reproduced and developed through the practices of their participants. A figured world is populated by the (imagined) characters and types who carry out its business and who have ways of interacting within it as well as orientations towards it. Below, I am interested in the figured worlds that are made relevant to Daniel and his friends and family, as well as the markers of identity in those particular worlds. Gee's *cultural models* and *discourses* (Gee, 1999, 2001), Wenger's *communities of practice* (Wenger, 1998) and Bakhtin's *speech genres* (Bakhtin, 1986) are akin to figured worlds. Just as one inhabits more that one community of practice, one inhabits more than one figured world. Figured worlds are meaning systems which mediate our behaviour, they are traditions of apprehension which gather us up and give us form as our lives intersect them (Holland *et al.*, 1998: 41). Some figured worlds, suggest Holland, are denied us and some we deny to others, some we miss by accident while others we learn fully.

Positionality or relationality is about the way behaviour signals the nature of social relations with others. It has to do with relations of power, prestige, entitlement, influence, affiliation and status. Positional identities therefore depend upon who is present in the interaction (Davies and Harré, 2001; Holland *et al.*, 1998). As expressed by Jill Johnston (1973 in Kitzinger, 1989: 83), 'identity is what you can say you are according to what they say you can be'. People develop a sense of their relative social position in a given social context. Positional identities refer to a view of oneself in relation to others in a given situation, how one can enter a conversation, what one can say, what emotions one can express; in sum, one's fitness for certain claims and rights (Holland *et al.*, 1998). Day-to-day, moment-by-moment encounters therefore are the stuff of identity formation.

The twin and overlapping notions of figurative identities and positional identities provide a conceptual frame for considering the shaping of selves, while the notion of mediational means or cultural tools invites an exploration of the resources (e.g. styles of language, dress and so on) that people recruit to enact identities. The rest of the chapter draws on these concepts in seeking to account for the ways in which children move themselves out of childhood and into adolescence.

Constructing a common identity: recruiting class and gender

Very early in the project, the participating boys construct a shared view of themselves and their neighbourhood, an identity that is assumed to be a given, to be normal and natural. This confers a sense of belonging to a community, a common sense of identity and a shared perspective on the world. This is achieved by distinguishing themselves and their neighbourhood from other people and other neighbourhoods. Class and gender are recruited as stabilizing forces, conferring a coherent identity for them and the people who live in their neighbourhood. The following two episodes reveal how a common identity is discursively constructed. The first is a social class identity that is different from and superior to the one they jointly afford others in other places; the second is a heterosexual male identity, which they distinguish and separate from the one they recognize as fitting others.

In Excerpt 1, the boys, Norman (11 years) and Daniel (12 years) who have been both neighbours and friends for several years, make class salient. They construct themselves as coming from a particular neighbourhood – of normal (turn 4), law-abiding, responsible, well-adjusted people who know how to behave and dress appropriately (turn 4). Although they don't know a single individual from the neighbourhood they castigate, they are absolutely certain that they are 'all knackers' (turn 4), definitely not 'normal people', and they can't imagine themselves ever having friends from that part of town (turns 12–15). That they might ever befriend someone from Esker is so shocking and unthinkable that the suggestion of it prompts a prayer ('Oh God, Oh my God'). They position themselves as the dominant class and other than those from Esker, characterizing them as deviant and rough.

The identity work is accomplished linguistically through the use of the plural pronoun we (e.g. turn 22), talking for each other, e.g turn 3, 'Norman and me are friends with the normal towny people', and through repetitions (turns 2 and 3: 'They're all knackers'; turns 5 and 6: 'They light bonfires'; turns 9 and 10: 'hash and ecstasy'; turn 12: 'Oh God, Oh my God'; turns 13 and 15: 'no way, no way'; turn 21: 'they know it … they know it'). Further, they don't at any point disagree or contradict each other, as there is no doubt about their categorization and recognition of themselves and others. Such linguistic moves index a shared, coherent world view. They jointly construct themselves as belonging to a particular community of practice that they can unproblematically distinguish from other communities. The people in Esker can never take up positions of normality, much less coolness – they are consigned to positions of deviance.

Yet this positioning is not total and straightforward. At the outset, Daniel suggests that Norman 'has a problem', inferring that perhaps he himself doesn't. Further, he is reluctant to utter the derogatory label 'knackers' aloud (turn 1). However, he is unable to resist for long and is very quickly drawn into the Esker bashing by explaining what Norman means by 'townies' (turn 3). Daniel takes his cue from Norman, expanding and embellishing his initiations in the early moves. Later in the conversation, however, he adjusts his utterances somewhat to appear more tentative and moderate. The *they* shifts from the inference that all of them sell drugs to 'one person does' (turn 8), and in turn 10 there is a further distancing from the claim that all of them are rough to the claim that it's mostly teenagers and 'they're not that bad'. And in the same turn, Daniel uses the more acceptable label, 'settled travellers'. This slight tempering on his part does not extend to the possibility of ever having friends there (turn 11). Nevertheless, Daniel's linguistic modifications allow him to be heard by me, the adult (but not Norman), as more mature and balanced in his views than Norman. He accomplishes this without compromising his Esker-bashing identity with Norman. All this requires careful attending to the self he is making available to his two different listeners. Daniel draws on evidence to support his claims about drugs – he knows someone who knows someone there, thus safely distancing himself from such undesirables. Together, they recognize themselves as quite distinct and in a separate category from that afforded all those who live in Esker. What is clear even from this short exchange is how people's representations of themselves in the flow of everyday life can reveal more than one self.

Excerpt 1: Esker estate – class mediation

Turn	Speaker		Annotation
1	D	He has a problem with townies. No, he hasn't problem with townies, he has a problem with ... I can't say it on the recorder ... knackers. Do you know a place called Esker?	Whispers
2	K	I do.	
3	N	Well, they just beat you up if you went there; they're all knackers.	Derogatory term for settled travellers
4	D	They're all knackers yeah there and that's what Norman means by townies. They wear their hats back like this. They don't have p-caps like normal people. Like Norman and me are friends with the normal towny people like that live in the town like in Churchtown or places like that. But the people in Esker and yyy – they act like townies. They go around beating up people they don't like.	C stands up to demonstrate, using 'townies' here as a derogatory term
5	N	And they light bonfires on beaches and hills and everything like that.	
6	D	Yeah, they light bonfires. They throw stuff in windows and rocks and everything like that. They rob people like they're always breaking into cars and they have a special place where they throw things like handbags after they rob them; they throw everything down the Protestant graveyard.	
7	N	That's where Daniel's mother's handbag was found when her ...	

(Continued)

Turn	Speaker		Annotation
8	D	Yeah, when me Mam's car was robbed. And they even sell drugs down in Esker. Well, one person does. They have drugs like hash and ecstasy.	
9	K	Do they?	
10	D	Yeah, hash and ecstasy, there's one guy there and they're selling 'extra ecstasy' and they all know he's doing it but they won't ever say they get them from their cousins in the Bronx in America, they hide them in the towels or something … but Kurtis's cousin who lives there told me he got caught and now he's in jail. … They're just real rough like criminals. But they're not that bad, the adults, it's mostly the teenagers. Most of the people there are settled travellers.	Information is second-hand (tempering)
11	K	Could you see yourself having friends from Esker?	
12	D	Oh God, Oh my God.	Shocked tone
13	N	No way.	
14	D	You wouldn't expect to have friends there.	
15	N	No way.	
16	K	Tell me why.	
17	D	'Cos they're rough.	As if it's obvious
18	N	They know they're from a rough place, they know.	
19	D	Yeah.	
20	K	Maybe they think the same about ye?	

(Continued)

Turn	Speaker		Annotation
21	D	No they don't, they know they're rough. They know it.	Indignant
22	N	They know we're from a normal place.	
23	N	And they think everyone is scared of them.	
24	D	Say if you knew a person from Esker and say you had a row with him or started spreading rumours about him, well the whole place, they'd all come after you and start beatin' you up.	
25	K	And would that ever happen out here?	
26	D	No never, never. We never got beaten up before, never.	Indignant again
27	N	Never, touch wood.	
28	D	And you'd never get anyone selling drugs in the town or anywhere outside that place.	

Throughout the data there are many examples of the mediation of gender. Indeed, a heterosexual male identity would appear to be salient for Daniel and Norman in nearly all encounters. They work hard, for instance, to ensure they could never be recognized as gay. On one occasion, they were presented with accounts of how same-age boys who they didn't know spend their time, one of whom travels a lot, swims, plays football and learns the piano and the mandolin. Learning to play a musical instrument is deemed highly troublesome – an unsuitable activity for both of them, since they would run the risk of being perceived as 'a bit bendy', a risk that they agreed they could not afford to take. It's far safer to just listen to pop music, especially to know about pop bands like Eminem (but not Westlife since they are for children). Learning to play any musical instrument is made into an activity that is inconsistent with being a heterosexual male.

Excerpt 2 also evidences how gender is made relevant, how together both boys claim not to like girls (turn 7), at least not 'girlie girls' (turn 12). And here Daniel in particular positions himself as someone, who although not liking girls (turn 7), will play with *anyone* (turn 12), even girls. There is also ambiguity and contradiction here (turns 7 and 12) where girls in the town and in the country are positioned as different, girls from the town apparently being more willing to reject traditional stereotypical female roles. However, there is other identity work going on in this excerpt. We see Daniel resisting an identity of not being liked (turns 6 and 7) by positioning those talked about as 'fighting with everybody' and so repairing the attack on his identity by Norman; and then quickly shifting the topic to new discursive territory where he attempts to speak for himself and Norman; we see him distinguishing himself from his friend by claiming greater experiences and access to other places not available to Norman, e.g. the town and the world of popular boys where shopping is taken for granted and where boys and girls hang out together freely (turn 12). In the country, where both boys live, only girls who are cousins are suitable girl contacts (turn 10). Moreover, we see Daniel claiming Norman as a friend only because there is nobody else (turn 1), a point that perhaps Norman is mindful of in turn 6. Norman's attempt to claim 'a few girlfriends' is reinterpreted by Daniel to mean not real girlfriends – Norman's bid to position himself as not a child is thwarted; his testing out of a heterosexual self is contested (turn 10), and he is denied access to the figured world of popular teenage boys, as that is Daniel's domain. In this episode, Daniel is more agentic than Norman, seeming to have the capacity to make Norman act as an instrument of his agency (Holland et al., 1998).

Excerpt 2: Girlie girls – gender mediation

Turn	Speaker		Annotation
1	D	The only reason why we got to be sooo best friends is because Donal wasn't living down the road because he's from America and …	
2	K	Is he?	
3	D	Yeah, he's from San Francisco.	
4	K	Oh.	
5	D	Me and Donal are real good friends now. He always stays in my house now. And then there's Amanda and Liam, they moved …	A and L are Norman's cousins
6	N	Yeah, they don't like Daniel.	He ignores this affront from his friend about his popularity
7	D	They moved into my, I mean, their house; they're always fightin' with everyone. See, we don't get along with girls. And Amanda is …	Amanda is Norman's cousin
8	K	So you don't get along with girls, neither of you?	

(Continued)

9	N	Well, I have a few girlfriends.	
10	D	Well, he means girl friends – he's talkin' about his cousins, same way I like my cousins. We get on with Liam obviously 'cos …	D prevents him from explaining, but later his friend insists that he has girl-friends and that he meets them

The figured world of popular teenage boys

Daniel marks himself out to others as belonging to the figured world of popular teenagers. He uses a range of cultural tools and mediating devices to pull off this identity – from physical markers, particularly expensive designer trainers and subtly highlighted hair, to significant experiences like going to discos, clubs and pubs, having older friends who party and drink alcohol, knowing about pop music, and having the freedom to plan his own time. Using these tools of identity, he and others legitimate him in the figured world of popular teenagers. He has actively chosen the figured world of popular males by which to grow and transform himself into a teenager. He finds it particularly seductive, and over time he has developed a certain expertise in demonstrating himself as this kind of person. Membership of this world enables him to relinquish childish things and childish ways. But this popular identity has to gain legitimacy afresh every time he is in the company of peers – despite his relative expertise in doing popularity, it can never be assumed or taken for granted. This valued identity is never finally won and requires constant endeavour because participation – the essential process of transformation/learning – is dynamic and unpredictable. As Lave (1996: 18) observes, with reference to positional identities, '[d]ifferences in power, interests, and possibilities for action are ubiquitous', which means actors have to be ever vigilant and attentive.

Excerpt 3: Friends and the town

Turn	Speaker		Annotation
1	D	I need to be with me friends in town. We talk about normal things like soccer and block.	
2	K	What's 'block'?	

(Continued)

Turn	Speaker		Annotation
3	N	(long explanation)	
4	C	We play that over and over. … Norman wouldn't know anybody over in Churchtown, would you, Norman?	
5	K	Churchtown is in town, is it?	
6	N	Churchtown is in town at the xxx side.	
7	D	My granny lives in Bayview so whenever my Dad goes in there I say hi and then bye and then I'm off down the road to Seaside, my auntie lives down the road in Seaside and they have four kids like Aoife is only 2, Sinead is 13. Adam is 17 but I wouldn't be really hangin' around with him that much.	
8	K	'Cos he's older than you?	
9	D	No, 'cos he doesn't really like playstation. He just goes playing with all his friends. Jason now he's 21. He's his other brother and Jason like he couldn't live without his playstation or PC. On a Saturday night they'd get a few cans and stuff and then they'd just have a party and they'd play FIFA all night. He's not into like …	
10	K	What is it, Norman?	
11	N	We usually watch the Simpsons on Sky One or …	
12	D	You would think we were the same age. We're all big fans of Man	D ignores N, he stands up to

(Continued)

Turn	Speaker		Annotation
		United. Norman's never been in Old Trafford but Jason and me are goin' to Old Trafford. We're big fans of Man United so we'd be playing together and we'd be goin' to the pub to watch the matches. Every weekend I'd nearly go into the pub with them.	ensure he keeps the floor
13	K	Would you?	
14	D	Yeah.	
15	K	So you spend a lot of time in town as well as around here.	
16	D	Yeah, I couldn't just stay in this country for say a whole week.	Sits down again
17	K	Do you mean in the country?	
18	D	I'd always like to go into the shopping centre and hang around with Donal.	
19	N	Yeah and buy CDs or something.	
20	D	Yeah, buy CDs.	
21	K	So you spend a lot a time with people who are older than you?	
22	D	Well, just one. [*Pauses a bit*] But with his friends as well, yeah. Well, they have all these friends like Grieve, and they all have these nicknames like Minki, Gravo.	Stands up, especially enthusiastic relating this
23	N	Cool.	Howling with laughter

(Continued)

| 24 | D | Hilljo, Jay we call 'em, they all have nicknames you can ask *anybody* like. I don't know how I'm such good friends with all them. They'd be ringing me an' all. And they're 21. The only reason we all get on so well is because we all love FIFA and we all love the PC. And we all love like goin' to the matches and everything like that. We just get on grand all the time. | |

In Excerpt 3, Daniel manages to make his world socially relevant and to ensure that he is heard as different to Norman. And Norman affords him the identity he so desires by his remark 'cool' in turn 23. Norman's bid for an exciting life is overtaken/denied by Daniel (turns 11 and 12) who has the power to make his version prevail. Throughout this short extract, Daniel uses the first person singular and verb phrases to position himself as active agent, whereas Norman uses noun phrases, uses first person plural once (turn 11) and never uses first person singular. In such slices of life, Daniel makes himself into a cool, popular teenager and his listeners legitimate this position – at least on this occasion. He is and feels popular – that identity is internally persuasive (Bakhtin, in Holquist, 1990) for him – he has made it his own and he feels completely validated in this scenario. He can do popularity with style – at least with Norman and one adult. In this scenario, he is an actor with more entitlement, power, influence and status than Norman who is invited by Daniel's positioning of him to enact a subject position of inferiority. To the extent that 'the inter-personal becomes the intrapersonal' (Holland et al., 1998: 235), Daniel has been *inhabited* by coolness. What is clear is that identity is performed and relational, it can't be viewed as the possession of an individual or simply an immutable internal state. The 'I', as Holland and Lave (2001: 8) observe, 'is by no means a freewheeling agent, authoring worlds from springs of meaning and insight within'.

Despite his animated talk, there are uncertainties regarding the extent to which he really feels he belongs to this world. In turns 9 and 22, he refers to *they* (not *we*); in turn 12, he says 'I'd *nearly* go into the pub with them'; and finally in turn 24, he admits 'I don't know how I'm such good friends with all them'. His popular self remains fragile and vulnerable. For Daniel, there is considered social work involved in maintaining his position. He admits in another conversation with his friends that '*I made myself* like Eminem, *I made myself* crazy about [some other pop group] and *I made myself* stay up all night'. Liking these things required effort over time; he didn't just learn to like them overnight. Moving out of childhood and into his valued version of teenhood requires hard work; it is far from a nat-ural, spontaneous process of maturation.

Having an extensive network of friends helps one to be more powerfully agentive in the figured world of cool teenager. Boys and girls who have 'no' or 'hardly any friends' are talked about. On one occasion, Norman, his cousin, Liam, and Daniel talk freely (and cruelly) about people in (primary) school 'who have no friends'. Norman says how one such girl, Hilda, 'fancies Daniel'. He is aware of this apparently and proceeds to describe the strategies he has for avoiding her. They all agree she is someone who must be shunned. When I ask about this girl, Daniel says, 'she has no friends, only a few girl friends'. He is unable to explain how this constitutes friendlessness, but the boys discursively make her into a non-popular person and condemn her to remain in this position. Such positions are needed however to facilitate the distinction between the popular and non-popular categories. When he came back from his holiday in Spain in August 2005, he enthused with several friends and cousins that he had made 40 friends and was constantly texting them on his mobile phone. The high point of this holiday, he explained to his audience, was going to 'adult night clubs' where once he kissed a girl. But such accounts of being active and experienced couldn't be easily verified by his peers nor did they go unchallenged. In his absence, Norman and some of his cousins accused him of 'using Norman', of 'boasting about all his friends', and they predicted that very likely he would 'fall in with a bad crowd' when he goes to secondary school. So a disruption is emerging at a collective level to Daniel's status in the group. His positional identity as popular and having lots of friends is being contested which could in the future result in alternative social arrangements.

The pivotal media associated with the world which Daniel so desires include pop music, clothes, especially tracksuits and trainers, mobile phones, computers, computer games, TV programmes, football, and, above all, friends and now night clubs. All these help to position him as a member of this category – they are his props or pivots in extending his identity. He transforms himself through the use of these resources. For example, one evening he spent over an hour bitterly arguing with his father about a pair of designer trainers that were not the right colour – the right colour in the same brand would have cost 30 euros more and his father didn't buy them for him, buying a cheaper pair instead. The endless energy expended on getting the right look and arguing relentlessly with his father all make sense in the world he was figuring but not in the value-for-money world his father was figuring. Trainers here are refigured objects used to affect others, to author a self, and so orient behaviour. These mediating devices enable him to gain a perspective on himself as popular, as cool, as trendy. Without them, his popular identity might evaporate.

Agency: Choosing an identity to grow by

Why does Daniel invest in this identity in preference to others? How is it that the popular teenage male identity is compelling for him, especially when it is plainly so exhausting and demanding? The first point to make here is that not choosing is not an option (until one is dead!). Bakhtin's notion of addressivity (Holquist, 1990; Shotter, 1989) – the quality of turning to someone else – is relevant. He suggests that the world must be answered – authorship is not a choice but the answer is never determined – this is the space for the author (see also Holland et al., 1998) or, expressed differently, this is where agency lies. Drawing on James Gee's (2001) notion that positions are on a continuum and can be taken up with varying degrees of commitment, it would seem that Daniel agentively commits to popularity. He has developed a certain level of expertise in this world so he finds it motivating. It has become personally meaningful for him. Other identities are not typically afforded him, for example, the learned boy, the successful-in-school identity. He does not feel valued in such worlds. For most of the period of this research, Daniel was in primary school. He hated his teacher who had a reputation for being strict and rather traditional in her teaching approach. He spent much of his time in his final year in primary school sitting apart from others in the classroom, as he was perceived by his teacher as 'a talker' and a 'disruptive influence'. She 'can't wait for him to leave the school' (and nor can he). His friends bother him because of this, pathologizing him ('he has a problem with talking'). His mother frequently affirms his dislike of school by admitting that she too hated it. They also talk about school subjects at home, and she pointed out to me in his presence that she was always 'hopeless' at maths and how Daniel too is 'hopeless'. School is not a place where Daniel can author himself. Primary school was a place where he was literally silenced, where he couldn't represent himself and where he was represented in terms of his failings rather than his successes. To strive for social significance in school would be futile. There appears to be no successful school identity available to him, other than as cool teenager who is quite good at football. He and his companions talk a lot about school but he feels he can do nothing about how constrained his life is in school. He copes by looking forward to the weekend. One Friday evening, this is how he expressed his plans for the days ahead:

> Today I just want to do what I want to do. I don't want to mow the lawn though me Dad might want me to. I have to clean out the dog's pen every day – it takes about ten minutes. Today I just want to have freedom. I'll go into town, stay with me cousin – he's 16, his brother is 21, and he's after applying to get into the guards and my other cousin, she's a girl, she's 14. We'll go to the pub, play snooker and watch the match on telly tomorrow. Tonight we'll go for a pizza and generally hang around and play on the playstation. I love that – freedom, freedom, freedom is what I want.

I would suggest that, while no agent position is ever inevitable, the figured world of popular teendom that Daniel has chosen fits, not only with the images and messages he gets from popular culture (television, pop groups, football, etc.), but generationally. Family ties are deeply significant for him. His parents (mostly) approve of his behaviour, seeing it as natural and normal. His father spoke admiringly of his ability to make friends in Spain despite language barriers, and both parents comment approvingly, occasionally teasing him, on his dress, as he transforms himself to go to the (secondary) school disco in the local town. Moreover, both his parents have a tradition themselves of dressing up, going out on weekend nights to meet their friends and frequently not getting home from the pub until very late. So what is personally meaningful to Daniel, what he has chosen (and what has chosen him), accord with his past and present life and with future possibilities as he sees them. He is not entirely a newcomer, therefore, to the figured world of cool teenhood – his desire for a not dissimilar figured world to his parents has been formed over time, a lifetime in a process of recruitment and identification. He is moving towards generational inclusion. The extent to which people identify with a figured world depends on their social histories. In Daniel's trajectory, we get a sense of self in history and a history in self (Holland and Lave, 2001). Holland et al. (1998) argue that it is difficult to understand a person's behaviour without knowing something of 'the opportunistic history of its formation' (p. 6). Insofar as he has had the opportunity to develop at least a certain expertise with the cultural system – what some identity researchers claim is a prerequisite to finding that world or system motivating (Dreyfus, cited in Holland et al., 1998) – it is not surprising that he finds it authentic, compelling and relevant. Daniel is agentive within limits, the limits set by the available figured worlds on the one hand (though new figured worlds can be constructed by him and his co-participants), and by the limits of the positions made available in the moment-by-moment interaction on the other.

Daniel makes a judgement about when it's really important to do popularity and when it's OK to do caring, learned boy or child. So far I have emphasized one dimension – one that appears to be salient to him when in the presence of peers. In other situations, other identities assume significance for him. For example, when in the presence of his parents in the living room of their house, he is quite prepared to be positioned as child, being stroked and cuddled by his father and mother, as they watch TV (including a football match), called *pet*, and having to be cajoled into eating his dinner. His parents ignore his interjections into their conversations, perceiving them as trivial, childish and inconsequential. Here, he seems to take a break from heavy-duty *impression management* (Lave, 1996: 14), reverting to a familiar subservient-to-adult, child position.

Caring as an identity is not internally persuasive for Daniel, especially when among his male peers. He has talked about paid work, which includes babysitting his young cousin who is three years old, but he feels obliged to stress that he only does this for the money, how he really doesn't like doing it, but how it's easy to do as he can watch TV. A neighbour (Amanda's mother, above) asked him to 'watch out for Amanda' on the bus to secondary school. Amanda is Norman's cousin and is prone to fainting and getting blackouts due to a medical condition (then under investigation). Daniel agrees to do this and tells other adults (including me) how he walks with Amanda every day to the bus (about half a mile) and back again in the evening. However, while on the bus, according to Amanda herself, he shuns her. He can however recruit a caring identity when it serves his preferred identity. On spending an afternoon and evening at a christening party in a neighbour's house, he put his arms around a six-year-old boy as they watched an adult horror movie, telling him not to look and covering his eyes at the most scary parts. The adults were not in the room at the time. He justified this by saying, 'he will only get nightmares tonight'. Daniel was able to engage in this act of caring in view of his peers as it didn't unduly compromise his macho cool image. In doing this, he was also marking his own fitness for such adult watching.

The popular teenage identity is one that he has selected as the dominant one by which to grow. Where other identities conflict with this, he usually resolves in favour of the former. For example, since the study began, Daniel has talked about the importance of 'paid work' and future work possibilities that would not involve physical labour (an essential condition in the light of his father's arthritis due to building work), all designed to provide him with the necessary financial resources to 'have fun' which translates to football, matches, the pub and holidays. Being a policeman/guard seemed to fit the bill and he had worked out a detailed rationale for this choice which he frequently discussed in the company of peers. However, he has recently shifted from this view explaining that it would be too difficult to do this job since he would run a huge risk of not remaining popular with his peers. He would have to stop people for speeding, having no tax and so on, and some of these people would likely be his mates who he would meet in the pub later. This job would simply not fit with his image of himself as a popular adult and so despite its many benefits otherwise, had to be abandoned. He no longer wants to be a guard.

A further incident which forced him to reconcile conflicting identities occurred when he moved into secondary school and was faced with having to choose between different subjects – business studies and home economics. 'Unlike his experience of primary school, he claims to love his secondary school – a school which is rather exceptional in its emphasis on sport in particular and on developing the *all round person* in general'. He deliberated about this early in September 2005 when he first went to the school. It was made dilemmatic for him because his mother advised him not to do business studies as he wouldn't be able to do the maths involved. As she is a cook and as he likes cooking, he reasoned that he didn't need to do home economics, as he already knew enough. At no point was he concerned that 'home ec', as he calls it, wouldn't fit with his male image, since he had already developed an interest in cooking from home and from watching cookery programmes on TV where the chefs are usually male. He eventually resolved this by managing to do media and graphic design, a subject that wasn't initially on offer to him.

Identity: the opportunity cost

Identities and agency trace our participation in activities. Identities are meaningless in the absence of participation in activities; we must participate in activities, even vicariously, in order to take them up. It follows therefore that identities can be both privileging and oppressive, as there is always an opportunity cost. Daniel has found a salient identity by which he can negotiate his way out of childhood and into teenhood. In agentively evolving a particular identity and making it dominant and central to his display of self, he has sacrificed other ways to grow and other potentially liberating ways to live a life. For example, we saw above how he will not allow himself to commit to learning how to play a musical instrument, this activity being perceived to conflict with his current identity. For the moment, this is the price he has to pay for a semblance of a coherent self. Furthermore, Norman is denied the more grown-up identity afforded to Daniel – he is not allowed to step into this popular space. He has to accept an inferior positioning, agreeing to listen while Daniel performs his expert, cool self.

Since moving into secondary school in September 2005, Daniel has tempered his dread of teachers, class work and school subjects. In conversation, he has initiated the possibility of being successful in school, occasioned by his evaluation of his new school as *cool*, insofar as: talk in class is allowed, some teachers don't object to note passing, school trips (to Alton Towers and Old Trafford this year) are exciting, discos are organized by the school at weekends, subjects are far more interesting than in primary school, especially science and other subjects that involve laboratories and workshops, and sport is highly regarded by teachers and pupils alike. The teachers here are perceived to be more lenient (and incidentally, by implication, 'not as smart') than their primary counterparts. The school itself is recognized locally as more liberal and progressive in orientation than either of the two single-sex secondary schools and far superior, in his view, to the technical school, the latter assumed to be a suitable school for those people who live in Esker. So at the end of his first year in secondary school, there is a hint of an emerging new identity, a potential turning point, and a consequent relinquishing of or disruption to the old one – the one that hated all things to do with school (except friends and football). There have been moments of resourcefulness when he reimagines himself as possibly a person who 'might go to college', thus pushing back the boundaries for identity. These moments are always couched in practical terms, such as the job this enterprise might lead to and the potential of such a job enabling him do what he thinks he wants to do leisure-wise. The key point, however, is that there is a change in Daniel's self-understanding in a new figuration of the world. How and whether this reinterpretation of himself leads to him questioning the validity of the popular identity remains to be seen.

Conclusion

This chapter has tried to illustrate how identity is occasioned in the everyday, how the everyday or moment-by-moment encounter is the means by which people learn, grow and transform themselves, how (like this chapter) it is ever a work in progress, and how agency is the phenomenon that allows the taking up of new and the relinquishing of old identities. It is evident that the self Daniel can negotiate is dependent on the others around him. He is figured by the world (Holland and Lave, 2001; Holland et al., 1998) of the cool teenager and this world grants him the semblance of a coherent identity; it is a guide to his actions. Since identity or self is jointly constructed and can only be given legitimacy in interaction with others, the self is ever relational and dynamic; it is socially distributed and can't ever be possessed by an individual. The self is a self in practice. The chapter sought to reveal the effort and activity involved in identity work, as well as the interdependence of opportunity and constraint in identity formation.

From the point of view of learning and development, it shows how children and adolescents test out, construct and shift their identities. I am interested in the processes of learning and development in the long term while accepting that the long term happens in the everyday. It is noteworthy that Daniel (and his friends) have picked socially acceptable ways by which to grow; they clearly reject deviance as an option, rejecting others who they view as deviant. Resources permitting, this work will continue over the next year or so, during which time it is proposed to attend more specifically to the meanings of gender. As others have demonstrated (e.g. Gulbrandsen, 2003: 113; Rolon-Dow, 2004), the ways that children move forward are basically gendered and in Daniel's world gender is becoming increasingly prominent.

References

Bakhtin, M. M. (1986) *Speech Genres and Other Late Essays*. Austin: University of Texas Press.
Bamberg, M. (2006) Biographic-narrative research, quo vadis? A critical review of 'big stories' from the perspective of 'small stories'. In K. Milnes, C. Horrocks, N. Kelly, B. Roberts and D. Robinson (Eds) *Narrative, Memory and Knowledge: representations, aesthetics and contexts*. Huddersfield: Huddersfield University Press.
Bruner, J. (1986) *Actual Minds, Possible Worlds*. Cambridge, MA: Harvard University Press.
Bruner, J. (1990) *Acts of Meaning*. Cambridge, MA: Harvard University Press.
Davies, B. and Harré, R. (2001) Positioning: the discursive production of selves. In M. Wetherell, S. Taylor and S. Yates (Eds) *Discourse Theory and Practice*. London: Sage, pp. 261–71.
Gee, J. (1999) *An Introduction to Discourse Analysis: theory and method*. London: Routledge.
Gee, J. (2001) Identity as an analytic lens for research in education, *Review of Research in Education* 25, 99, 412–20.

Gulbrandsen, M. (2003) Peer relations as arenas for gender construction among young teenagers, *Pedagogy, Culture and Society* 11, 1, 113–31.

Holland, D., Lachicotte, W., Skinner, D. and Cain, C. (1998) *Identity and Agency in Cultural Worlds*. Cambridge, MA: Harvard University Press.

Holland, D. and Lave, J. (2001) History in person. In *Enduring Struggles: contentious practice, intimate identities*, pp. 1–32. Sante Fe: School of American Research Press.

Holquist, M. (1990) *Dialogism: Bakhtin and His World*. London: Routledge.

Kitzinger, C. (1989) Liberal humanism as an ideology of social control: the regulation of lesbian identities. In J. Shotter and K.J. Gergen (Eds) *Texts of Identity*, pp. 82–98. London: Sage.

Lave, J. (1996) The practice of learning. In S. Chaiklin and J. Lave (Eds) *Understanding Practice: perspectives on activity and context*, pp. 3–32. Cambridge, MA: CUP.

Lave, J. (2008) Everyday life and learning. In P. Murphy and R. McCormick (Eds) *Knowledge and Practice: representations and identities,* pp. 3–14. London: Sage.

Murray, K. (1989) The construction of identity in the narratives of romance and comedy. In J. Shotter and K. J. Gergen (Eds) *Texts of Identity*, pp. 176–205. London: Sage.

Penuel, W. and Wertsch, J. (1995) Vygotsky and identity formation: a sociocultural approach, *Educational Psychologist* 30, 83–92.

Rolon-Dow, R. (2004) Seduced by images: identity and schooling in the lives of Puerto Rican girls, *Anthropology and Education Quarterly* 35, 1, 8–29.

Shotter, J. (1989) Social accountability and the social construction of 'you'. In J. Shotter and K. J. Gergen (Eds) *Texts of Identity*. London: Sage.

Wenger, E. (1998) *Communities of Practice: learning, meaning and identity*. Cambridge, MA: CUP.

Wertsch, J. V. (1991) *Voices of the Mind: a sociocultural approach to mediated action*. London: Harvester Wheatsheaf.

Wertsch, J. V., del Rio, P. and Alvarez, A. (1995) Sociocultural studies: history, action and mediation. In J. V. Wertsch, P. del Rio and A. Alvarez (Eds) *Sociocultural Studies of Mind*. Cambridge, MA: CUP.

7

Identity in Practice

Etienne Wenger

There is a profound connection between identity and practice. Developing a practice requires the formation of a community whose members can engage with one another and thus acknowledge each other as participants. As a consequence, practice entails the negotiation of ways of being a person in that context. This negotiation may be silent; participants may not necessarily talk directly about that issue. But whether or not they address the question directly, they deal with it through the way they engage in action with one another and relate to one another. Inevitably, our practices deal with the profound issue of how to be a human being. In this sense, the formation of a community of practice is also the negotiation of identities.

The parallels between practice and identity are summarized in Figure 7.1. To highlight them in this chapter, I will […] recast them in terms of identity. This exercise will yield the following characterizations:

- Identity as *negotiated experience*. We define who we are by the ways we experience our selves through participation, as well as by the ways we and others reify our selves.
- Identity as *community membership*. We define who we are by the familiar and the unfamiliar.
- Identity as *learning trajectory*. We define who we are by where we have been and where we are going.
- Identity as *nexus of multimembership*. We define who we are by the ways we reconcile our various forms of membership into one identity.
- Identity as *a relation between the local and the global*. We define who we are by negotiating local ways of belonging to broader constellations, and of manifesting broader styles and discourses.

These parallels constitute a level of analysis that presents identity and practice as mirror images of each other. […]

Negotiated experience: participation and reification

[…] Engagement in practice gives us certain experiences of participation, and what our communities pay attention to reifies us as participants. Becoming a claims processor, for

---

practice as …	identity as …
• negotiation of meaning (in terms of participation and reification)	• negotiated experience of self (in terms of participation and reification)
• community	• membership
• shared history of learning	• learning trajectory
• boundary and landscape	• nexus of multimembership
• constellations	• belonging defined globally but experienced locally

Figure 7.1   Parallels between practice and identity

instance, is both taking on the label "claims processor" and giving this label specific meanings through engagement in practice. It is doing what claims processors do, being treated the way they are treated, forming the community they form, entertaining certain relations with other practices, and – in the details of this process – giving a personal meaning to the category of claims processor. If […] Ariel is treated rudely by a customer, her engagement in practice suddenly brings into focus the humble status of her position in a striking way. She is working the front line and can be yelled at without compunction. Events like these can jolt our experience of participation and bring our identity into focus. Our very participation becomes reified, so to speak, and the labels we use take on deeper meanings.

The experience of identity in practice is a way of being in the world. It is not equivalent to a self-image; it is not, in its essence, discursive or reflective. We often think about our identities as self-images because we talk about ourselves and each other – and even think about ourselves and each other – in words. These words are important, no doubt, but they are not the full, lived experience of engagement in practice. I am not trying to belittle the importance of categories, self-images, and narratives of the self as constitutive of identity, but neither do I want to equate identity with those reifications. Who we are lies in the way we live day to day, not just in what we think or say about ourselves, though that is of course part (but only part) of the way we live. Nor does identity consist solely of what others think or say about us, though that too is part of the way we live. Identity in practice is defined socially not merely because it is reified in a social discourse of the self and of social categories, but also because it is produced as a lived experience of participation in specific communities. What narratives, categories, roles, and positions come to mean as an experience of participation is something that must be worked out in practice.

An identity, then, is a layering of events of participation and reification by which our experience and its social interpretation inform each other. As we encounter our effects on the world and develop our relations with others, these layers build upon each other to produce our identity as a very complex interweaving of participative experience and reificative projections. Bringing the two together through the negotiation of meaning, we construct who we are. In the same way that meaning exists in its negotiation, identity exists – not as an object in and of itself – but in the constant work of negotiating the self. It is in this cascading interplay of participation and reification that our experience of life becomes one of identity, and indeed of human existence and consciousness.

Community membership

I have argued that practice defines a community through three dimensions: mutual engagement, a joint enterprise, and a shared repertoire. Because a community of practice is not necessarily reified as such, our membership may not carry a label or other reified marker. But I have argued that our identity is formed through participation as well as reification. In this context, our membership constitutes our identity, not just through reified markers of membership but more fundamentally through the forms of competence that it entails. Identity in this sense is an experience and a display of competence that requires neither an explicit self-image nor self-identification with an ostensible community.

When we are with a community of practice of which we are a full member, we are in familiar territory. We can handle ourselves competently. We experience competence and we are recognized as competent. We know how to engage with others. We understand why they do what they do because we understand the enterprise to which participants are accountable. Moreover, we share the resources they use to communicate and go about their activities. These dimensions of competence [...] become dimensions of identity.

- *Mutuality of engagement.* In a community of practice, we learn certain ways of engaging in action with other people. We develop certain expectations about how to interact, how people treat each other, and how to work together. We become who we are by being able to play a part in the relations of engagement that constitute our community. Our competence gains its value through its very partiality. As an identity, this translates into a form of individuality defined with respect to a community. It is a certain way of being part of a whole through mutual engagement. For instance, I have reported that among claims processors it is more important to give and receive help than to know everything oneself. This results in a definition of individuality that differs from, say, forms of individuality in certain academic circles, where knowledge is a form of personal power and not knowing is largely construed as a personal deficit.
- *Accountability to an enterprise.* As we invest ourselves in an enterprise, the forms of accountability through which we are able to contribute to that enterprise make us look at the world in certain ways. Being a claims processor, doctor, parent, social worker, salesperson, beggar, folk dancer, or photographer gives us a certain focus. It moves us to understand certain conditions and to consider certain possibilities. As an identity, this translates into a perspective. It does not mean that all members of a community look at the world in the same way. Nonetheless, an identity in this sense manifests as a tendency to come up with certain interpretations, to engage in certain actions, to make certain choices, to value certain experiences – all by virtue of participating in certain enterprises.
- *Negotiability of a repertoire.* Sustained engagement in practice yields an ability to interpret and make use of the repertoire of that practice. We recognize the history of a practice in the artifacts, actions, and language of the community. We can make use of that history because we have been part of it and it is now part of us; we do this through a personal history of participation. As an identity, this translates into a personal set of events, references, memories, and experiences that create individual relations of negotiability with respect to the repertoire of a practice.

This translation of dimensions of competence into dimensions of identity has its inverse. When we come in contact with new practices, we venture into unfamiliar territory. The boundaries of our communities manifest as a lack of competence along the three dimensions I just described. We do not quite know how to engage with others. We do not understand the subtleties of the enterprise as the community has defined it. We lack the shared references that participants use. Our non-membership shapes our identities through our confrontation with the unfamiliar.

In sum, membership in a community of practice translates into an identity as a form of competence. An identity in this sense is relating to the world as a particular mix of the familiar and the foreign, the obvious and the mysterious, the transparent and the opaque. We experience and manifest our selves by what we recognize and what we don't, what we grasp immediately and what we can't interpret, what we can appropriate and what alienates us, what we can press into service and what we can't use, what we can negotiate and what remains out of reach. In practice, we know who we are by what is familiar, understandable, usable, negotiable; we know who we are not by what is foreign, opaque, unwieldy, unproductive.

Trajectories

I have argued that identity in practice arises out of an interplay of participation and reification. As such, it is not an object, but a constant becoming. The work of identity is always going on. Identity is not some primordial core of personality that already exists. Nor is it something we acquire at some point in the same way that, at a certain age, we grow a set of permanent teeth. Even though issues of identity as a focus of overt concern may become more salient at certain times than at others, our identity is something we constantly renegotiate during the course of our lives.

As we go through a succession of forms of participation, our identities form trajectories, both within and across communities of practice. In this section, I will use the concept of trajectory to argue that:

1. identity is fundamentally temporal
2. the work of identity is ongoing
3. because it is constructed in social contexts, the temporality of identity is more complex than a linear notion of time
4. identities are defined with respect to the interaction of multiple convergent and divergent trajectories.

In using the term "trajectory", I do not want to imply a fixed course or a fixed destination. To me, the term trajectory suggests not a path that can be foreseen or charted but a continuous motion – one that has a momentum of its own in addition to a field of influences. It has a coherence through time that connects the past, the present, and the future.

In the context of communities of practice, there can be various types of trajectories:

- *Peripheral trajectories.* By choice or by necessity, some trajectories never lead to full participation. Yet they may well provide a kind of access to a community and its practice that becomes significant enough to contribute to one's identity.

- *Inbound trajectories*. Newcomers are joining the community with the prospect of becoming full participants in its practice. Their identities are invested in their future participation, even though their present participation may be peripheral.
- *Insider trajectories*. The formation of an identity does not end with full membership. The evolution of the practice continues – new events, new demands, new inventions, and new generations all create occasions for renegotiating one's identity.
- *Boundary trajectories*. Some trajectories find their value in spanning boundaries and linking communities of practice. Sustaining an identity across boundaries is one of the most delicate challenges of this kind of brokering work.
- *Outbound trajectories*. Some trajectories lead out of a community, as when children grow up. What matters then is how a form of participation enables what comes next. It seems perhaps more natural to think of identity formation in terms of all the learning involved in entering a community of practice. Yet being on the way out of such a community also involves developing new relationships, finding a different position with respect to a community, and seeing the world and oneself in new ways.

Learning as identity

The temporal dimension of identity is critical. Not only do we keep negotiating our identities, but they place our engagement in practice in this temporal context. We are always simultaneously dealing with specific situations, participating in the histories of certain practices, and involved in becoming certain persons. As trajectories, our identities incorporate the past and the future in the very process of negotiating the present. They give significance to events in relation to time construed as an extension of the self. They provide a context in which to determine what, among all the things that are potentially significant, actually becomes significant learning. A sense of trajectory gives us ways of sorting out what matters and what does not, what contributes to our identity and what remains marginal.

For claims processors, being on a trajectory is an important aspect of their job. They know that improvement in their performance will mean advancement, and they value the fact that advancement is automatic because it gives them some degree of control over their trajectory. More over, their sense of trajectory extends beyond claims processing. Some of them view the job as their profession, hoping to move on to technical or managerial positions in due time; some are just paying their way through college and have no interest in a professional career in claims processing. These different trajectories give them very different perspectives on their participation and identities at work. So for them, processing a claim is not just a self-contained activity. Understanding something new is not just a local act of learning. Rather, each is an event on a trajectory through which they give meaning to their engagement in practice in terms of the identity they are developing.

Learning events and forms of participation are thus defined by the current engagement they afford, as well as by their location on a trajectory. A very peripheral form of participation, for instance, may turn out to be central to one's identity because it leads to something significant.

Paradigmatic trajectories

The progression of a career offered by the company is not the only way claims processors define their identity as a trajectory, even within the confines of their job. Their community, its history, and its evolution shape the trajectories they construct. More experienced peers are not merely a source of information about processing claims; they also represent the history of the practice as a way of life. They are living testimonies to what is possible, expected, desirable.

More generally, any community of practice provides a set of models for negotiating trajectories. These "paradigmatic" trajectories are not simply reified milestones, such as those provided by a career ladder or even by communal rituals. Rather, they embody the history of the community through the very participation and identities of practitioners. They include actual people as well as composite stories. Exposure to this field of paradigmatic trajectories is likely to be the most influential factor shaping the learning of newcomers. In the end, it is members – by their very participation – who create the set of possibilities to which newcomers are exposed as they negotiate their own trajectories. No matter what is said, taught, prescribed, recommended, or tested, newcomers are no fools: once they have actual access to the practice, they soon find out what counts.

From this perspective, a community of practice is a field of possible trajectories and thus the proposal of an identity. It is a history and the promise of that history. It is a field of possible pasts and of possible futures, which are all there for participants, not only to witness, hear about, and contemplate, but to engage with. They can interact with old-timers, who offer living examples of possible trajectories. A community of practice is a history collapsed into a present that invites engagement. Newcomers can engage with their own future, as embodied by old-timers. As a community of practice, these old-timers deliver the past and offer the future, in the form of narratives and participation both. Each has a story to tell. In addition, the practice itself gives life to these stories, and the possibility of mutual engagement offers a way to enter these stories through one's own experience.

Of course, new trajectories do not necessarily align themselves with paradigmatic ones. Newcomers must find their own unique identities. And the relation goes both ways; newcomers also provide new models for different ways of participating. Whether adopted, modified, or rejected in specific instances, paradigmatic trajectories provide live material for negotiating and renegotiating identities.

Generational encounters

As a process of negotiating trajectories, the encounter between generations is much more complex than the mere transmission of a heritage. It is an interlocking of identities, with all the conflicts and mutual dependencies this entails; by this interlocking, individual trajectories incorporate in different ways the history of a practice. Different generations bring different perspectives to their encounter because their identities are invested in different moments of that history. With less past, there is less history to take into consideration. With less future, there is less urgency to reconsider history. Yet, the perspectives of old-timers and newcomers are not so simply delineated.

If learning in practice is negotiating an identity, and if that identity incorporates the past and the future, then it is in each other that old-timers and newcomers find their experience of history. Their perspective on the generational encounter is not simply one of past versus future, of continuity versus discontinuity, or of old versus new.

- While newcomers are forging their own identities, they do not necessarily want to emphasize discontinuity more than continuity. They must find a place in relation to the past. In order to participate, they must gain some access – vicarious as it may be – to the history they want to contribute to; they must make it part of their own identities. As a result, newcomers are not necessarily more progressive than old-timers; they do not necessarily seek to change the practice more than established members do. They have an investment in continuity because it connects them to a history of which they are not a part. Their very fragility and their efforts to include some of that history in their own identity may push them toward seeking continuity.

- Conversely, old-timers have an investment in their practice, yet they do not necessarily seek continuity. Embroiled in the politics of their community and with the confidence derived from participation in a history they know too well, they may want to invest themselves in the future not so much to continue it as to give it new wings. They might thus welcome the new potentials afforded by new generations who are less hostage to the past.

Depending on how a community negotiates individuality, the generational encounter can have different effects – with different degrees of emphasis on continuity and discontinuity as old-timers and newcomers fashion their identities in their encounter. This encounter is always a complex meeting of the past and the future, one in which generations attempt to define their identities by investing them in different moments of the history of a practice. The new will both continue and displace the old. In each other, generations find the partiality as well as the connectedness of their personal trajectories, that is, new dimensions of finitude and extension of their identities.

The temporality of identity in practice is thus a subtle form of temporality. It is neither merely individual nor simply linear. The past, the present, and the future are not in a simple straight line, but embodied in interlocked trajectories. It is a social form of temporality, where the past and the future interact as the history of a community unfolds across generations.

In summary, the temporal notion of trajectory characterizes identity as:

1. a work in progress
2. shaped by efforts – both individual and collective – to create a coherence through time that threads together successive forms of participation in the definition of a person
3. incorporating the past and the future in the experience of the present
4. negotiated with respect to paradigmatic trajectories
5. invested in histories of practice and in generational politics.

Nexus of multimembership

As I mentioned, we all belong to many communities of practice: some past, some current; some as full members, some in more peripheral ways. Some may be central to our identities while others are more incidental. Whatever their nature, all these various forms of participation contribute in some way to the production of our identities. As a consequence, the very notion of identity entails:

1. an experience of multimembership
2. the work of reconciliation necessary to maintain one identity across boundaries.

Identity as multimembership

Our membership in any community of practice is only a part of our identity. Claims processors do not form their identities entirely at work. They came to their jobs as adults or youths, having belonged to many communities of practice. Some have other jobs concurrently; some are students in community colleges; some are parents; some are church-goers; some are bar-goers; some have engrossing hobbies. In fact, for many of them, their work is a part of their identity that they tend to disparage.

Because our identities are not something we turn on and off, our various forms of participation are not merely sequences in time. Claims processors who are parents come to the office without their children, and they will return home at the end of the afternoon to be with them. Though there are sequential phases in their engagement in different locations, they certainly do not cease to be parents because they are at work. They talk about their kids; and, more generally, the tidbits of conversation they interweave with their exchanges of work-related information continually reflect their participation in other practices.

Our various forms of participation delineate pieces of puzzle we put together rather than sharp boundaries between disconnected parts of ourselves. An identity is thus more than just a single trajectory; instead, it should be viewed as a nexus of multimembership. As such a nexus, identity is not a unity but neither is it simply fragmented.

- On the one hand, we engage in different practices in each of the communities of practice to which we belong. We often behave rather differently in each of them, construct different aspects of ourselves, and gain different perspectives.
- On the other hand, considering a person as having multiple identities would miss all the subtle ways in which our various forms of participation, no matter how distinct, can interact, influence each other, and require coordination.

This notion of nexus adds multiplicity to the notion of trajectory. A nexus does not merge the specific trajectories we form in our various communities of practice into one; but neither does it decompose our identity into distinct trajectories in each community. In a nexus, multiple trajectories become part of each other, whether they clash or reinforce each other. They are, at the same time, one and multiple.

Identity as reconciliation

If a nexus of multimembership is more than just a fragmented identity, being one person requires some work to reconcile our different forms of membership. Different practices can make competing demands that are difficult to combine into an experience that corresponds to a single identity. In particular:

1. different ways of engaging in practice may reflect different forms of individuality
2. different forms of accountability may call for different responses to the same circumstances
3. elements of one repertoire may be quite inappropriate, incomprehensible, or even offensive in another community.

Reconciling these aspects of competence demands more than just learning the rules of what to do when. It requires the construction of an identity that can include these different meanings and forms of participation into one nexus. Understood as the negotiation of an identity, the process of reconciling different forms of membership is deeper than just discrete choices or beliefs. For a doctor working in a hospital, making decisions that do justice to both her professional standards and institutional bottom-line demands is not simply a matter of making discrete decisions; she must find an identity that can reconcile the demands of these forms of accountability into a way of being in the world.

The work of reconciliation may be the most significant challenge faced by learners who move from one community of practice to another. For instance, when a child moves from a family to a classroom, when an immigrant moves from one culture to another, or when an employee moves from the ranks to a management position, learning involves more than appropriating new pieces of information. Learners must often deal with conflicting forms of individuality and competence as defined in different communities.

The nexus resulting from reconciliation work is not necessarily harmonious, and the process is not done once and for all. Multimembership may involve ongoing tensions that are never resolved. But the very presence of tension implies that there is an effort at maintaining some kind of coexistence. By using the term " reconciliation" to describe this process of identity formation, I want to suggest that proceeding with life – with actions and interactions – entails finding ways to make our various forms of membership coexist, whether the process of reconciliation leads to successful resolutions or is a constant struggle. In other words, by including processes of reconciliation in the very definition of identity, I am suggesting that the maintenance of an identity across boundaries requires work and, moreover, that the work of integrating our various forms of participation is not just a secondary process. This work is not simply an additional concern for an independently defined identity viewed as a unitary object; rather, it is at the core of what it means to be a person. Multimembership and the work of reconciliation are intrinsic to the very concept of identity.

Social bridges and private selves

Multimembership is the living experience of boundaries. This creates a dual relation between identities and the landscape of practice: they reflect each other and they shape each other. In weaving multiple trajectories together, our experience of multimembership replays in our identities the texture of the landscape of practice. But this replay is not a passive reflection. On the contrary, as the boundaries of practice become part of our personal experience of identity, the work of reconciliation is an active, creative process. As we engage our whole person in practice, our identities dynamically encompass multiple perspectives in the negotiation of new meanings. In these new meanings we negotiate our own activities and identities, and at the same time the histories of relations among our communities of practice. The creative negotiation of an identity always has the potential to rearrange these relations. In this regard, multimembership is not just a matter of personal identity. The work of reconciliation is a profoundly social kind of work. Through the creation of the person, it is constantly creating bridges – or at least potential bridges – across the landscape of practice.

And yet, the work of reconciliation can easily remain invisible because it may not be perceived as part of the enterprise of any community of practice. Across boundaries, the parallelism between histories of practice and personal trajectories no longer holds. The experience of multimembership can require the reconciliation of a nexus that is unique and thus very personal. Indeed, this nexus may not, in its entirety, be relevant to any practice or even to any relationship we have with anyone. Even though each element of the nexus may belong to a community, the nexus itself may not. The careful weaving of this nexus of multimembership into an identity can therefore be a very private achievement. By incorporating into the definition of the person the diversity of the social world, the social notion of a nexus of multimembership thus introduces into the concept of identity a deeply personal dimension of individuality.

Local–global interplay

An important aspect of the work of any community of practice is to create a picture of the broader context in which its practice is located. In this process, much local energy is directed at global issues and relationships. For Ariel, belonging to the profession of claims processing or to an organization like Alinsu constitutes relations whose meanings she negotiates through her participation in her community of practice. For instance, when one of her colleagues was fired for speaking against the company at a radio show, claims processors used each other as resources for making sense of this event. Their local community of practice became a productive context in which to discuss whether it was right for the claims processor to criticize her employer publicly or for the company to respond by firing her. Similarly, sports events and TV shows are the topics of frequent animated conservations in the office. Although these conversations reflect outside interests and allegiances, they become part of the processors' participation in their local community. If the baseball fans or the television watchers worked among people for whom allegiance to a baseball team was a trivial concern and watching television a waste of time, their interests may well take on very different meanings for them.

More generally, what it means to be left-handed or right-handed, a woman or a man, good-looking or plain, a younger person or an older person, a high-school dropout or the holder of a doctorate, the owner of a BMW or of a beat-up subcompact, literate or illiterate, outcast or successful – these meanings are shaped by the practices where such categories are lived as engaged identities. Broader categories and institutions attract our attention because they are often more publicly reified than the communities of practice in which we experience them as part of a lived identity. Affiliation with a political party is more public than membership in a group that discusses politics over lunch, but the lunch discussions may have more impact on our thinking than the party's platform.

In the same way that a practice is not just local but connected to broader constellations, an identity – even in its aspects that are formed in a specific community of practice – is not just local to that community. In our communities of practice, we come together not only to engage in pursuing some enterprise, but also to figure out how our engagement fits in the broader scheme of things. Identity in practice is therefore always an interplay between the local and the global.

In summary, drawing a parallel between practice and identity has yielded a perspective on identity that inherits the texture of practice. Indeed, our identities are rich and complex because they are produced within the rich and complex set of relations of practice. [...]

8

Funds of Knowledge for Teaching in Latino Households

Norma González, Luis Moll, Martha Floyd Tenery, Anna Rivera, Pat Rendón, Raquel Gonzales and Cathy Amanti

"Home visits are not new. I was doing home visits 20 years ago in the Model Cities program," asserted the principal of one elementary school. Her point is well-taken. The notion of home visits is neither novel nor unusual. Teachers may opt to visit the home of a student to discuss a particular problem, such as a student's disruptive behavior in the classroom, or to pinpoint difficulties with a particular subject matter. The teacher may simply introduce him- or herself to parents and elicit their cooperation. Some school programs require home visits for the teachers to mentor parents on the teaching of reading or math to their children, to provide suggestions on how to help the students with their homework, or to distribute books and supplies.

In this chapter, we describe a very different type of household visit by teachers. These are research visits, for the express purpose of identifying and documenting knowledge that exists in students' homes. In contrast to other visits, these visits are part of a "systematic, intentional inquiry by teachers," as Lytle and Cochran-Smith (1990, p. 84) define teacher research. We are convinced that these research visits, in conjunction with collaborative ethnographic reflection, can engender pivotal and transformative shifts in teacher attitudes and behaviors, and in relations between households and schools and between parents and teachers (see González & Amanti, 1992; Moll, Amanti, Neff, & González, 1992).

Instead of presenting the (university-based) researchers' interpretations of ongoing work, as is common in these reports, we have chosen to emphasize the participating teachers' insights on the project: what they consider relevant and important to communicate to others, especially to other teachers, as a result of their own inquiry. Lytle and Cochran-Smith (1990) have noted that:

> Conspicuous by their absence from the literature of research on teaching are the voices of teachers themselves – the questions and problems teachers pose, the frameworks they use to interpret and improve their practice, and the ways teachers themselves define and understand their work lives. (p. 83)

From: Gonzalez, N., Moll, L.C. & Amanti, C. (eds.) *Funds of Knowledge: Theorizing Practices in Households, Communities and Classrooms* (New Jersey 2005: Lawrence Erlbaum Associates), pp. 89–118. Reproduced with permission.

[…] In what follows, we first present an overview of the research project, highlighting what we refer to as funds of knowledge, a key theoretical concept in our work. This section is intended to provide the general context of the research and the goals of the investigation. A critical assumption in our work is that educational institutions have stripped away the view of working-class minority students as emerging from households rich in social and intellectual resources. Rather than focusing on the knowledge these students bring to school and using it as a foundation for learning, the emphasis has been on what these students lack in terms of the forms of language and knowledge sanctioned by the schools. This emphasis on "disadvantages" has provided justification for lowered expectations in schools and inaccurate portrayals of the children and their families.

We then introduce the teachers in the project and describe their participation in the study, including selected aspects of their research training. We follow with a summary of their insights, gained from their research efforts, regarding three key domains of change:

1. The development of teachers as qualitative researchers.
2. The formation of new relationships with families.
3. The redefinition of local households as containing important social and intellectual resources for teaching.

We conclude with a discussion of the minimal conditions necessary to conduct this work in other settings. As we emphasize, we offer no "recipes" for replication elsewhere. Instead we suggest the importance of developing at each site a community of learners, where teachers are offered a format to think, reflect, and analyze with others and to produce the knowledge necessary to transform their teaching in positive ways. In describing such communities of learners, Ayers (1992) remarked that "people learn best when they are actively exploring, thinking, asking their own questions, and constructing knowledge through discovery" (p. 20). As teachers actively coconstruct the theory and practice behind research-based household visits, the challenging sense that knowledge is open-ended, active, and continuous can create new and meaningful environments of learning for all concerned.

The research project

A central goal of our project is to draw on the knowledge and other resources found in local households for the development of classroom practice. We can summarize our three main project components as follows:

1. *Community*: Featuring an ethnographic study of the origin, use, and distribution of funds of knowledge among households in a predominantly Mexican, working-class community of Tucson, Arizona.
2. *After-school "lab" or study groups*: These are settings especially created to enhance the collaboration between teachers and researchers; to discuss research findings; and to plan, develop, and support innovations in instruction.
3. *Schools*: Featuring classroom studies to examine existing methods of instruction and implement innovations based on the household study of funds of knowledge and conceptualized at the after-school sites.

These three components allow us to conduct research simultaneously in several related areas and to shift our primary unit of study from classrooms to households or shift from a focus on teachers to a focus on the students, without losing sight of the interconnectedness of the settings or of the activities we are analyzing.

In terms of the community component, our emphasis has been on understanding local households historically. This approach involves understanding the sociopolitical and economic context of the households and analyzing their social history (see, e.g., Vélez-Ibáñez, 1988). This history includes their origins and development and, most prominently for our purposes, the labor history of the families, which reveals some of the accumulated funds of knowledge of the households. Funds of knowledge refers to those historically developed and accumulated strategies (skills, abilities, ideas, practices) or bodies of knowledge that are essential to a household's functioning and well-being (for details, see Greenberg, 1989; Vélez-Ibáñez & Greenberg, 1992). A key finding from our research is that these funds of knowledge are abundant and diverse; they may include information about, for example, farming and animal husbandry, associated with households' rural origins; or knowledge about construction and building, related to urban occupations; or knowledge about many other matters, such as trade, business, and finance on both sides of the U.S.–Mexico border.

We are particularly interested in how families develop social networks that interconnect them with their environments (most importantly with other households) and how their social relationships facilitate the development and exchange of resources, including funds of knowledge (see, e.g., Moll & Greenberg, 1990; Vélez-Ibáñez & Greenberg, 1992). A key characteristic of these exchanges is their reciprocity. As Vélez-Ibáñez (1988) has observed, reciprocity represents an "attempt to establish a social relationship on an enduring basis. Whether symmetrical or asymmetrical, the exchange expresses and symbolizes human social interdependence" (p. 42). That is, reciprocal practices establish serious obligations based on the assumption of confianza (mutual trust), which is reestablished or confirmed with each exchange, and they lead to the development of long-term relationships. Each exchange with kinsmen, friends, neighbors, or teachers in our case, entails not only many practical activities (everything from home and automobile repair to animal husbandry and music), but constantly provides contexts in which learning can occur – contexts, for example, where children have ample opportunities to participate in activities with people they trust (Moll & Greenberg, 1990).

Parameters of teacher participation

Another key feature of the project is the close collaboration of anthropologists and educators, especially in the work with classroom teachers. We have been experimenting with after-school teacher study groups (labs) as contexts for informing, assisting, and supporting the teachers' work – contexts, in other words, for the exchange of funds of knowledge between teachers and researchers (for details, see Moll et al., 1990).

These after-school settings function as mediating structures in forming strategic connections between the household fieldwork and classroom practice. After-school lab meeting locales alternate among the four schools and the university. Participants include the four teachers involved; a teacher-researcher who is on leave of absence from the school district and is pursuing graduate work in anthropology; university researchers in education, anthropology, and math education; and graduate students in education. Meetings take place every two weeks, although they are sometimes preempted because of school activities. Within the study group framework, a combination of ethnographic field methods are analyzed, and participant observation, open-ended interviewing strategies, life histories, and case studies are incorporated into the joint inquiry of household and community ethnography. In this way, the ethnographic experience becomes a collaborative endeavor, not based on a lone researcher venturing out into the field, but a multiauthored discourse constructed out of experiences as participant, field-worker, teacher, and anthropologist. Mentoring functions switch back and forth as researchers and teachers each manipulate their own sphere of expertise. As teachers enter the households as learners, so the researchers enter the teacher study groups as learners. As previously noted, reciprocity as theoretical construct has formed the basis for the exchange between households and schools, and this construct has been paralleled to incorporate the relationships between teachers and researchers. Within this interactive and constitutive process, the role of teacher is defined in nontraditional ways. The redefined relationship is that of colleagues, mutually engaged in refining methodology, interpretation, and practice (see González & Amanti, 1992). In this way, "curriculum, research and learning become matters of authorship rather than authority" (Woodward, 1985).

As is often the case with anthropological research, certain insights and conclusions came in a post hoc fashion, and the evolution of the teacher study groups is a case in point. The original prototype of the teacher labs consisted of the discussion of household visits and data. However, the actual fieldwork was not conducted by teachers, but by anthropologists. Ironically, although a participatory model of learning was advocated in work with children, the original teacher labs relied on a transmission model: information was presented, and teachers received it without actively involving themselves in the production of this knowledge (see Moll et al., 1990). It became apparent that although worthwhile information about the forms and functions of the households was being transmitted to the teachers through the study groups, true ownership of the data was not taking place. Teachers were disconnected from the actual context of the household. The admonition suggested by Spindler and Spindler (1990) – that "learning about human cultures must occur empathetically and emotionally as well as conceptually or cognitively" (p. 108) – began to take on transcendent importance. The connection of the household and teacher could not come about through a field researcher as intermediary: the bond had to be formed interpersonally, evocatively, and reciprocally.

On the few occasions when teachers did accompany field researchers into homes, the teachers had a noticeably ready access to the households, which the anthropologists had to labor to achieve. For a child's teacher, entrée into the household in a position of respect and honor was the standard. The households evinced no suspicion of motives, nor mistrust of how the information was to be used, circumstances which had at times plagued the anthropologists. The common bond of concern for the child overrode most constraints. In addition, it was found that once the teachers were involved in a dialog with the households, they were effortlessly asking much better learning questions about the child's activities. It became apparent that for the teachers to know the households, an ethnographic method of approaching the households could be productive. Thus, the stage was set for the entrance of teachers as ethnographers into the households of their students.

The teachers

Four teachers were recruited to work as teacher-researchers. Recruitment of teachers was carried out through personal and previous research contacts. The number of teachers was purposely limited in order to maintain a small, tight-knit group which would remain together for a prolonged amount of time. Initially the four teachers represented two schools, but by the beginning of the second year, two had moved to new schools. All of the schools are located within working-class, predominantly Mexican neighborhoods. Two Mexican-origin and two Anglo teachers participated in the study, all of them fluent in Spanish:

Anna Rivera, a bilingual classroom teacher for 15 years, is presently an elementary school principal, although she was a bilingual first-grade teacher at the time of the study. She completed her doctorate in elementary education and has taught the full range from prekindergarten to graduate courses at the university.

Patricia Rendón has been teaching since 1969. She received her undergraduate degree in Ohio and taught there for 4½ years. With a background in languages, she moved to Medellín, Colombia, and later to Bogotá. She taught K–8 in different bilingual settings in Colombia for 9 years. Since moving to Arizona, she has been both a monolingual and bilingual teacher. She received her MA in 1991 and presently teaches fourth and fifth graders in a bilingual classroom.

Martha Floyd Tenery has been a teacher in various settings for 9 years. She has taught as an elementary classroom teacher, a bilingual resource teacher, an English as a second language (ESL) teacher for Spanish speakers, a teaching assistant in the Japanese Department, and as an English teacher at Anhui University in China. She recently completed her doctoral studies in language, reading and culture.

Raquel Gonzales has been a bilingual kindergarten teacher for 6 years. She is presently finishing her MA in counseling and guidance.

Teachers as learners

Once teachers entered households as learners – as researchers seeking to construct a template for understanding and tapping into the concrete life experiences of their students – the conventional model of home visits was turned on its head. No attempt would be made to teach the parents or to visit for punitive reasons. This shift constituted a radical departure from household visits carried out in other programs that incorporate the home visit concept (Vélez-Ibáñez, Moll, González, & Amanti, 1992). The after-school labs were restructured to accommodate these shifts, and the ethnographic method, rather than household visits, emerged as the vehicle for participant observations. Within the lab setting, ethnography surfaced as more than techniques. It became the filter through which the households were conceptualized as multidimensional and vibrant entities. This new perspective reflected a corresponding shift in teachers' theoretical paradigms. As has been noted (Spindler & Spindler, 1990), in teaching anthropology "a state of mind is more important than specific technique"; or as Segal (1990, p. 121) put it: "The question is: How can we go about teaching an anthropological imagination?"

Through the mediating structure of the after-school study groups, teachers were provided with the forum to engage in reflexive thought. Although specific techniques in participant observation, fieldnote writing, interviewing, and eliciting of life histories were presented, the focus was continuously on the discourse, on the joint construction of knowledge. Ethnographic fieldwork became not one lone researcher grappling with overwhelming data, but a collaborative and reflexive process in which teachers and researchers shared insights and information.

However, reflexivity in fieldwork is not unproblematic. Indeed one of the missions of the study groups became overcoming the paradox of gaining understanding without falling into the trap on inaction. In the face of the sometimes overwhelming social and structural factors that face the students and their families, it would be easy to simply "give up". One teacher (Martha Floyd Tenery) voiced this sentiment as she reflected on her initial pessimism:

> I did not realize it at the time, but I used to believe that my students had limited opportunities in life. I thought that poverty was the root of many of their problems, and that this was something too big for me to change as a teacher.

Through the reflexive discourse of the study groups, this hopelessness was short-circuited. The teachers no longer felt isolated from each other, or the community, as this same teacher explained:

> This fatalistic obsession of mine has slowly melted away as I have gotten to know my students and their families. I believe this transformation is the most important one I have made. Its ramifications have reached far beyond the classroom.

Teaching an "anthropological imagination": teachers as reflective practitioners

This is not to say that the road has been smooth. Initially, teachers reported a struggle with shedding notions of educational research based on quantifiable variables that must be meticulously controlled. Yet a realization gradually emerged that reflexively oriented work needs to "begin with the understanding that systematic thinking about one's own experiences is a valid source of some knowledge and insight" (Segal, 1990). A reliance on anything but empirical data and a shift to reflexive observation, in many cases, left the teachers feeling overwhelmed with the sheer complexity of the task.

Anna Rivera reported feeling "like a private investigator – like you're watching everything. What are they cooking? How do you make this, how do you do that? The home visit was totally different from what I had done before." The myriad of details, of participating and observing, of interviewing and audiorecording and note taking, of being both the teacher and ethnographer, was at the outset of the first interview a numbing experience. This hesitance soon wore off as teachers became more and more comfortable with the process. Martha Floyd Tenery reported after her series of interviews:

> I remember at first I was scared to death. Would the family be skeptical? What would they think of me? Would they feel uncomfortable? I remember thinking all kinds of things. And now, it seems, like, what is the big deal? I can do this, and I can do it well.

When questioned about their own particular transformations, teachers overwhelmingly cited two factors: the orientation to the households as containing funds of knowledge and the reflexive process and debriefings after the visits. Anna Rivera affirmed that "most of the change had come during the study groups. I heard something, or I said something during the study group." Teachers in the study group affirmed their theoretical development as an aftermath of the actual practice of household visits. They reiterated that theory and practice are really two sides of the same coin, and one without the other is limited.

The reflexive mode injected into the study groups noticeably altered the ways in which participants viewed their own participant observation as it engendered an examination of underlying beliefs and rationalizations. As other qualitative researchers have stated, "people who have never before articulated their beliefs and customs now are asked to do so and what may never before have been examined has now become verbally objectified, so that it is at least present for examination" (Ely, 1991, p. 197). One teacher, commenting on the reflexive process, stated:

> That was the only time I had ever talked about how I was teaching and why I was teaching that way, and how that related to how I perceive children to learn. At all the other in-services or teacher meetings I had ever attended, I was talked at, I was fed information, and it was more technique, how to do something, not why.

The study groups offered a safe, nonjudgmental environment for thinking out loud about classroom practice as well as about household functions. Participants in the study groups were able to voice their changing ideas about households and the subsequent transformation that the observations and reflection provoked.

Throughout the study groups, anthropological inquiry was presented as more of a state of mind than a technique. However, the theoretical implications of technique became conspicuous in several ways, and an effort to systematize reflexivity emerged. As part of the ethnographic experience, teachers were asked to select two to three students from their classrooms. No formal attempt at representativeness was made. Households were visited three times, and the interviews lasted an average of two hours each. An interview of the target child was also conducted. Ages of the students ranged from kindergarten through to fifth grade. Teachers were asked to tape-record the interviews (if the family was comfortable with it) and to conduct the interviews as conversationally as possible. Teachers were paid (when possible) as project participants for their extra duty time.

Following their forays into the field, teachers were asked to write fieldnotes based on each interview, and these fieldnotes became the basis for the study group discussions. Teachers overwhelmingly remarked on the time-consuming nature of this process. After a hectic school day, taking the time to conduct interviews that often stretched two or three hours and to later invest several hours in writing fieldnotes was an exacting price to pay for a connection to the households. They cited this one factor as precluding wholesale teacher participation in this project. Yet, in spite of the strain of the task, the teachers felt that the effort was worth it. The reflexive process involved in transcription enabled the teachers to obtain elusive insights that could easily be overlooked. As they replayed the audiotapes and referred to notes, connections and hunches began to emerge. The household began to take on a multidimensional reality that had taken root in the interview and reached its fruition in reflexive writing. Writing gave form and substance to the connection forged between the household and the teacher.

A second ethnographic technique involved the writing of a personal field journal. Not all teachers opted to do this. One teacher who kept an extensive journal noted:

> Transformation occurs over a long period of time and is quite subtle in its nature. Elements of my transformation would have been elusive had I not documented them along the way. I recognize this as I look back and cannot remember having those feelings/beliefs.

Another teacher lamented the fact that she had not kept the journal. She did not follow the suggestion and bemoans the fact in retrospect:

> I don't remember when I stopped feeling and thinking this way or that way. I don't think it was an overnight thing. I think all of that is just changing little by little. If I had kept a journal, I could go back and read and say, okay, this is where I first started thinking about it.

These comments highlight that an awareness of the documentation of the reflexive process began to take shape.

A third field technique involved questionnaires. Teachers felt that the use of questionnaires signaled a shift in approaching the households as learners. Entering the household with questions rather than answers provided the context for an inquiry-based visit, and the teachers considered the questionnaires a meaningful resource. They addressed such diverse areas as family histories, family networks, labor history, educational history, language use, and child-rearing ideologies. Within each topic, questions were left open-ended, and teachers probed and elicited information as the interviews proceeded. Interviews were, as teachers commented, more of a conversation than an interview, and one teacher noted that with tape-recording the interview, she was free to be a conversational partner without the task of furious note-taking. Teachers used the questionnaire as a guide rather than a protocol, suggesting possible areas to explore and incorporating previous knowledge into formulating new questions. Interviews were not conducted as a unilateral extraction of information, as teachers were encouraged to make connections with their own lives and histories as they elicited narratives from the families.

These issues illustrate the critical effect that methodology had in learning a different way of visiting homes. Teachers often voiced the notion that "methodology helps to implant theory and represents its embodiment particularly in this project, which is very experiential." The theoretical orientation to the households as containing funds of knowledge was critical in teacher transformation. But equally as important in the transformative process was the reflection generated by the collaborative effort of a collective ethnographic experience.

Funds of knowledge as transformative principle

Teachers voiced two underlying transformative potentials in viewing the households as repositories of funds of knowledge. The first concerns a shift in the definition of culture of the households, and the second concerns an alternative to the deficit model of households.

The first shift owes its genesis to the prevailing trends in anthropological literature away from an integrated, harmonious, univocal version of culture. It seemed to us that the prevailing notions of culture in the schools center around observable and tangible surface markers: dances, food, folklore, and the like. Viewing households within a processual view of culture, rooted in the lived contexts and practices of their students and families, engendered a realization that culture is a dynamic concept and not a static grab bag of tamales, quinceañeras, and cinco de mayo celebrations (see González, 1992). Instead teachers learned how households network in informal market exchanges. They learned how cross-border activities made "mini-ethnographers" of their students. And, most importantly, they found that students acquired a multidimensional depth and breadth from their participation in household life (Moll et al., 1992).

Cathy Amanti, a teacher who participated in an earlier pilot phase of this project and is now on leave pursuing a graduate degree in anthropology (and is a researcher on the project), evoked what this realization signified (from González & Amanti, 1992):

> The impact of participating in this project went far beyond my expectations. My approach to curriculum and my relationship with my students are two areas where the impact was most profound. In the area of curriculum, as a teacher of predominantly Mexican and U.S. Mexican students, I believed in the importance of acknowledging and including aspects of my students' culture in my classroom practice. However, though teachers are trained to build on students' prior knowledge, they are given no guidelines for how to go about eliciting this knowledge. Also, the multicultural curriculum available in schools perpetuates an outdated notion of culture as special and isolated ritual events and artifacts, the kind featured in *National Geographic*. Its focus on holidays, "typical" foods and "traditional" artifacts covers a very narrow range of my students' experiences and ignores the reality of life in the borderlands, which often falls outside the norms of traditional Anglo or Mexican culture.

> Participating in this project helped me to reformulate my concept of culture from being very static to more practice-oriented. This broadened conceptualization turned out to be the key which helped me develop strategies to include the knowledge my students were bringing to school in my classroom practice. It was the kind of information elicited through the questionnaires that was the catalyst for this transformation. I sought information on literacy, parenting attitudes, family and residential history, and daily activities. But I was not looking for static categories, or judging the households' activities in these areas according to any standards – my own or otherwise. I simply elicited and described the context within which my students were being socialized. What this meant was that if the father of one of my students did not have a "job" I did not stop the inquiry there. The format of the questionnaires encouraged me to continue probing to discover any type of activity that the father and mother were doing to ensure the survival of the household.

> If we were simply eliciting labor history associated with categories of work in the formal economic sector, we would risk both devaluing and missing many of the experiences of our students and their families. This has clear implications for how we approach culture. If our idea of culture is bound up with notions of authenticity and tradition, how much practice will we ignore as valueless and what will this say to our students? But if our idea of culture is expanded to include the ways we organize and make sense of all our experiences, we have many more resources to draw upon in the classroom.

The second transformative effect of the funds of knowledge perspective deals with debunking the pervasive idea of households as lacking worthwhile knowledge and experiences. Teachers were particularly concerned about reiterating this theme, as they felt that many educators continue to hold an unquestioning and negative view of the community and households. Closely related to this point, teachers said that some educators approach the community they work in with an attitude of "How can they help *me*? This places the entire burden on the community to reach out to the school." One teacher (Martha Floyd Tenery) stated:

> It's never "How can I do this?" They feel if parents don't show up for school events it means they don't care. But there could be many reasons why the parents can't come to these meetings such as conflicts with work, or not knowing the language.

However, this same teacher recognizes that she still thinks and says many things that could be construed as emanating from a similar mindset. "You have to disprove what you've been taught," she said. Another teacher (Anna Rivera) remarked on "unlearning" her previous training in household visits: "Can you imagine what kind of subtle message comes across when someone comes into your home to teach you something?"

Each teacher, as she came to know the households personally and emotionally, came away changed in some way. Some were struck by the sheer survival of the household against seemingly overwhelming odds. Others were astonished at the sacrifices the households made in order to gain a better education for their children. They all found parents who were engineers, teachers, and small business owners in Mexico, who pulled up stakes and now work in jobs far below their capabilities in order to obtain a "better life and education" for their children. They found immigrant families living with 15 people in a household, with all the adult men and women working, in order to pay for rent and everyday necessities. As Raquel Gonzales noted:

> I came away from the household visits changed in the way that I viewed the children. I became aware of the whole child, who had a life outside the classroom, and that I had to be sensitive to that. I feel that I was somewhat sensitive before the visits, but it doesn't compare with my outlook following the visits.

What follows are two brief case study examples[1] based on the teachers' experiences in doing research in their own students' households.

The Estrada Family (Anna Rivera)

I have been in contact with the Estrada family since August 16, 1991. During the last year and a half, I have visited the family during five formal interviews, two birthday parties, one *quinceañera* (an adolescent girl's debutante party), and several informal visits. I summarize here what I have learned about this family, describe how I used that knowledge in my teaching, and reflect on what changes I have undergone.

My first contact with the family occurred before the first day of school. I was preparing the classroom for the first day of school when I heard a knock at the door. In walked a family who wanted to introduce themselves to their new school. Mr. and Mrs. Estrada wanted their third-grade daughter to become acquainted with the school and the teacher, me. In Spanish, they shared that they believed education to be important and that they decided to visit their third-grade daughter's classroom and their kindergarten daughter's classroom in order to make the transition to a new school a positive experience. They had in tow a 4-year-old son because they wanted him to know what was expected.

Through the interviews, I learned that the family was quite extensive. I met the middle-school-age son, two high-school-age daughters, a maternal grandfather, and a maternal uncle, all of whom shared the same household. The trailer they lived in was located among 14 other trailers in a recently developed trailer park.

The living room included a bookcase of reference books in Spanish. The father had been trained in Hermosillo, Sonora, Mexico, as an electrical repairman. He worked on refrigerators, air conditioners, and other appliances while in Hermosillo. In Tucson, he works for a local tortilla factory delivering tortillas to grocery stores.

The living room bookcase also includes recipe books and craft books. The family had owned and operated a small convenience store in Hermosillo. Mrs. Estrada was in charge of managing the store, including ordering, bookkeeping, and selling. In fact, they had named the store in honor of the third-grade daughter.

They moved to Tucson because they wanted to improve the opportunities for their children. Mrs. Estrada had family in Tucson and had lived here for a while as a child. Mr. Estrada came in search of a job and living quarters and then made arrangements for his family to join him about 6 months later. The children left their schoolmates and moved here in 1988.

During my visits, I have observed each family member take responsibility. The three older children are assigned the care of a younger sibling. The two sisters in high school are each responsible for one of the two younger sisters, and the brother in middle school is responsible for the youngest brother. The family is very resourceful. Everyone helps with the household chores, including producing tortillas for eating and for selling. The males are the ones in charge of maintenance, and the father shares his tools with the sons.

During a birthday party, I observed that the family had choreographed their duties. The father and the son in middle school took care of the *piñata*, which meant that the son had to stand on the roof of a van to hold one end of the line while the other end was attached to the roof of the trailer. The daughters organized the children for the *piñata* breaking. Each family member served food and beverages. What do these observations have to do with my teaching? Specifically, I used the knowledge about owning and managing a store to create a math unit on money. For three weeks, we explored the social issues of money, along with mathematical concepts about money.

Beyond that, I used the information I learned about the home in incidental matters that color the curriculum. I knew where my student lived and who her neighbors were. I made connections in class: "I want you to practice hitting a softball. I bet you can use that empty lot near your home to practice with your classmate who lives across the street"; and, "How about if you work on your science project with your classmate who lives next door to you?"

The knowledge I gleaned also had an impact on the student. She knew I had been at her home to talk with her parents. She understood that her parents and I communicated. This influenced the other students also. They recognized me in the trailer park. They came over to chat with me. They knew I knew where they lived and played.

What changes have I undergone? Fundamentally, I have redefined my conception of the term home visit. I was trained during my first years of teaching (some 15 years ago) that my goal during a home visit was to teach the parent. I had an agenda to cover. I was in control.

Now I go to learn. I have some questions I want to explore, and I might want to learn about some particular home activities like what the family does for recreation. However, these questions are open-ended. I start an interview and follow the conversation to wherever it might lead. I am an active listener. I am a listener who returns to pick up the conversation from the last visit.

Most significantly, I am becoming a listener who reflects. During the last year and a half, I have made time to do the visits and have made time to reflect about what I have learned. I have firsthand knowledge that I have gained through my research with the families. I use this knowledge as background when I am reading about minoritized families in books or articles. I read an article and compare what it states to the knowledge gained from my work. I contrast and sometimes confirm, but more often challenge what I read.

I must admit that this whole process is a demanding one. I am choosing to place myself in situations where I have to listen, reflect, communicate, act, and write. I believe I am learning, developing, and creating, and that is what makes this research worthwhile.

Reflecting on change (Martha Floyd Tenery)

As I reread some of the early journal entries I made for this project, I realize how I have changed my views of the households. As I read these entries, I realized that I had discussed my students in terms of low academics, home-life problems, alienation, and socioeconomic status, and that I was oriented toward a deficit model. I no longer see the families I visited that way. Since I am looking for resources, I am finding resources, and I recognize the members of the families for who they are and for their talents and unique personalities. We now have a reciprocal relationship where we exchange goods, services, and information. I have also dispelled many myths that are prevalent in our region.

One example of a dispelled myth is that Mexican immigrants have poor educational backgrounds. To the contrary, I discovered that some schools in Mexico were academically ahead of the United States, and discipline was stricter. Instead of finding parents who do not emphasize education, parents wanted more homework, more communication with the schools, and stricter discipline. All five families (that I interviewed this year) informed me that education was one of the reasons they came to the United States. Another myth dispelled by the interviews is that Mexicans have limited work experience. The parents of my five students had held the following occupations: grocery store owner, bank executive, carpenter, mechanic, dairyman, grave digger, military, factory supervisor, farm worker, international salesman, mason, and domestic worker.

Strong family values and responsibility are characteristics of the families I visited. In every case, the household included extended family membership. Fifteen family members lived in one house, including the student's grandmother, mother, two aunts, and their husbands and children. My students were expected to participate in household chores such as cleaning the house, car maintenance, food preparation, washing dishes, and caring for younger siblings. I learned what this insight meant when one of my students was unable to attend school drama and chorus rehearsals one day. In my journal entry detailing this project, I noted the following incident:

Wednesday (11/25/92). The music teacher commented (to me), "You know, Leticia has missed two chorus rehearsals." Before I could answer, the school drama teacher stepped in to add, "Oh, she's very irresponsible." She had signed up to be in the Drama Club and had only been to two meetings. I said "Wait a minute. …" The drama teacher corrected herself, and said, "Well, she's acting irresponsibly." I then told her how Leticia's younger brother was being hospitalized for a series of operations, and when the mother had to leave, she left Leticia in charge of caring for her two younger siblings. In fact, her missing after-school rehearsals was an act of responsibility, obedience, and loyalty to her family.

I believe that this episode, and many other similar occurrences, help me to separate truths from myths by relying on what I have seen and heard from my students. [...]

One of the more important connections to be made concerns the tapping of the funds of knowledge for use within classroom pedagogy. Although all of the teachers are convinced that these funds exist in abundance, extracting their potential for teaching has proven to be an intricate process. Curriculum units based on the more conspicuous funds, such as an ethnobotanical knowledge of medicinal herbs and the construction of buildings, have emerged, but developing a tangible, systemic link to classroom practice has been more elusive (however, see Moll et al., 1990, 1992). The general consensus is that teachers are in need of time and support to move from theory to practice, or from field research to practice. They strongly affirmed that the labs or study groups provide an important way of maximizing time and combining resources, and of conceptualizing the pedagogical connection between classrooms and households.

A final dilemma concerns the evaluation of the project. The assessment of the ethnographic process, the study groups, and the curriculum units cannot be carried out along conventional (experimental or quasiexperimental) lines. Transformation does not have a time frame. Qualitative evaluation methods have been most amenable to the methodology, and teachers were willing to document their own intellectual journeys through the use of personal journals, debriefing interviews, analysis of fieldnotes, study group transcripts, and classroom observations. In sum, how to provide convincing evidence of positive change is a constant project issue.

Conclusion

At the end of a presentation in a local school district, one educator remarked cynically, "We don't need teachers to learn to be anthropologists. We need them to learn to teach." We suggest that the point is not whether teachers learn to become anthropologists or good ethnographers. The teachers themselves have made this very clear, as Pat Rendón comments: "I don't want to be an anthropologist. I want to use what resources I can to become a better teacher." The issue is how to redefine the role of teachers as thinkers and practitioners. We have argued in this chapter that it begins by teachers themselves redefining the resources available for thinking and teaching through the analysis of the funds of knowledge available in local households, in the students they teach, and in the colleagues with whom they work.

As the teachers' field research has evolved in such a way as to provide ownership of the process, they have been able to construct themselves as agents of change. In significant ways, these teachers have begun to fuse the role of technicians in their practice as educators. As Giroux (1985) indicated, educators as transformative intellectuals can recognize their ability to critically transform the world. In a parallel fashion, as teachers have transcended the boundaries of the classroom walls, so have parents transcended the boundaries of the household. In a few but significant instances, parents have come to view themselves as agents capable of changing their child's educational experiences. As parents responded with personal narratives concerning their own unique and singular life course, a heightened historical consciousness began to emerge. The welcome communicative event of articulating the trajectory that brought parents to be where they are facilitated an awareness of the historical character of their experiences. In this way, the notion of dialog as an emancipatory educational process (Freire, 1981) was injected into the households. As other researchers (Lather, 1986; Savage, 1988) have stated, ethnography can be seen as a tool for social action that can enable persons to transform the confines of their circumstances. In the powerful dialog that this ethnographic interview can engender, parents can and did find a passageway to the schools. As the teacher validates the household experience as one from which rich resources or funds of knowledge can be extracted, parents themselves come to authenticate their skills as worthy of pedagogical notice. Most significant, teachers have reported that parents have felt an increased access to the school. No longer is the institution viewed as an impenetrable fortress ensconced on foreign soil. Rather, the teachers' incursion into previously uncharted domains has been reciprocated by the parents. Parents have felt the surge of *confianza* which has unlocked doors and overcome barriers.

Clearly the project"s payoffs are multifaceted and complex. The emergence of teachers as qualitative researchers is clearly one by-product. A second involves the increased access to the school felt by parents. A third is the changed relationships between teachers and the students whose households they visited. A fourth, and for our purposes significant, goal is the emergence of curriculum units based on the household funds of knowledge. Teachers have been able to sift through the household resources and have found multiple elements that can be used as the bases for math, science, language, arts, or integrated units. The classroom application is an evolving portion of the funds of knowledge inquiry. We have opted not to focus on this aspect in this chapter because of its multiple dimensions. However, teachers have invariably noted that each household contains an array of activities, strategies, and topics that can form the kernel of units to engage students. For example, teachers have formed mathematical units based on construction knowledge, ecology units based on ethnobotanical knowledge of the home, a unit titled "Sound and Its Properties" based on music, and a comparative history of clothing, including topics such as an inquiry into the absorbency of fabrics, among other instructional activities.

For teachers interested in developing a similar project in other locations, we propose the following minimal conditions based on our experiences, and as discussed in this chapter:

1. *Theoretical preparation*: The theoretical concept of funds of knowledge provided a new perspective for the study of households as dynamic settings with abundant social and intellectual resources.
2. *Home visits as participant observers*: The key is to enter the homes in the role of "learner," willing to interact and prepared to document what one learns, to produce new "firsthand" knowledge about the families and community.
3. *Study groups*: These meetings become the centers for discussion, reflection, and analysis of the household visits and a catalyst for ideas about teachers.
4. *Voluntary participation*: All teachers agreed that participation in the project must remain voluntary, so that teachers have maximum control over the project and the work does not become an undesirable imposition on teaching.

The teachers identified other aspects of the project as being important to its success, although not necessarily essential, such as the use of questionnaires to help guide the household interviews and observations, the collection and elaboration of fieldnotes, and collaboration with anthropologists or other educational researchers. There was also consensus that the project must be reinvented anew at each site, in relation to its social and historical conditions.

We suggest that these minimal conditions can engender a dialog of change and collaboration among teachers, parents, students, and researchers. The dialog of the ethnographic interview can provide a foundation for the development of critical consciousness. The discourse that the interview sparks highlights the theoretical assertion that knowledge is not found but constructed, and that it is constructed in and through discourse (Foucault, 1970, 1972). As the participants in this project become colearners and coconstructors of knowledge, environments for a probing disposition of mind can be meaningfully and effectively created.

[...]

Note

1. All household and family names have been changed to preserve anonymity.

References

Ayers, W. (1992). Work that is real: Why teachers should be empowered. In G. A. Hess, Jr. (Ed.), *Empowering teachers and parents: School restructuring through the eyes of anthropologists* (pp. 13–27). Westport, CT: Bergin & Garvey.

Ely, M. (1991). Reflecting. In M. Ely, M. Anzul, T. Friedman, D. Gardner, & A. Steinmetz (Eds.), *Doing qualitative research: Circles within circles* (pp. 179–226). New York: Falmer.

Foucault, M. (1970). *The order of things: An archeology of the human sciences.* New York: Pantheon.

Foucault, M. (1972). *Archeology of knowledge and the discourse of language.* New York: Pantheon.

Freire, P. (1981). *Education for critical consciousness.* New York: Continuum.

Giroux, H. (1985). Teachers as transformative intellectuals. *Social Education, 2,* 376–379.

González, N. (1992). *Child language socialization in Tucson U.S. Mexican households.* Unpublished doctoral dissertation, University of Arizona, Tucson, AZ.

González, N., & Amanti, C. (1992, November). *Teaching ethnographic methods to teachers: Successes and pitfalls.* Paper presented at the Annual Meeting of the American Anthropological Association, San Francisco, CA.

Greenberg, J. B. (1989, April). *Funds of knowledge: Historical constitution, social distribution, and transmission.* Paper presented at the Annual Meeting of the Society for Applied Anthropology, Santa Fe, NM.

Lather, P. (1986). Research as praxis. *Harvard Educational Review, 46,* 257–277.

Lytle, S., & Cochran-Smith, M. (1990). Learning from teacher research: A working typology. *Teachers College Record, 92,* 83–103.

Moll, L. C., Amanti, C., Neff, D., & González, N. (1992). Funds of knowledge for teaching: Using a qualitative approach to connect homes and classrooms. *Theory Into Practice, 31,* 132–141.

Moll, L. C., & Greenberg, J. (1990). Creating zones of possibilities: Combining social contexts for instruction. In L. C. Moll (Ed.), *Vygotsky and education* (pp. 319–348). Cambridge, UK: Cambridge University Press.

Moll, L. C., Vélez-Ibáñez, C., Greenberg, J., Whitmore, K., Saavedra, E., Dworin, J., & Andrade, R. (1990). *Community knowledge and classroom practice: Combining resources for literacy instruction* (OBEMLA Contract No. 300-87-0131). Tucson, AZ: University of Arizona College of Education and Bureau of Applied Research in Anthropology.

Savage, M. (1988). Can ethnographic narrative be a neighborly act? *Anthropology and Education Quarterly, 19,* 3–19.

Segal, E. (1990). The journal: Teaching reflexive methodology on an introductory level. *Anthropology and Education Quarterly, 21,* 121–127.

Spindler, G., & Spindler, L. (1990). The inductive case study approach to teaching anthropology. *Anthropology and Education Quarterly, 21,* 106–112.

Vélez-Ibáñez, C. G. (1988). Networks of exchange among Mexicans in the U.S. and Mexico: Local level mediating responses to national and international transformations. *Urban Anthropology, 17,* 27–51.

Vélez-Ibáñez, C., & Greenberg, J. (1992). Formation and transformation of funds of knowledge among U.S. Mexical households. *Anthropology and Education Quarterly, 23,* 313–335.

Vélez-Ibáñez, C., Moll, L. C., González, N., & Amanti, C. (1992). *Funds of knowledge for educational improvement. An elaboration of an anthropological and educational collaborative dissemination project* (Report submitted to the W. K. Kellogg Foundation). Tucson, AZ: Bureau of Applied Research in Anthropology.

Woodward, V. (1985). Collaborative pedagogy: Researcher and teacher learning together. *Language Arts, 62,* 770–776.

9

'This is Our School': Provision, Purpose and Pedagogy of Supplementary Schooling in Leeds and Oslo

Kathy Hall, Kamil Özerk, Mohsin Zulfiqar and Jon Tan

[…]

Background and context

Ethnic minority groups in England have been furthering their children's education through their supplementary schools since before the Second World War. More recent immigration in Norway means that supplementary schools there have a shorter history. While these community initiatives in both countries have had some attention from scholars and researchers (Tomlinson, 1985; Chevannes & Reeves, 1987; Dove, 1993; Özerk, 1995; Reay & Mirza, 1997; Zulfiqar, 1997) and some unpublished accounts exist of the scale, scope and funding of provision in some areas (e.g. Bastiani, 2000), after-school educational provision for minority ethnic children is an underresearched and undertheorised field.

Several writers (e.g. Stone, 1981; Chevannes & Reeves, 1987; Zulfiqar, 1997) have argued that the growth of supplementary schooling is a direct result of the failure of the mainstream system to cater for the cultural and educational needs of minority ethnic children, that it is inadequately supported by the state and local education authorities (LEAs), and that it is often regarded with suspicion by the mainstream system. This line of argument is that supplementary schooling seeks to counter the hegemony of the mainstream sector, challenging notions of education and knowledge as being emancipatory. In this way, the existence of supplementary schools is indicative of the alternative actions of individuals in response to the perceived inability of mainstream schooling to provide meaningful experiences for their community/client group (Popkewitz & Brennan, 1998). The meanings and understandings of those who participate in supplementary schools are of particular interest in this study. […]

Research on race and underachievement in England by Gilborn & Gipps (1996) reveals that, rather than seeking to render invisible differences between races (an assimilationist approach), schools need to recognise cultural differences between pupils. Not to do so, they argue, may reinforce racist practices. They say, '[f]ailure to address ethnic diversity has proved counter-productive at the school level. Where schools have adopted "colour-blind" policies, for example,

From: *British Educational Research Journal*, 28 (3), 2002, pp. 399–418. Reprinted by permission of the publisher (Taylor & Francis Ltd, http://www.informaworld.com).

inequalities of opportunity have been seen to continue' (p. 80). These authors demonstrate that a disproportionately high percentage of children from ethnic minority backgrounds are allocated to lower streams, are deemed to have learning difficulties and are excluded from school. Unsurprisingly, they also disproportionately underachieve in examination results both in England (Gilborn & Gipps, 1996) and in Norway (Lauglo, 1996; Özerk, 1997; Lodding, 1998). It should not be surprising, therefore, that ethnic minority groups *resist* by providing their children with opportunities, outside of the mainstream sector, to learn their own language, culture and traditions. Far from mainstream schools operating to instil self-regulation, discipline and a sense of individuals as members of a community, their particularity in delivering *one* sociocultural educational message can be seen to continually dislocate experiences of community and school/education for certain groups. The effects of such marginalisation and exclusion on the educational progression and life chances of such groups have been well documented (Office for Standards in Education [OFSTED], 1996, 1999). The establishment of supplementary, community-based educational sites thus represents the ways in which individuals operationalise power through 'individual actions to vision and re-vision [themselves] as acting, thinking and feeling persons' (Popkewitz & Brennan, 1998, p. 16). Thus, while such organisations may not be viewed as a threat, they offer a critique of mainstream provisions. From their deployed position, they not only renegotiate the organisation of education, but effect change in areas of curriculum, knowledge and the teacher–student relationship (Gore, 1998; Green, 1998; Shutkin, 1998). The lack of systematically documented evidence in the public domain means that the nature of this resistance is little understood. A comparison of England and Norway in this regard would be especially illuminating in view of the different emphases in social policy in both countries on community and local interests and initiatives.

Our previous comparative work on curricular policy demonstrates that Norway is more explicit than England in its acknowledgement of and desire to cater for cultural and ethnic diversity in schools. Yet, the literacy policy texts of both countries could be described as assimilationist in that the official assumption is that, to make progress, ethnic minorities need to assimilate the language of the mainstream, thereby losing their own linguistic identity (Hall *et al.*, 1999; Özerk, 1999). Yet, literacy, it is arguable, is the most potent cultural code for representing reality and positioning people. Volosinov (1973), for example, says that consciousness and experience have no existence outside of a culture's codes and several cultural theorists have argued that the literacy one practices not only influences and reflects but produces one's beliefs, values, assumptions and related behaviour (see Hall [1998] for a review). As the education administration theorist, Greenfield (in Ribbins & Greenfield, 1993) has argued in relation to how organisations invent social reality, there are many ways of knowing, and individuals create the world in which they live. Supplementary schooling, with its emphasis on different cultural codes to those offered in mainstream schooling, offers the potential to construct a different set of meanings, values and constructions of self. Whether and how this occurs is explored in the following. [...]

Research design

Two techniques were used to explore the functions of supplementary schools in both cities. First, we assembled existing, mostly unpublished documentation to ascertain the scale and nature of provision in the two cities. In the next and more substantial component of the project, we conducted a more in-depth study of specific supplementary schools in both cities.

A fundamental principle that informed our study is our view of curriculum and peda-gogy as phenomenological (Bronfenbrenner, 1979; Pinar & Reynolds, 1992). This means that the curriculum, teaching and learning taking place in supplementary schools cannot necessarily be understood in terms of the external or 'objective' features of the learning context. Rather, they have to be understood in relation to how they are interpreted and made sense of by those involved. An advocate of subjectivism, Greenfield argues that a focus on human action and intention (Ribbins & Greenfield, 1993) is required in order to understand the values and assumptions underlying any organisation. Most important, then, is the interrelation of the 'external', structural frameworks of educational policy and the ways in which individuals manipulate such frames in the course of their day-to-day lives. What becomes significant in our understanding of educational processes and peda-gogy within supplementary schooling is the way those involved position their own prac-tice and school/education's purpose in relation to the mainstream. Drawing on the concepts of '*structuration*' (Giddens, 1984, 1991; Giddens & Pierson, 1998), and '*gov-ernmentality*' (Burchell *et al.*, 1991), our view of curriculum, pedagogy and educational change thus emphasises the complex and inextricable nature of the relationship between external, objective and individual-centred drivers of change. Such a view involves indi-viduals as contributors to the relative positioning of mainstream/supplementary educa-tion, both through resistance and re-visioning of mainstream educational policy and practice.

To reflect these conceptual themes of structure and individual action, it was decided to use case study methodology. Such a flexible and interpretive research approach would enable us to understand the practices, dominant ideologies and social processes that struc-ture the workings of supplementary schools, as well as understand how attendance at and working in supplementary schools help learners and teachers make sense of their own life world. We are interested in the relationship between supplementary and mainstream schooling, and whether, for example, the pedagogy of supplementary schools is seen by the participants as *oppositional* and if so, what the implications of this might be for the state and what counter-resistances, if any, might be anticipated.

Four schools–two in each city–were chosen for study. Obtaining access to schools in both cities did not present any difficulty, and indeed, participants were keen to be involved, freely and generously giving of their time. Three of the schools did not necessarily want the kind of anonymity and confidentiality normally assured in such research situations and the two Leeds schools wished their schools to be named. However, because of the sensitive nature of some of the teacher narratives, specifically the occasional references (positive and negative) to teachers and schools they had encountered in their own main-stream schooling, we decided to protect the identity of all schools and participants. Therefore, the account that follows uses pseudonyms. All the participants cooperated fully with our requests for teacher and leader/founder interviews, conversations with pupils and parents, and observations of lessons.

Over a period of two months, six day-long visits took place in the two supplementary schools in Oslo and over a four-month period, five evening and two day-long visits took place in the two schools in Leeds. While teachers, pupils, school leaders and parents were interviewed in both cities and while we had designed semi-structured interview and observa-tional schedules, in practice, we adopted a more unstructured, informal and interactive style in which we were able to take advantage of opportunities as they arose. Interviewees were encouraged to talk about what mattered to them in relation to their role in the school. Some interviews involved groups, especially those with pupils and parents; some, specifically the teacher interviews, were individually based; some were of short duration, perhaps only 10 minutes, while others lasted up to two hours. All were audio-recorded and later transcribed. Five lessons were observed in each city and these, too, were audio-recorded and field notes made to contextualise the interactions.

On two occasions in Leeds, two of us observed the same lessons, both of us met and conversed informally with all the Leeds participants, and both of us listened to all the Leeds audio-recordings. We considered these processes vital means of authenticating and cross-checking our interpretations of participants' comments and of the teaching we observed. The lack of Norwegian prevented this in the case of the Oslo database but the researchers compensated for this by sharing and discussing all the transcripts of interviews and the field notes of observation and interactions—all of which were presented in English. The analysis of a combination of documentation, observation and interviews (with adults and children) offered an important means of enhancing the validity of our evidence. Communication among the researchers took place by e-mail and telephone, and one face-to-face meeting was convened to develop the analysis. This chapter is the result of our collaborative interpretation.

Documentary evidence on supplementary schools in Leeds and Oslo

A common feature currently across supplementary schools in Leeds and Oslo is the nature of their organisation—they are all community based and they rely on volunteers (Quddus, 1986, 1989; Oslo Kommune, 1998, 1999; Kempadoo & Abdelrazak, 1999). Although most schools perform multiple roles and there is considerable overlap in curriculum provision, supplementary schools in Leeds and Oslo can be classified into four main groupings:

(i)   mother tongue schools;
(ii) religious schools;
(iii) those focusing on the teaching of culture and history; and
(iv) supplementary mainstream schools (only in Leeds). [...]

The main features of supplementary schools in both cities can be summarised as follows:

- voluntary status with little financial support from local authorities;
- poor accommodation and mostly untrained teachers, some of whom lack bilingual competence;
- high levels of parental and community involvement;
- learners grouped according to mixed ability and mixed ages, and in some ethnic groups, according to gender;
- relatively rigid discipline and formality in teacher–pupil relations;
- a curriculum designed to generate pride and knowledge in home culture, roots and history;
- a curriculum delivered in community languages; and
- 'low key' operation which the mainstream society often views with some susupicion. [...]

Profile of case study schools

School AL

This supplementary Punjabi school is an integral part of a Sikh *Gurdwara* (temple) in a district of Leeds. The school was established in 1991 in response to parental requests to promote linguistic and cultural development. The intention is that children will be able to participate actively in the life of the *Gurdwara*, heighten their interest in religious writings and Sikh history, and learn Punjabi. [...]

School BL

This school was established in 1998 by a group of young Pakistani professionals to provide support to Pakistani pupils in National Curriculum subjects (primarily English and mathematics). Key individuals include a university lecturer, a secondary school teacher, a computer consultant and a community education worker. [...]

School CO

The Kosovo-Albanian Immigrant Association (KAIA) established this school in 1992. The school has a Steering Committee which monitors all organisational and financial aspects of provision. [...] The school caters for 78 children between the ages of 6 and 16 and has four volunteer teachers. The predominant activity of the school is mother tongue teaching—Albanian.

School DO

This Tamil school was established in 1992 by the parents of some 22 children to provide mother tongue teaching. Currently, it has 428 children aged 4–16 years and 30 students aged 16–19, totalling 458 students benefiting from provision here, constituting the largest supplementary school in Oslo. [...]

Overarching function: group solidarity

Unsurprisingly, each school's curricular activity reflected its particular orientation, whether language teaching or mainstream subjects. However, regardless of the schools' particular curricular orientation and regardless of city, all four supplementary schools operated in a way that reinforced group solidarity. This was evidenced through the variety of groupings, celebrations, meetings, interactions, contacts and ceremonies that take place in each school. This quotation from a conversation with a 16-year-old Tamil boy in his supplementary school (DO) illustrates the point well:

> Look at these people, so many people here, they like to be here. They bring their children here, small children ... look at the adults chatting, look at those who are standing

there, one, two three … nine men talking together for two hours. They cannot find such a place anywhere else. What are they talking about? I think everything from politics to shopping, maybe about cars, who knows? It is good to meet each other, Tamil people are like that. They like to visit each other, to work together. Here they have to help sometimes, to clean the school, they help the children. Now we bought a new place, I do not know where it is but I saw drawings. It is good so we are going to use it every day … every day. We can have a canteen there and parties, we can buy things, such facilities are not here. Folklore is good, Tamil folklore and dance is different. I like it, you cannot do such things at the Norwegian school, they would laugh at you, here we do it, no problem.

School AL is used for religious ceremonies that mark important life events, e.g. weddings, it is used for formal meetings to plan the work of the Gurdwara, it is used as a cafeteria, it is used for informal socialising and interaction by all age groups from babies to older members of the community, for intra- and inter-generational events, and, of course, for teaching. On our first evening visit to this school, we were invited to join over 100 men, women and children at a regular Sunday celebratory meal (*langar*) which the women had prepared. One of the teachers in this school spoke about the place of the supplementary school in her life, now and in the past. For her, the school, which is synonymous with the temple, provided opportunities to learn, to socialise but, especially, to belong:

> If I don't attend the Sikh Temple on a regular basis I do feel a bit lost. I feel as if I know a lot of the community that come here and if I haven't been for a couple of weeks someone will say 'you haven't been'. It's important for me to attend the Temple socially as well as to teach. It's about how we were brought up. I always had a supplementary school in my life … for the youth club, the girls' group and that's where I learned to play the harmonium and where I learned Punjabi. One way or another the supplementary school has always been in my life so I like to come here. It stayed with me. The supplementary school is your link to the community.

Similarly, School CO in Oslo fulfilled a variety of functions. During the second day visit to this school, we observed that, apart from the variety of teaching sessions that were ongoing, the Kosovo-Albanian Immigrant Association (KAIA) was hosting a steering committee meeting for Kosovo-Albanian immigrant teachers during which the teachers discussed common problems and issues they encountered in their work and reflected on ways of addressing some of them. Their discussion ranged from children's bilingual development to problems experienced by children in mainstream schooling. A conversation with three of the teachers in School CO that evening confirmed that the school is multifunctional. It is a place where the Kosovo-Albanian band can practise, it is a place for religious events, including wedding ceremonies, it is a place where community members can enjoy Albanian television broadcasts, it is place where adult members who have limited competence in Norwegian can be supported by other, more linguistically proficient speakers of Norwegian, a place where children are safe, under adult supervision, and a place where adults can discuss the local and national politics from their perspective and where they can discuss strategies for negotiating with the Norwegian authorities. In relation to children, one teacher said, 'this is a place where children with the same language background can meet, take mother-tongue lessons together and play together'.

The following field notes were made during a day visit to School DO:

I counted 89 men and 103 women. Some of them sitting and talking with each other, others selling cokes, biscuits and snacks on behalf of the school. Others were selling tickets (fund-raising), two men were selling VCRs, another group was discussing the architect's drawings of the new centre. … I have never seen so many immigrant parents in one place. There were about 430 children participating in mother-tongue classes and other activities. In addition to this there were about 70 very young children (0–3 years old) who were with their parents.

The pupils we interviewed were even more direct than the adults about the sense of empowerment and belonging that attendance at their supplementary school brings them. This response from a 15-year-old boy in School DO is not unusual:

I have been going here for nine years, all the time … my father was among the founders. I like this place. We get help here, we meet each other.… what we learn here is good. We learn many things about history, culture, geography, about Sri Lanka and Norway, we even have mathematics here you know and other subjects. If you go here you do not encounter with problems at Norwegian school … There is a kind of party every week, with many parents, many children, music and dance. We, Tamil people, like to keep contact with each other. Sometimes some boys at the school and where we live try to show racist attitudes towards us but we are not afraid. We are strong in the class, we work hard and they understand that they cannot break us. This weekend school is *our* school. It makes us strong … strong people with strong identity. (our emphasis)

Another 15-year-old boy contrasts his experience in School AL with his mainstream school in terms of solidarity. He says:

we have like Indian friends here, which I think is good. And it's like most people get on with you here and you know them a really long time. It's a bit different to normal school because in the classes, it's like you're speaking your own language, it's a bit different. I like it.

Several comments from other pupils, teachers and parents confirmed this sense of solidarity. Two points are noteworthy in relation to this theme. One is how our interviewees participated in and construed their participation in their school: it was not merely physical, intellectual or instrumental, it was also emotional, spiritual and deeply meaningful. They did not speak about their involvement in their school in dispassionate terms but in a way that could be described as 'fervent'. The second is about clarity of purpose. There is no doubt that the people we interviewed share the same set of values about the importance of pride in one's own culture and of knowledge of one's roots and history. In addition, they are clear that the purpose of their supplementary school is to inculcate pride, to support each other, and to further their sense of themselves and their community. In this sense, participants may be seen to utilise their individual power to negotiate the means by which they can gain meaningful educational and sociocultural experiences. Attendance at supplementary schools was thus a way of reclaiming the specificity of cultural and social identity that was missing from mainstream schooling. Their school provided an educational climate that was empowering in an inclusive sense—promoting a general feeling of solidarity and common purpose. This shared understanding and appreciation of the purpose of their school must be a factor in the success of these institutions, since it is now well established that one of the key features of a successful school (however 'success' is defined) is that stakeholders are aware of and share its purposes (Rutter *et al.*, 1979).

The most striking message, then, from our evidence is that the supplementary school imbues its participants with a sense of belonging to a community that supports them practically, culturally, socially, emotionally and spiritually. Whether the curriculum focus of the school is mother tongue teaching or mainstream school subject teaching, or a combination of curricular foci, the underlying principle in operation is the same—support through strong ethnic identity and community attachment. [...]

Curriculum, pedagogy and links with mainstream schooling

As indicated on several occasions so far in this chapter, the impetus for the development of supplementary schools stemmed from the mainstream's inadequacy of addressing the educational needs of ethnic community members. Several teachers, pupils and parents talked passionately, about, for example, the links between their mother tongue and a sense of self and community identity and how their home language is not supported in the mainstream system. While community leaders in both cities are acutely aware of how their culture is marginalised by the mainstream system, teachers in Oslo made more overt reference to this. For example, one particular teacher in School CO returned to this point several times in interview:

> The Government does not understand the situation of our children. The state school authorities do not respect the background of our children ... Lack of support for the development of the minorities' mother tongue in the ordinary school system and lack of bilingual support for our minority children in the Norwegian school system is a conscious policy from the majority society to keep our children at the bottom of society ... The system functions to discriminate against our children.

However, all the teachers interviewed, regardless of their particular curricular focus in the supplementary school, shared a desire to promote their pupils' progress in the mainstream school. To illustrate, although the focus was mother tongue teaching in School CO, another teacher explained to the researcher how he links his teaching directly to what his pupils are studying during the week in their ordinary school:

> As you see, some of the children brought their Norwegian textbooks with them. I know roughly the main topics the children do at the Norwegian school. I have seen

their books. Many times I relate the mother tongue lessons to those topics, like Health, European Geography, the Seasons, you know, there are many standard topics. I try to touch some of them.

Students in School DO were keen to succeed in their mainstream school. One 14-year-old boy explained what he learns in the supplementary school and why he attends:

> What we learn here is good. We learn a lot about the world. We become knowledge-able. It helps us to be better at the Norwegian school … I want to get good marks and go to a good secondary school and get a chance to get into a university … I want to be a doctor.

Another pupil at this school perceived that he had 'to work harder than Norwegians to be successful.' Pupils appreciated the pragmatic nature of their curricular experience. As far as they were concerned, what they did had immediate relevance for them—getting their homework done, passing examinations, understanding their mainstream textbooks. One boy, for instance, in School AL explained that he thought he would not continue attending after he had taken Punjabi in his General Certificate of Secondary Education (GCSE) examination:

> I think I will stop [attending], because that's what I want. That's the reason I come to Punjabi classes, I want my GCSE. So after I get that qualification, I'll stop coming.

In all four schools, pupils were in mixed-gender and mixed-ability groups, but the age differences were minimised. All the lessons we observed involved high levels of pupil–teacher interaction, teacher questioning, some pupil-initiated questions, individual attention and small group work. Teachers were definitely in control: they decided the content, sequence, pace and tasks to be completed. Although authoritative, teachers were not authoritarian and relations between them and their students were friendly, sensitive and cheerful. The nature of teaching and learning was dictated largely by textbooks, worksheets and homework exercises. Textbooks provided a structure for the syllabus and the lessons we observed in Schools BL and DO (both mainstream curriculum oriented) used them extensively and systematically, but not exclusively. Teachers themselves elaborated on themes in the textbooks; they frequently created worksheets and designed activities and tasks for pupils to do in class or for homework that consolidated or extended pupils' understanding and knowledge.

Teaching in Schools AL and CO—being mother tongue oriented—tended to be largely whole-class based and tended to involve the development of vocabulary, grammar, comprehension and oral work. Homework was set and marked in relation to the theme of the lesson. School CO also emphasises Albanian history, especially its more recent history and the situation of Albanian immigrants in Norway today. Main textbooks in School CO are imported from abroad. School DO used one textbook for each grade and this acted as a core syllabus. These were worked out in Norway by the DO teachers. Some other reference books were also used. These were imported from either Sri Lanka or London. Teaching in schools BL and DO involved more group and individual work and here mainstream textbooks played a much greater role. Here teachers (more than one per class) moved around the class offering individual support, explaining specific points in the textbook. Teachers in both these schools talked about how the terminology in the textbook sometimes acts as a barrier to learning and how they see their role as unpacking that language for pupils and developing their conceptual understanding. As one teacher in Leeds said in relation to tests as well as to textbooks, 'often the barrier to learning is just one word'.

Mother tongue literature was shared and discussed in both Schools AL and CO. Interestingly, School CO had only a limited amount of books in Albanian, with each child possessing, at most, two books in Albanian. One of the teachers movingly described an occasion when they received some storybooks from Kosovo. Such was their excitement that, in his words, 'they almost ate the books'. Field notes from an observational session in this school are consistent with this point:

> Both before the lesson, during the lesson, during the break and after the break and when the lessons were over, the pupils handled their mother tongue books—all had two books, a textbook/reading book and an exercise/workbook—very gently. So gently and carefully that one could not avoid registering it.

Teachers in both cities commented on how unaware they perceived mainstream teachers to be of all their pupils' lives. While teachers in the supplementary schools made every effort to familiarise themselves with life in mainstream classrooms, the opposite did not appear to be the case. One incident related to us by a teacher in School CO powerfully exemplified this. In the teacher's own words:

> A few months ago two of my pupils went to Macedonia to visit their relatives. They were away from the school for five days. That trip was their first trip abroad since they came to Norway as babies. I was told that the headmaster of the Norwegian school and their teacher were not happy about the children's absence and when they came back they criticised their parents. When I heard about this episode, I asked the two children whether their teachers asked them to tell about their trip or to tell their friends about it. The answer was 'no' from both of my pupils. Can you imagine a situation where your positive experiences were underestimated, undercommunicated? I did the opposite. I asked them to tell us about their trip. They had a lot of things to say and they were proud of doing that. It was fascinating to see them telling about their trip. The same children were criticised at their Norwegian school but applauded at their Albanian school, you see the difference?

Our conversations with the pupils in Oslo confirmed that they distinguished very clearly between their mainstream and supplementary schools in terms of loyalty and attachment. Of significance, as indicated in the chapter's title, was the way they referred to 'our' school and 'the ordinary school' or 'the Norwegian school'. A 10-year-old girl in School CO revealed: 'We are all friends here, I like to be here. This is our school.' It is significant that pupils spend between 22 and 28 hours per week attending 'the ordinary school' but they do not feel a sense of ownership of that place; they spend a mere three hours per week at their supplementary school but they do feel that sense of ownership and belonging. This must be an issue of interest to the mainstream system, where some pupils clearly feel emotionally excluded though they are physically integrated and included. These pupils are seen and see themselves as 'other' in their mainstream school. The apparent unawareness of teachers in the mainstream system of the lives of their pupils from ethnic minority backgrounds merits further investigation.

Conclusion

This final section considers the rhetoric and the reality of official policy and practice in the two countries along with the implications of the evidence presented in this chapter.

Sprinkled throughout official educational documentation in England/Wales and Norway are references to and endorsements of pluralism, multiculturalism, cultural and linguistic diversity, and bilingualism. Principles of integration, inclusion and respect for diversity are counselled. In the case of policy texts on language, the important role of pupils' mother tongue in relation to learning and to ethnic identities is confirmed. However, as the first part of this chapter explained, practice in mainstream schools diverges enormously from this rhetoric. In reality, mainstream schooling, at best, neglects, and at worst, denies cultural and linguistic diversity to such an extent that communities so affected mount their own provision at considerable cost to themselves. These schools seek to develop capacities and values that children already have but which mainstream schools appear to underrate or ignore. It is arguable that the mainstream system is geared to assume deficits in students while the supplementary school locates and teaches to strengths. In our view, this state of affairs is patronising and condescending and, more seriously, is indifferent and lacking in respect. What is paradoxical is that despite purporting to be inclusive and supportive of diversity, mainstream schooling is, in practice, exclusive and insensitive to diversity, while supplementary schools welcome any students who wish to attend them. For example, School DO in Oslo had two Pakistani pupils who did not understand Tamil but who, nevertheless, benefited from the support available to them at the school with the Norwegian mainstream textbooks and homework. It is arguable that this supplementary school is more in tune with the state's official rhetoric than the state's own schools!

In Oslo, there is a further paradox. We have already mentioned the limited resources available from the state for supplementary schools in both countries. However, in Oslo, there is no funding at all available for supplementary schools that support bilingualism or mother tongue learning but there is for religion learning. We term this *theologisation* of ethnic minority children's needs. There is no principled reason for not applying the same rule to language and religion, in our view. The current position in both England and Norway is assimilationist with regard to the dominant language—English and Norwegian, respectively. In both countries, the aim of the state is that all pupils *fit into* an established social and economic order. In practice, this means that they learn a common language and this is not contentious, but that they learn it in a subtractive way is. As Tove Skutnabb-Kangas (1997) and Robert Phillipson (1992) demonstrate, a common language, learned in a subtractive, rather than additive, way is a most important mechanism of control.

Skutnabb-Kangas (1997) makes a helpful distinction between 'necessary language rights'—the right to learn one's mother tongue (and to an official language if that is not the mother tongue)—and 'enrichment-oriented rights'—the right to learn any foreign language. It is arguable that in the case of minorities in mainstream education in England and Oslo, the more fundamental 'necessary language rights' are accorded less status than 'enrichment-oriented rights'. Policy-makers in both countries need to recognise how current practices not only do not promote but actually prevent positive language rights in education for some pupils. Supplementary school teachers make it clear that their pedagogical philosophy is not in opposition to that of the mainstream but that it acts as a *corrective* to the *subtractive* approach of that system. Their approach to language is 'additive'. It is vital that policy-makers not just engage in dialogue with supplementary school leaders, but ensure that they become part of the policy-making machine so that the mainstream system can offer the kind of education that is respectful of *all* children. This, at a minimum, means mother tongue support and bilingual education. There is an urgent need to reconstruct the mainstream to incorporate the interests of ethnic minority groups.

Our study shows that supplementary schools are aware of the routines and demands of the mainstream system. Thus, while offering a learning environment that is conducive to the reclamation of individual and collective senses of sociocultural identity and power, supplementary schooling also communicates notions of traditional authority, self-regulation and knowledge. In this sense, their position—while containing elements of cultural resistance—is additive, filling in the gaps of cultural specificity that mainstream schooling neglects. The apparent lack of awareness or benign neglect on the part of mainstream teachers of the realities of the lives of minority pupils exists in stark contrast. In this sense, we would argue that these children do not enjoy 'equality of respect' (Lynch, 1999) with their majority counterparts since they experience their schooling as denying their identities. Their best interests are not being served by the mainstream. In this regard, it is worth noting that childhood is a part of life and not just a preparation for it—the quality of the experience in the *here and now* of the child's life matters. In addition, as other researchers remind us (Connell, 1993; Lynch, 1999), we must not view schooling as some kind of unproblematic good, where more is better—schooling itself is, for some, a place where one's identity is denied or one's voice is silenced. Given its lengthy duration and its formative impact, schooling must be meaningful for *all* young people. If mainstream schooling were more meaningful culturally for these children, then supplementary schools would be unnecessary.

While the evidence presented here portrays a positive picture of supplementary schools, we are aware of potential difficulties and we believe that further research is needed on their impact. Of interest, for example, is the extent to which members of minority ethnic groups remain within the confines of their community during and after their school years, thus possibly creating barriers in terms of their ability and willingness to participate fully in mainstream society. The question is: to what extent do supplementary schools inadvertently encourage ghettoisation? Moreover, the possible link between supplementary schools and fundamentalism merits examination, although we found no evidence of such a link in our four schools. Also, of interest is the extent to which attendance at supplementary schools impacts on other aspects of development and other possible activities, specifically physical development, individual-initiated activity and free play. The total amount of time spent in school is obviously higher for those children who attend supplementary school—indeed, it is noteworthy that many children, particularly those of Muslim faith, attend more than one supplementary school.

There would appear to be more continuity than discontinuity across all four schools than between schools in each city. All four supplementary schools reflect the desire of respective ethnic minority communities to provide an instrument for cultural continuity and enrichment. Language development and associated religious and educational activities become tools for self-determination and the maintenance of cultural identity as defined by ethic minority communities. This encourages self-respect and a sense of cultural security in what many perceive as a hostile environment riddled with racist practices in the mainstream education system and the society at large. These elements of identity and self-respect are key components in individual ability to negotiate obstacles that exist structurally in the mainstream, and to blur the edges of what may be considered predictable educational progressions. Supplementary schooling thus becomes a defensive and empowering mechanism in a society that often does not positively register the existence of 'others' and negates the culture and languages of ethnic minority communities. [...]

References

Bastiani, J. (2000) *A Report on Supplementary Schooling in the Lambeth Education Action Zone* (London, Institute for Public Policy Research).

Bronfenbrenner, U. (1979) *The Ecology of Human Development: experiments by nature and design* (Cambridge, MA, Harvard University Press).

Burchell, G., Gordon, C. & Miller, P. (Eds) (1991) *The Foucault Effect: studies in governmentality, with two lectures by and an interview with Michel Foucault* (Chicago, IL, Chicago University Press).

Chevannes, M. & Reeves, F. (1987) The black voluntary school movement: definition, context and prospects, in: B. Troyna (Ed.) *Racial Inequality in Education* (London, Tavistock).

Connell, R. W. (1993) *Schools and Social Justice* (Philadelphia, PA, Temple University Press).

Dove, N. E. (1993) The emergence of black supplementary schools, *Urban Education*, 27, p. 449.

Giddens, A. (1984) *The Constitution of Society: outline of the theory of structuration* (Cambridge, Polity Press).

Giddens, A. (1991) *Modernity and Self-identity: self and society in the later modern age* (Cambridge, Polity Press).

Giddens, A. & Pierson, C. (1998) *Conversations with Anthony Giddens: making sense of modernity* (Cambridge, Polity Press).

Gilborn, D. & Gipps, C. (1996) *Recent Research on the Achievements of Ethnic Minority Pupils* (London, HMSO).

Gore, J. M. (1998) Disciplining bodies: on the continuity of power relations in pedagogy, in: T. A. Popkewitz & M. Brennan (Eds) *Foucault's Challenge: discourse, knowledge and power in education*, pp. 231–251 (New York, Teachers College Press).

Green, B. (1998) Born again teaching? Governmentality, grammar and public schooling, in: T. A. Popkewitz & M. Brennan (Eds) *Foucault's Challenge: discourse, knowledge and power in education*, pp. 173–204 (New York, Teachers College Press).

Hall, K. (1998) Critical literacy and the case for it in the early years of school, *Language, Culture and Curriculum*, 11, pp. 183–194.

Hall, K., Özerk, K. & Valli, Y. (1999) Curriculum reform in contemporary English and Norwegian official documents with particular reference to literacy, *European Journal of Intercultural Studies*, 10, pp. 85–104.

Kempadoo, M. & Abdelrazak, M. (1999) *Directory of Supplementary and Mother-tongue Classes 1999–2000* (London, Department for Education and Employment).

Lauglo, J. (1996) *Motbakke, men mer driv? Innvandrerungdom i norsk skole* (Oslo, Ungforsk Report no 6).

Lodding, B. (1998) *Med eller uten rett. Evaluering av Reform 94: Underveisrapport 1997 fra prosjektet Etniske minoriteter* (Oslo, NIFU).

Lynch, K. (1999) *Equality in Education* (Dublin, Gill & Macmillan).

Ofsted (1996) *Recent Achievements of Ethnic Minority Pupils* (London, OFSTED/HMSO).

Ofsted (1999) *Raising the Attainment of Minority Ethnic Pupils: schools and LEA responses* (London, OFSTED/HMSO).

Oslo Kommune (1998) *Oversikt over grupper, flyktninge og innvandrerorganisasjoner i Oslo og omegn pr 01.02.98* (Oslo, Oslo kommune Flyktninge og innvandreretaten).

Oslo Kommune (1999) *Statsbudsjettet 1999, kap. 521 post 73: Tilskud til frivillig virksomhet i lokalsamfunn* (Oslo, Oslo kommune Byradsavdeling for eldre og bydelene).

Özerk, K. (1995) *Modeller for undervisningsorganisering for minoriteter.* Report nr 2 (Oslo, Universitetet i Oslo, Pedagogisk forskningsinstitutt).

Özerk, K. (1997) Forholdet mellom språklig utvikling, erfaringsmessig utvikling og skolefaglig utvikling, in: T. Sand (Ed.) *Flerkulturell virkelighet i skole og samfunn*, pp. 176–200 (Oslo, Cappelen Akademisk forlag).

Özerk, K. (1999) *Oppturingsteori og lareplanforstaese* (Vallset, Opladske bokforlag).

Phillipson, R. (1992) *Linguistic Imperialism* (Oxford, Oxford University Press).

Pinar, W. F. & Reynolds, W. M. (Eds) (1992) *Understanding Curriculum as Phenomenological and Deconstructed Text* (New York, Teachers College Press).

Popkewitz, T. A. & Brennan, M. (Eds) (1998) *Foucault's Challenge: discourse, knowledge and power in education* (New York, Teachers College Press).

Quddus, A. (1986) *Leeds City Council and Supplementary Schooling.* Unpublished report.

Quddus, A. (1989) *Supplementary Schools in Leeds. Report to the Education Committee, Leeds City Council.* Unpublished report.

Reay, D. & Mirza, H. S. (1997) Uncovering genealogies of the margins: black supplementary schooling, *British Journal of Sociology of Education*, 18, pp. 477–503.

Ribbins, P. & Greenfield, T. B. (Eds) (1993) *Greenfield on Educational Administration: towards a humane craft* (London, Routledge).

Rutter, M., Mortimore, P. & Ouston, J. (1979) *Fifteen Thousand Hours: secondary schools and their effects on children* (London, Open Books).

Shutkin, D. (1998) The deployment of information technology in the field of education and the augmentation of the child, in: T. A. Popkewitz & M. Brennan (Eds) *Foucault's Challenge: discourse, knowledge and power in education*, pp. 205–230 (New York, Teachers College Press).

Stone, M. (1981) *The Education of the Black Child: the myth of multi-cultural education* (London, Fontana).

Skutnabb-Kangas, T. (1997) Human rights and language policy in education, in: *Encyclopedia of Language and Education, vol. 1: language policy and political issues in education*, pp. 55–65 (Dordrecht, Kluwer).

Tomlinson, S. (1985) The 'Black Education' movement, in: M. Arnot (Ed.) *Race and Gender* (Oxford, Pergamon Press).

Volosinov, V. N. (1973) Marxism and the philosophy of language, cited in: J. Donald (1983) How illiteracy became a problem (and literacy stopped being one), *Journal of Education*, 165, pp. 35–52.

Zulfiqar, M. (1997) Beyond the national curriculum: development of supplementary schooling in Britain, *Development Education Journal*, 4, pp. 33–34.

Section 3

Shaping Identities

10

Gender, Assessment and Students' Literacy Learning: Implications for Formative Assessment

Patricia Murphy and Gabrielle Ivinson

[...]

Introduction

In the late 1990s, there were a significant number of classroom interventions to enhance boys' literacy achievement. These interventions arose because of widespread concern about boys' achievement locally and globally. This concern emerged in the United Kingdom (UK) with research to evaluate the impact of new assessment procedures introduced in the General Certificate of Secondary Education (GCSE) (Stobart et al., 1992). Coursework was introduced into the new examination to improve the 'fitness for purpose' of the assessment. Two-thirds of entries in English were for 100% coursework syllabuses. There was considerable mistrust of this non-standard form of assessment and it began to be construed as detrimental to boys. In 1994, coursework was limited to 40% in English with 20% given over to oral assessment. In spite of these changes, girls continued to outperform boys in English at 16+ with nearly 17% more girls than boys gaining A*-C grades in English in 1995. National assessments showed this performance advantage emerged at age 7 and continued through schooling (Murphy & Elwood, 1998).

A joint report from the Office for Standards in Education (Ofsted) and the Equal Opportunities Commission, *The Gender Divide* (1996), highlighted the achievement gap, raised questions about gender mediation of learning, and speculated about single-sex grouping as a possible ameliorating strategy.

> Should mixed schools experiment more with single-sex grouping for specific purposes, or would this be expensive and difficult to justify? (p. 26)

The source of this advice was the evidence, although conflicting, about the enhanced performance of girls and boys in single-sex schools compared with their counterparts in mixed schools. The problem with these findings was the very different nature of the student intakes and

From: *Teacher Development*, 9 (2), 2005, pp. 185–200. Reprinted by permission of the publisher (Taylor & Francis Ltd, http://www.informaworld.com).

the schools themselves in terms of their history and ethos. To extrapolate to single-sex groupings was even more problematic. The Basic Skills Agency evaluated skill-based strategies in English to support boys' literacy development (Frater, 1997). The research concluded that mixed-ability and mixed-sex groupings were used with equal success to single-sex groupings. A review of research commissioned by Ofsted (Arnot et al., 1998) looked in some detail at research into single-sex groupings. Although the evidence was inconclusive, the authors suggested that experimenting with the strategy was worthwhile but with the caution that it should be in the 'particular circumstances of particular schools' (p. 83). In 1998, local education authorities were required to set up strategies to improve boys' achievement, and to evaluate their effectiveness. The pedagogic solution that was foregrounded was single-sex groupings.

In the chapter, we discuss case-study data from settings where teachers in a mixed comprehensive school focused attention on the needs of low-achieving boys in English. To address the needs of these boys, they employed a strategy whereby the boys were grouped with mixed-ability girls and gendered seating (boy-girl-boy) was enacted which potentially placed girls in the role of peer tutors. The remaining high and average achieving boys were grouped together to maintain and enhance their learning in English. We examine the data from a socio-cultural perspective on gender and assessment to exemplify the dynamic social process of knowledge reconstruction. We describe how educational achievements emerge and are a consequence, in part, of the interrelation between gender and assessment as social forces operating in settings. We argue that this interrelationship needs to be considered in thinking about what to pay attention to in formative assessment. Sociocultural theories of situated cognition provide a broader conceptualisation of formative assessment and what that might imply for practice.

Background

Learning and gender

Schools as social arenas (see Lave, 1988) are socially situated and mediated by practices beyond their boundaries (Bruner, 1996; Wenger, 1998). The term 'setting' was defined by Lave to foreground subjective experiences within local contexts. Nespor (1997) similarly suggests that settings within school are 'intersections in social space, knots in a web of practices that stretch into complex systems beginning and ending outside the school' (p. xiii). Teachers, through their practice, orchestrate classroom settings. Simultaneously, students create, enact and experience settings. The distinction between arena and setting recognises that social, historical, and political forces shape activities enacted in schools. Students and teachers bring beliefs and knowledge to settings as a consequence of their participation in a multitude of other social contexts. One such set of beliefs involves gender, which can be viewed as a hegemonic social representation that circulates as a set of norms, ideas and conventions and provides the resources from which individuals construct social identities (Lloyd & Duveen, 1992; Ivinson & Murphy, 2003).

The social representation of gender comprises a bi-polar construct that divides social life into masculine and feminine marked activities, objects and attributes. Football, for example, is socially marked as masculine and 'romantic fiction' is marked as feminine. In English classrooms, a student's written text can be seen as an extension of self open to the interpretive gaze of others (Zittoun et al., 2004). The way the text is interpreted acts back on the student and extends an identity, which the student may or may not wish to appropriate. If a writing genre has a feminine valence, and the writer is a boy, he may experience conflict. Students have to manage such conflicts and one solution is to abandon a troublesome writing genre and revert to one that is congruent with expressing a social gender identity. Therefore, learning has social and identity consequences for students.

Underlying the debate about the gender gap in literacy achievement is the assumption that equal outcomes for boys and girls are an indication of gender neutrality and imply equality in treatment and opportunity. This position implies that gender is interchangeable with sex group and that essentialist generalisations can be made about girls and boys. Furthermore, the social and cultural contexts in which actions and outcomes are produced remain unchallenged. We are concerned with the way gender-based inequalities are produced within settings and the pedagogic practices that may reinforce, challenge or transform social representations of gender.

Assessment and gender

Gorard (2004) has challenged the interpretation of national and international data about English that there is a systematic difference between boys and girls at the lowest levels of attainment. He argued that the performance gap emerged only at the higher levels of attainment and suggested that UK schemes that target low-attaining boys to overcome the gender gap in literacy performance were 'based on an incorrect diagnosis' (p. 29). He speculated that the gap at age 15 may mean that boys and girls may 'simply be differently literate'. Although we agree with Gorard's interpretation of the gender gap (see Murphy & Ivinson, 2004), we take issue with his assumption that equal outcomes indicate that assessment is functioning in the same way for girls and boys. This fails to recognise assessment as a sociocultural process and reduces assessment processes and instruments to technical devices. Underlying assessment practices, such as judging which tier to enter students in the GCSE examination, are sociocultural processes in which representations of gender shape teachers' perceptions of 'success'. For example, more boys than girls are allocated to the higher tiers in science and mathematics (Stobart et al., 1992; Elwood & Murphy, 2002).

The research found that this was due to teachers' beliefs that girls would be uncomfortable with the challenges that higher tiers represent. 'Weaker girls feel more secure in the middle tier'. Girls are also seen to be more motivated than boys and can be relied on to continue to work even though ceilings have been placed on their achievements in contrast with boys: 'low ability girls are generally better motivated than low ability boys'. Boys tended to be located more in the higher tiers to meet the challenges they relish and to avoid disaffection: 'at higher tier boys are more arrogant, girls are more worried' (Stobart et al., 1992, cited in Elwood & Murphy, 2002, p. 403). Teachers and others tend to fall back on common-sense beliefs about gender while their practices reinforce and give substance to them. It is in this way that assessment technologies become social technologies and shape our cultural understandings (Hanson, 2000).

Formative assessment is understood generally to be about enhancing learners' capacity to learn, though it is often more narrowly understood as the means by which students' learning needs are identified and teaching is shaped to address them (Organisation for Economic Co-operation and Development, 2005). If, as is assumed in policy directives, gender mediates learning and educational achievements, then formative assessment needs to take account of the influence of hegemonic social representations of gender on knowledge construction. Relationships between teaching, learning and assessment need to embrace a view that thinking, knowing and remembering are distributed phenomena undertaken between people, and between people and tools in specific settings.

Traditionally, formative assessment emerged from a behaviourist perspective where neither assessment nor learning was understood as social in nature. More recently it has been aligned with constructivist views of learning in that it was recognised that students actively construct meaning rather than receive it. The locus of control for learning shifts from the teacher to the student as learners evaluate their efficacy in the tasks they undertake and increasingly take on board these personal evaluations (Bruner, 1996). As part of this view of the agentive mind, students' prior knowledge was seen as a major determinant of new learning. Hence, teachers and students needed access to this if the teaching and learning process was to be effective, a central aim of formative assessment.

Many of the writings about formative assessment appear to be directed largely at the students', as opposed to the teachers', needs. It follows from a constructivist perspective, however, that a teacher can never 'know' a student's mind but can only model it. Therefore, to guide students, teachers need to understand the sense that students make of the learning opportunities provided. To make effective sense of learning opportunities, students have to know what they are learning, its value and purpose. It has been noted that a constructivist perspective is necessary but insufficient for the optimal definition of formative procedures (Allal & Mottier Lopez, 2005). By focusing attention on individual sense making and how the teacher and students jointly reconstruct knowledge through interaction, constructivist approaches tend to lose sight of the wider social and cultural context of learning. While some researchers refer to Bourdian concepts to analyse the role of socialisation in knowledge construction (Ecclestone & Pryor, 2003), we call upon Rogoff's work which recognises that practices in local settings are embedded within 'the institutions, technologies, norms and practices developed by and appropriated from previous generations' (1990, p. 138). This is congruent with Lave's (1998) view that the arena encompasses the individual in settings in which 'agent, activity and the world mutually constitute each other' (Lave & Wenger, 1991, p. 33).

The theoretical framework of situated learning offers a broad perspective for conceptualising formative assessment yet theorising about formative assessment should not be cut off from the realities of classroom practice (cf. Allal & Mottier Lopez, 2005). In making the case for a broader conceptualisation of formative assessment, we turn to teachers' practice to highlight the role that formative assessment could play in helping teachers to recognise how beliefs about gender influence teaching and assessment in situ.

Gender and the reconstruction of English

We draw on data from two settings in the case-study school. The students were in Year 10 and aged 14–15, studying for their GCSE examination. In the first setting, the students were mixed-ability girls and boys identified as low achievers in English ($n = 19$). The ratio was 3:2 girls to boys and the seating was boy-girl-boy-girl. The seating was chosen with two purposes in mind. The first was to use the girls to engage boys in dialogue about their English and through peer interaction to model 'successful' practice in English. The second was to control the boys so that they were not disruptive and off-task. Both purposes were seen to increase boys' participation and therefore improve their achievement. In the other setting, the remaining boys were organised into a single-sex grouping ($n = 27$). The organisation of the settings made visible representations of both boys and girls. Thus, there were 'good' boys to be nurtured and 'problem' boys to be controlled and changed. Girls were characterised as successful and to be emulated.

We wanted to observe 'everyday' practice and negotiated only that the teachers used the same activity and that it had an identifiable end product. The activity they selected was a creative writing task to produce three different novel openings to be submitted as part of the students' coursework portfolio for the public examination at the end of Year 11. The activity took place over a three-lesson period. In the first lesson, students were introduced to different literary techniques relating to different genres. Extracts from novel openings were read out and exercises from an in-house booklet on creative writing were discussed and the whole class considered group feedback. In the second lesson, drafts were written as an individual activity and the teachers selected students to read out their drafts and feedback was provided to inform the whole class. In the third lesson, the students continued with their individual writing and the writing, including the decisions about which drafts to submit as final pieces, was completed at home.

Data collection

We observed in both settings and took field notes of teachers' interactions with the students and audio-taped classroom discourse as well as interviewing each teacher. We observed and audio-recorded student interactions and interviewed selected students and had access to their written drafts and their final submitted texts. In our analysis, we draw on Rogoff's (2001) concept of three planes of analysis that are mutually constituting and inseparable – the institutional, interpersonal and personal. These represent different analytical lenses on sociocultural activity. We foregrounded the interpersonal and intrapersonal planes to consider how the teacher orchestrated the setting and how students in turn enacted and experienced it. In selecting the data for the article we have three aims. First, to exemplify how the teachers' practice and the orchestration of the setting were influenced by their perceptions of the students and how to enable their participation. Second, to illuminate the construction and reconstruction of knowledge in settings and, finally, how settings influence students' enactments, the decisions they made and the consequences for social identities and learning.

The settings

Both teachers introduced the task by modelling 'successful' writing through published work from established authors. In the second lesson, both groups were engaged in drafting their first novel openings. The teacher in the mixed setting explained how in order to 'model' successful writing, she chose students with 'good' pieces of work in English to read our drafts, predominantly girls. Her practice may have been influenced by the school-wide policy to provide models of success for boys. In her mind, there was a strong need to guide the low-achieving boys because she was responsible for students who were being failed in English, which is how the media and government policy were representing the problem.

'Classroom Rescue for Britain's Lost Boys' (*The Independent, 1998*)
'Cissy English Lessons May Hinder Boys' (*Daily Telegraph, 1998*)

In the all-boys group the pedagogic strategy was different. All boys read out a novel opening; this both reflected the teacher's view of these boys as succeeding at English and her concern to heighten their participation in the subject. There was no selection process in her mind, rather a concern to embrace the boys' interpretation of the activity.

In the mixed setting, the majority of girls selected to read out a draft they had written in the romance genre. Numerous surveys note that girls choose to read romance or stories that involve relationships, subjective experiences and emotions and that their writing mirrors their reading habits (White, 1988; Millard, 1997). The drafts reflected what students were familiar with and by choosing girls to model successful writing, the teacher unwittingly made the romance genre a high status and legitimate realisation of English subject knowledge. This was not necessarily reflected in her grading of the final submissions, however. In the boys' class, a wider range of genres such as adventure and action-orientated genres, including crime, horror and science fiction were read out and thus legitimated. As with the girls, the boys were reflecting their knowledge of familiar texts (Millard, 1997). No boy in the single-sex group drafted a first novel opening in the romance genre. Romance was not discussed, valued or legitimised in this setting. Consequently, hegemonic social representations of gender were consolidated through the teachers' practice. The teachers had little awareness that the boys and girls were actively reconstructing social representations of gender through their writing.

Students' experience and enactments

The mixed setting

Josie's novel opening 'Love Train' was selected and read out. She established a context for her novel and a background for her characters as she described embarking on a train journey with her future husband and mother. The main character was portrayed as a victim of a marriage arranged by her mother for financial reasons. She spoke of her hatred for her future husband, Tim. The excerpt from the middle of the opening is of the dramatic romantic encounter with a stranger:

> We walked up to the train and that's when I saw him a boy, I mean a man. He was already on the train sitting beside his small, tiny window. He was looking at me because I could feel his eyes burning through my skin. All my thoughts and emotions sank. All I was thinking about was that man. From what I could see, he was tall, dark and handsome. I could see the sweat trickling down his rusty skin coloured face. His clothes were shabby but clean … I noticed he needed a shave because I could see little hairs trying to push through his tough rusty skin. His eyes were dark brown like a tree trunk dying. His lips were moist from where he had licked them. I turned to look at Tim and his face and clothes. My emotions were not as high as for the man, I just saw. I turned to look at the stranger to see him and to feel his warm eyes burning through my skin again. But when I glanced he had vanished into thin air.

Other students in the mixed setting repeatedly mentioned Josie's novel opening as a good piece of writing. Josie herself was pleased with it and described how the idea came from the film *Titanic*:

Yeah I was happy because I read them out to my Mum and she thought, the first one which is called 'Love Train' – she thought it was very good. She just liked the feel of what I was writing, she is a great romantic herself it was a bit like the Titanic I suppose, except that it was on a train instead and it was right at the beginning where she sees him on the balcony.

Her choice of style and genre was validated and legitimised by her teacher, her peers and her mother. A social identity as a writer of romance was extended to her across contexts and was compatible with her feminine social identity. Sara also wrote a romance:

Her lilac cotton dress floated like a feather behind her as she started to jog. The weather was calm. The air was still. Phoebe saw something move. She heard a twig break. She waited for a moment … then heard laughing. It was Joey. He stepped out from the bush that he had been hiding behind and held Phoebe around her waist. Phoebe held his hands, then turned to face him, for what seemed like eternity, they stared into each other's eyes, a burning stare of love.

   Phoebe could stand the temptation no longer and pulled Joey's face towards hers. Their lips made contact. It was an intimate kiss. Joey ran his hands through Phoebe's hair. Phoebe pulled away and whispered in Joey's ear. She looked up at him and waited for his answer.

   He laughed,

   'I thought you'd never ask!'

   He took hold of her hand and led her back to his BMW.

Both Josie and Sara received positive feedback and achieved high Bs.

Her friend read out Katie's draft.

Last night was sensational. We made passionate love all night by the open fire. We touched and held each other all night. I'd never experienced anything like this before, his firm hands held me so tight. I felt so needed and wanted. As I ran my long finger nails through his soft dark hair, I stared into his big dark blue eyes. Soon the intense moment was over and we lay awake there most of the night holding and touching each other beneath the hot burning flame until we feel asleep.

Classmates speculated about the origins of this intimate writing. Josie was aware of the social identity that was being extended to Katie. Josie thought:

It was quite intimate – she put a lot of describing into it and perhaps she was a bit embarrassed by reading it out … It was really good describing though so … maybe it was from experience.

Katie in interview explained that she was not embarrassed about the content of her opening, but about the public nature of the task of reading out loud her draft. She was pleased by her work and felt that the teacher's feedback had validated her writing: 'She said well done and that it was good.' Katie's final draft was short and without context and was given a C grade. The grading process is private and open only to the teacher and the student. It is the performances of the texts and the public feedback that provide clues about legitimate and successful writing in a setting.

For example, three openings that were read out were from an action genre and Josie described the two boys' attempts:

> They were good but I think they could have been improved because they didn't actually describe what it was. Some of them just write 'a gun shot went off' and 'my brother got hit' ... when they should have written 'I heard a bang' and 'it hit my brother' then show where it hit, all the blood rushing out and what you did, what were the thoughts rushing through your head.

In contrast, Josie considered Lizzie's to be good because 'she was feeling what was going on and the atmosphere around her'. However, 'it was short and she had only just got started' so only a flavour of its potential was available as a model for the other students.

It was unsurprising that the students in the mixed setting generally associated good writing with description, feelings, emotions, and authenticity. Katie articulated what she thought the teacher valued:

> Lots of descriptive writing – imagination, describing the person and their thoughts.

The boys in the setting recognised that romance involved writing about feelings and had a high status as opposed to the 'action' openings. Boys in the mixed class did not write in the romance genre at first but two boys attempted to later in the lesson. Adam commented in interview that Josie's writing was very good and felt that he was 'actually getting into it [writing]'. He experimented with romance and drafted an opening. He drew on real life about a boy's attempt to get intimate with his girlfriend, rather than drawing on an example from a film or a book which were not readily available to him and used humour and actions as part of his style.

The teacher's view was that Adam had started to write romance because he discovered that he could write 'naughty things'. The teacher was unaware that Adam had recognised romance as 'good English' based on her practice and that he was taking a risk attempting a feminine writing practice. If the teacher had recognised this attempt to expand his writing repertoire, she could have encouraged him. Instead Adam said,

> The teacher read it and said, 'Make sure it doesn't get into an X-rated sort of thing' because it was actually starting to get a bit rough in there with the writing.

Dissuading Adam from writing romance was particularly pertinent given that she recognised that Katie's writing was 'a rather steamy Mills and Boon piece'. Yet, because Katie's writing was compatible with the teacher's social representations of femininity, it was not seen as problematic in the way that Adam's was. Adam reacted to the feedback by rejecting his draft as a failed piece of writing and fell back on what he understood were legitimate genres and styles for boys. He handed in three openings about war, horror and crime. The only other boy to hand in a romance opening worked on it at home using his mother's Jackie Collins novel as a model. Josie described what happened to this boy's attempt with a new genre:

> He gave his work in then got told off ... He said that he tried to write how it was. He said that he didn't mean to offend anybody but obviously the teacher just took it the wrong way.

He thought it was a bit unfair, she like warned him and then showed two other teachers … He was really embarrassed.

Josie made explicit the dilemma between writing that was 'rude' and writing that was 'intimate'. She made a very telling point about Martin's literacy difficulties: 'If you look in books about romance you don't find that much detail like in action, so I think it was a bit out of order'. The issue for Josie was then one of access to romance and its associated conventions rather than interpreting Martin's writing as a provocative act.

Both boys and girls recognised which genres were marked as masculine and feminine. Boys were reconstructuring the hegemonic that romance was not for them. Lawrence explained that having to express authentic knowledge about relationships was the problem:

because if you like something [the piece of writing] that is not good and it is bad but he's tried it as a romantic novel and it is pretty bad and the girls think it is bad then they are going to think that he did not have any clue at all about relationships and the boys are going to crack up at him and they are just going to really, really embarrass him.

The teacher's feedback to Martin left him with no insights about how to write in a style that was judged an appropriate expression of emotions. In his own words, he recognised the danger that his writing was 'going over the top' but the 'top' was left for him to define. Martin's participation in English was constrained rather than enhanced. Adam through self-regulation imposed constraints on his writing by falling back into 'safe' writing genres compatible with a masculine social identity. Both boys went to real life and action details to create authenticity rather than details about feelings. To help them, the teacher needed to first understand their situated experiences as writers and readers and second to consider how to create bridges between the genres and the conventions they were familiar with and those they were not. To do so though, she needed first to recognise how gender was influencing her pedagogic practice and second to be aware of practices that challenge rather than reconstruct hegemonic social representations of gender.

The all-boys' setting

In the all-boys' setting, we noted that the teacher accepted and praised the boys' attempts at first drafts and these reflected the genres they had experience of in their reading. No boy produced a romance opening. The performance of texts to an audience of male peers amplified hegemonic masculinity. Boys spoke about how boys policed each other's texts. James described the dangers of writing about feelings in an all-boys' setting:

I think it's harder to write about real things because if you were writing about them, then if people read them they would like know what your thoughts were about, things that were actually happening to you. But whereas if it is just a fantasy thing it is not going to really reveal anything unless you want to reveal it, so you could choose what does not really matter.

Two things struck us. First was the contrast in the exposure that girls like Josie and Katie risked in writing in ways that their teacher gave value to compared with 'boys' genres. Second, neither teacher was aware of the boys' concerns about sharing drafts with a public audience of boys. There were two overt consequences in the boys' setting. Typically, representations of successful English reflected those genres associated with boys. Paul, a successful writer, was given an A grade and his first opening was an adventure genre; there was considerable emotion expressed but about facing danger and death rather than about intimate relationships.

> The sand beat across my face. It dug into my cheeks like a thousand daggers, I pulled up my bandanna over my cracked lips and pulled my hat down so that only my eyes were showing. I held up my hand, trying to shield myself from the onslaught of sand to little effect. The searing heat was relentless. It jeered at me with a silent voice.
>
> The trees offered me no refuge now either. I fell to the floor and wept. I tried to pull myself up. I had to get up!
>
> I had started this thing. Now I had to finish it. So I went onward, to raw, stark death, I walked into the desert.

Although no reference had been made to the romance genre, four boys did submit romance openings. Don was one of these boys.

> 'He hasn't been around for two months. Why did I let him go like this? I've got to try and win him back after the two months I've felt totally lovesick. I've got to tell him that I've got feelings for him' said Shelly.
>
> 'We'll go and take the man who is rightly yours', said Sarah. 'I'll leave tomorrow, I'm sure he's staying at his parents in Dorset'. Shelly replied, 'I'll stay and look after the house'. 'I've got to show my feelings for him after seven years of love, I can't just let Matt go like that', Shelly sighed.

Don was awarded an F grade for his attempt. Unlike Martin and Adam, he tried to write as he imagined the genre was represented in texts, with his main characters as females. Needless to say, Don would not feel encouraged to write in this style again.

Steven managed his identity as a popular boy in the group by reconstructing texts that reflected characteristics of hegemonic social representations of masculinity. He knew the first text was for the public performance and he chose to write about a banana that had no friends because it was deformed. Predictably, the other boys found this hilarious. However, behind the comedic writing was another motive, which Steven revealed in interview. He had wished to explore the theme of rejection personified by 'deformity', but without risk of personal exposure. He did not pursue this because feedback from the teacher suggested the story was not 'particularly brilliant'. He described the use of comedy characters in the following way:

> It's like putting on a different pair of shoes … Experiencing something that would not normally happen … I like writing stories, I mean it's just like imagining what you are doing in your head you know, you train yourself in a different scenario.

Patrick used a similar distancing device in his first draft, choosing an 'alien' with human characteristics and explained why:

It can be sort of like a satire of the way humans are, in a way because it can do things which could seem stupid but comparing them to human things to make you think in a different way. It also gives you more freedom.

In the all-boys' setting, as James had noted, certain practices and genres were not legitimate for boys. In both cases, the boys were using their knowledge of gender and the need to maintain a masculine identity which resulted in devising distancing techniques as writing practices that neither teachers, nor girls, had access to. The need to create distance between the public and the private was not necessary to maintain a feminine gender identity; indeed, quite the opposite: self-exposure was deemed an appropriate and successful practice for girls in English.

Discussion

Sadler (1989) observes that formative assessment is concerned with how judgements about 'the quality of students' responses can be used to shape and improve student competence' (p. 120). If that is to happen then teachers need to understand how prior sociocultural experiences interact with classroom experiences to create romance texts such as Don's and Katie's. However, as Sadler notes, salience, i.e. what teachers and students take note of, is a 'function of both the condition of mind of the perceiver and the properties of the object being assessed' (p. 133). Therefore, what is noted is what is judged worth noticing. Formative assessment practices need to be expanded to provide tools for teachers to recognise and understand what knowledge students are bringing into settings, and to do so they need tools to understood gender processes. It is only when gender processes are understood by students and teachers that they can become resources for learning.

Although the romance genre was apparently privileged in the mixed setting, it is 'boys' texts that are generally privileged in grading as representative of more sophisticated writing. The three girls who achieved the highest grades A* and A in the mixed setting did not submit romance novel openings. Two of the girls submitted openings for adventure novels and the other girl a war novel opening. Yet, the grading process is not visible to students – it is a private act. The high status given to the texts of the three girls was not the subject of formative feedback to the students as a whole, nor were the drafts used to model ways of reconstructing successful English in the setting. The teacher's interactive feedback was motivated primarily to encourage students, and therefore gave them limited understanding of success criteria and left it to them to reformulate a holistic sense of a good novel opening. The single-sex setting heightened the significance of the peer gaze for boys, making it imperative not to attempt gender-transgressive behaviour. Gender researchers predicted this consequence: 'single sex provides new opportunities for old-style masculinity, for male bravado and bonding … in terms of gender reform such classes are bad news' (Kenway, cited in *Guardian Education*, 2000, p. 4).

A starting point to consider how to plan formative assessment that is not blind to gender would be to look at overt aspects of students' texts. Table 10.1 shows the percentages of the different genres submitted by the students in the two settings. More boys than girls selected the adventure genre, although a similar proportion of girls and boys engaged with crime and horror genres. Comparing boys' choices in the two settings, it appears that

Table 10.1   Percentage of submitted texts in different genres by boy/girl and setting

Genre	% frequency		
	Boys only	Boys mixed	Girls mixed
Crime/Murder	18	17	19
Horror	20	17	17
Diary	3	6	0
Adventure	22	22	14
Sci-fi	14	22	3
Romance	5	0	28
Children/Fairy tale	4	0	6
Teenage	6	0	8
War	4	10	6
Humour	4	0	0
Other	0	6	0

boys in the mixed setting had access to a narrowing range of genres compared with boys in the single-sex setting. Findings like these could suggest to teachers where their practices might inadvertently steer students towards some genres and not others. The findings can also inform teachers about what students may feel more familiar and comfortable with in their writing, and therefore which genres offer more of a challenge for them. It would allow teachers to choose the examples of novel openings with gender representations in mind and plan discussion that considers this. If an aim of activities is to explore genre, then students need to feel supported in taking such risks as well as needing access to cultural resources to extend what they are familiar with. It was in the mixed setting that boys chose to experiment, which in itself says something about the strategy of single-sex groupings. That this failed we felt was due to the way the grouping strategy focused teachers' attention on the students' attributes and not on the texts they were producing.

To help support students like Martin and Adam, teachers would need to be aware of how their own practice is mediated by social representations of gender. Furthermore, they would need to realise the task that school learning imposes on students to manage gender identities, particularly when subject cultures require public performances as part of the learning process. Learning requires that students move beyond established knowledge and cross into new domains. In both classrooms, hegemonic social representations of gender and genre were dominant because teachers were being given no formative tools or encouragement to recognise and challenge these processes. Josie, as was the case with many of the girls, experienced no tension between the reconstruction of successful English and her social gender identity. Formative feedback could have encouraged Josie to explore how emotions and feelings are treated within different genres, allowing her to write about what she was concerned with while extending her repertoire of skills and conventions.

Policy shapes practice. While developing the Maori Mainstream Programme in New Zealand, Bishop and Glynn recognised the need for a social and cultural dimension to formative assessment (Bishop & Glynn, 1999). They argued that teachers need to understand their 'preconceptions, goals, aspirations and cultural preferences' and to 'be prepared to listen to others in such a way that their previous experiences and assumptions do not close them off from the full meaning of students' description of their experience' (cited by

Looney & Poskitt, 2005, p. 180). To develop this understanding, teachers, like their students, need the autonomy to reformulate problems of practice for themselves rather than to have ameliorative strategies imposed. Furthermore, just as students need opportunities to learn beyond the boundaries of the familiar, so too do teachers. Without these opportunities, teachers will collude in creating students who are indeed differently literate even when the chimera of equal outcomes is achieved.

References

Allal, L. & Mottier Lopez, L. (2005) Formative Assessment of Learning: a review of publications in French, in *Formative Assessment: improving learning in secondary classrooms*, pp. 242–264. Paris: OECD Publishing.

Arnot, M., Gray, J., James, M., Ruddock, J. with Duveen, G. (1998) *Recent Research on Gender and Educational Performance*. London: Office for Standards in Education.

Bishop, R. & Glynn, T. (1999) *Culture Counts: changing power relations in education*. Palmerston North, New Zealand: The Dunmore Press.

Bruner, J. S. (1996) *The Culture of Education*. Cambridge, MA: Harvard University Press.

Daily Telegraph (1998) Cissy English Lessons May Hinder Boys, 11 February, p. 4.

Ecclestone, K. & Pryor, J. (2003) Learning Careers or Assessment Careers?: the impact of assessment systems on learning, *British Educational Research Journal*, 29, pp. 471–489.

Elwood, J. & Murphy, P. (2002) Tests, Tiers and Achievement: gender and performance at 16 and 14 in England, *European Journal of Education*, 37, pp. 395–416.

Frater, G. (1997) *Improving Boys' Literacy: a survey of effective practice in secondary schools*. London: Basic Skills Agency.

Gorard, S. (2004) The International Dimension: what can we learn from the PISA study?, in H. Claire (Ed.) *Gender in Education 3–19: a fresh approach*, pp. 26–32. London: Association of Teachers and Lecturers.

Guardian Education (2000) Clever Lad! 29 August, p. 4.

Hanson, A. F. (2000) How Tests Create What They are Intended to Measure, in A. Filer (Ed.) *Assessment: social practice and social product*. London: Routledge.

Independent (1998) Classroom Rescue for Britain's Lost Boys, 5 January, p. 8.

Ivinson, G. & Murphy, P. (2003) Boys Don't Write Romance: the construction of knowledge and social gender identities in English classrooms, *Pedagogy, Culture and Society*, 11, pp. 89–111.

Lave, J. (1988) *Cognition in Practice*. Cambridge: Cambridge University Press.

Lave, J. & Wenger, E. (1991) *Situated Learning: legitimate peripheral participation*. Cambridge: Cambridge University Press.

Lloyd, B. & Duveen, G. (1992) *Gender Identities and Education: the impact of starting school*. Hemel Hempstead: Harvester Wheatsheaf.

Looney, J. & Poskitt, J. (2005) New Zealand: embedding formative assessment in multiple policy initiatives, in *Formative Assessment: improving learning in secondary classrooms*, pp. 177–190. Paris: OECD Publishing.

Millard, E. (1997) *Differently Literate: boys, girls and the schooling of literacy*. London: Falmer Press.

Murphy, P. & Elwood, J. (1998) Gendered Experiences, Choices and Achievement – exploring the links, *International Journal of Inclusive Education*, 2, pp. 95–118.

Murphy, P. & Ivinson, G. (2004) Gender Differences in Educational Achievement: a sociocultural analysis, in M. Olssen (Ed.) *Culture and Learning*, pp. 365–386. Greenwich, CT: Information Age Publishing.

Nespor, J. (1997) *Tangled up in School: politics, space, bodies and signs in the educational process.* Mahwah: Lawrence Erlbaum Associates.

Office for Standards in Education & Equal Opportunities Commission (1996) *The Gender Divide: performance differences between boys and girls at school.* London: HMSO.

Organisation for Economic Co-operation and Development (2005) *Formative Assessment: improving learning in secondary classrooms.* Paris: OECD Publishing.

Rogoff, B. (1990) *Apprenticeship in Thinking: cognitive development in social context.* New York: Oxford University Press.

Rogoff, B. (2001) Problem-solving and Learning, keynote paper presented at International Conference on Communication, 25–29 June, University of Strathclyde.

Sadler, D. R. (1989) Formative Assessment and the Design of Instructional Systems, *Instructional Science*, 18, pp. 119–144.

Stobart, G., White, J., Elwood, J., Hayden, M. & Mason, K. (1992) *Differential Performance at 16+: English and mathematics.* London: School Examinations and Assessment Council.

Wenger, E. (1998) *Communities of Practice: learning, meaning, and identity.* Cambridge: Cambridge University Press.

White, J. (1988) *The Assessment of Writing: pupils aged 11 and 15.* Windsor: NFER-Nelson.

Zittoun, T., Duveen, G., Gillespie, A., Ivinson, G. & Psaltis, C. (2004) The Use of Symbolic Resources in Developmental Transitions, *Culture and Psychology*, 9, pp. 415–448.

11

New Ways of Knowing: Learning at the Margins

Colin Lankshear and Michele Knobel

[...]

Genesis of a project

In 1998, Language Australia funded an innovation project designed to generate research-based practical suggestions for how new technologies would be employed to help enhance literacy learning outcomes among disadvantaged students. Within these parameters we were free to develop our own approach. The main goal of the study was to design and implement an intervention that would employ an innovative pedagogical approach to using new technologies within classroom settings with disadvantaged learners. It was hoped that the approach to be employed would promote 'efficacious' learning and challenge traditional markers and experiences of disadvantage operating in the contexts of the study (cf. Rowan *et al.*, 2002: 146).

More specifically, the project was intended to address three main concerns we had collectively identified from our previous research and teaching experiences. [...]

First, teachers' cultural identities and experiences are often very different from those of their students. This makes it difficult for them to connect learning as closely as possible to students' varied cultural identities and experiences: that is, to teach for diversity and to minimize disadvantage. During recent decades, issues of diversity and disadvantage have largely been associated with ethnicity, social class, and language. These are important and ongoing dimensions. In addition, however, it must now be recognized that issues arise around how to relate teaching to the identities, experiences and perspectives of increasing numbers of 'screenagers' (Rushkoff, 1996) and 'insiders/natives'(Barlow in interview with Tunbridge, 1995) who have grown up amidst the saturation of daily life by the digital-electronic apparatus (Ulmer, 1987). Learners who 'are digital' may be disadvantaged by learning arrangements that marginalize or penalize the important forms of knowledge, understanding and practical proficiency they have acquired.

Second, low levels of technical and cultural knowledge on the part of teachers often result in computer-mediated learning activities being ineffective, inefficacious, or mystifying. This

From: Chapter 8 in Lankshear, C. & Knobel, M., *New Literacies: Changing Knowledge and Classroom Learning* (© 2003, published by Open University Press). Reproduced with the kind permission of the Open University Press Publishing Company.

may range from time being lost simply for want to knowing how to operate the machines, to students acquiring odd or confused notions of a practice because of the way it is represented within classroom activity.

Third, teachers often make well-intentioned uses of student 'savvy' with new technologies to get around snags at the technical operation level. If the practices within which these operations (and skill appropriations) are embedded are ineffectual or at odds with 'mature' versions of computer-mediated social practices, the result of drawing on student savvy might be to enlist 'insider' ('native') competence in the service of 'newcomer' (or 'immigrant') practices (Lankshear and Bigum, 1999).

The 'logic' of a new project

The project idea was to build four purpose-designed 'networks of practice', each of which was based in a school. Network activities would, however, occur as far as possible outside formal school hours and not be part of formal curriculum work. The learning groups would contain at least one teacher from the school and up to four students. Besides the resident teacher, it was hoped to include a teacher currently in training and one or more 'cultural workers'. These would be older youths or adults with insider knowledge of social practices employing new technologies, and who also were broadly open to the perspectives and concerns of young people. At least one researcher and research assistant would be assigned to each group. Ideally, the groups would contain a mix of mindsets, offering scope for negotiation and for developing mutual understandings within a relaxed learning environment. The plan was for each cluster to operate as a face-to-face entity for two hours a week over an eight- to ten-week period. It was hoped that between meetings participants would continue planning and implementing their activities.

The intention was to employ a learning strategy of 'scaffolded co-construction'. Working collaboratively and in accordance with their respective strengths, participants would negotiate a task to be completed during the time frame which would result in an authentic product – the kind of thing that would be produced within a mature form of social practice. The task would employ an electronic ICT and require the group collectively to design and implement learning activities of an expert-like nature. Ideally, the innovation would foment a 'pedagogical logic' that could work productively with participants whose mindsets, experiential backgrounds, and existing knowledge and competence were different. The researchers were hopeful that this pedagogical 'logic' would be adaptable to a wider range of educational settings. It was important that the activities and processes involving new technologies should contribute to developing an appreciation of the knowledge bases and mindsets of the other participants in the group, and that all participants would acquire new technical skills with the technologies they chose to work with. It was also important that participants would develop cultural and critical understandings of literacy practices involving these technologies.

An informal 'warm-up' phase was included, during which participants would get a chance to interact socially and get a feel for the 'operating principles' of the learning group while working with new technologies (e.g. playing a computer game, visiting and commenting on websites). After the warm-up activities, the groups would move on to the main agenda: negotiate what they were going to do, how they would do it, and then get on with doing it. Diverse kinds of activities were seen as possible indicative options to be negotiated within the networks. These included:

- designing a webpage for a client (such as an educator at a local university or a local industry group). Participants would be involved in page design, construction and publication;

- constructing a community database to be located in a particular school. The group would identify the kinds of information that are interesting, relevant, and important to the community, and then participate in the collection, organization and online publication of this data;
- engaging in a geographic information systems mapping activity, possibly using university facilities – for example, mapping local skateboarding venues;
- establishing a youth-culture or emergent-artists' network, and using online resources and facilities to inform the public about the network, to advertise events, and to facilitate activities.

Within each learning group, participants were to work together to decide exactly what it was they were going to do. This decision would take account of the means they had available to them within the group and via other resources (including expertise) they could access. The groups would be free to determine their own patterns of activity (if any) between sessions. It was important that in conceiving, shaping, and implementing their activities, participants would draw on their own skills and understanding *and* consciously pursue 'insider' interpretations of problems and productions of outcomes. Identifying and negotiating across different perspectives, values, experiences and the like in search of an expert-like production would be a key element of the learning and doing process.

The researchers were to play multiple roles in this process in the manner of participant observers. They would observe and document the activities in the manner of qualitative research fieldworkers. They would also, however, be available to act as knowledge and information resources if required and so far as they were able, and to monitor the extent to which authentic expert-like forms of practice were being pursued.

The Yanga headlands site

Yanga Headlands State High School is on Australia's north-east coast in what is officially designated a rural region in the state Education Department's documents. At the time of the study, the school had 975 students. Learning sessions were conducted in one of the school's staffrooms. The staffroom comprised two small adjoining rooms that contained two computers. These were all that were available for the first session, until the teacher participant (Lucy) found a laptop that was used in subsequent sessions. Lucy, who was the English coordinator and a deputy principal, made the decision to use these rooms for the sessions because she believed timetabling issues made it too difficult for the group to access any of the computer 'lab' classrooms. This decision upset the school's technology coordinator (who had initially been extremely supportive in setting up the network). The coordinator thought students should not be using computers that were designated for staff, and stated emphatically that students must *never* be allowed access to staff computers. As a deputy principal, however, Lucy managed to secure approval from the principal for continued use of these rooms and the computers.

At the time of the study, the school had four computer labs plus sundry networked computers spread throughout the school. All had Internet access. A system of Internet 'licences' operated in the school. Students were required to sign an agreement that they would not abuse their access to the Internet by visiting pornography and other prohibited sites, and by not downloading software. The four boys involved in the network had all lost their Internet licences for one reason or another prior to the project.

The participants

The project at Yanga Headlands ran between 21 April and 15 June 1999. It included Lucy (albeit in a peripheral role due to her time being taken up elsewhere in the school), a fourth-year education (honours) student from the nearby university, two of the principal researchers in the research team, a research assistant, and four boys all aged 14 and in Year 9.

Lucy was a particularly dedicated teacher. She had volunteered her own time to work with this group of boys, who – as we mentioned earlier – were regarded by their regular teachers as 'trouble' and had all been identified as 'having problems with literacy'. The boys did not attend the English sessions scheduled for their class each day. Instead, they spent that time with Lucy working on a range of projects. Prior to the study, they had most recently been involved in producing a magazine based on their shared passion for motorbikes. Collecting information for their magazine had included interviewing motorbike mechanics and enthusiasts in the region's main city, 40 kilometres away, about the various qualities of different motorbikes (e.g. evaluating the differences between 2-stroke and 4-stroke engines). The boys prepared their interview questions, wrote them out, and Lucy drove them to the city to conduct their interviews.

The postgraduate student, Pedro, knew two of the boys well from coaching them in soccer during their primary school years. His wife had taught one of them in Year 7. Pedro brought his baby daughter, Holly, with him to each project session. Initially, this was suggested as a solution to difficulties in arranging childcare. But the researchers soon realized that having the baby in the sessions would be valuable because of how she might help 'disrupt' conventional notions of classrooms and authority; and provide a model of a male taking an active role in childcare.

The two researchers from the university, Chris and Leonie, had not had any real contact with the school prior to this project. Neither had Lynn, the research assistant for the project.

The four student participants were Stuart, Kyle, Ben, and Jarrod.

Stuart was chatty, friendly and engaging. He had a smallish build for his age and was given to wearing oversized, slightly tatty shirts and shorts. Occasionally, he would be in school uniform, but even then he managed to look far more casual than other students. He had shoulder-length blonde hair shaved close to his scalp high above his ears. This cultivated 'tough look' contrasted with his rather high-pitched voice. He regarded himself as being about Year 6 level in most things at school, and openly stated his dislike of reading and writing. The other boys shared this sentiment. At home, he would strip down his motorbike and reassemble it correctly. He said that he learned to do this by first watching his dad work on his bike, then from being left to his own devices to figure out a problem, tune the engine, or to rebuild it once his father had taken it apart. When asked what he did when he encountered a difficult problem fixing his bike, he replied without hesitation: 'I read the manual when I get stuck'. Stuart did not see himself as being competent with computers. He said 'I didn't go very well with computer [studies at school]', even though he had a computer at home with an Internet connection which he used to look for pictures and information on motorbikes for their magazine.

Kyle had an olive complexion and long dark hair that he usually wore tied back in a ponytail. Like Stuart, Kyle has a 'tough' look to him. It is easy to imagine that (unlike Stuart) he could pack quite a punch if he wanted to. While not particularly tall, he had well-toned arms that were readily visible through the muscle shirts he liked to wear. Kyle had perhaps the most careworn look about him of all the boys. This disappeared, however, when he started to talk about anything that interested or mattered to him. On such topics he became articulate and entertaining. Based on his comments during sessions and that he tape-recorded for the researchers, we formed an impression that Kyle spent much of his time reflecting on people and events.

Ben lived outside Yanga on a farm of about 200 hectares. He was a fresh-faced kid whose general demeanour had a kind of impishness about it. He smiled readily, but was slow to look people in the eye and was constantly putting himself down and making jokes at his own expense. There was nothing of the tough or rough image to Ben. His family operated a dairy farm and Ben used his motorbike to help round the cows up for his parents. He too could strip his motorbike and reassemble it in working order. Ben had access to a computer at home. However, at school he referred to himself as a 'fast forgetter' and worried for several weeks that he would not remember how to do certain things (e.g. add a hyperlink to his webpage) once Pedro and the others had gone. Ben had a good sense of humour, and a range of lines that regularly drew laughs from the others in the network. For example, when Stuart was being somewhat slow in moving about the different *3D Moviemaker* control icons, Ben commented with friendly impatience, 'C' mon Stu. You move like my grandmother. And she's in a home!'

Jarrod was tall with blond hair, and was regarded by Lucy and the three boys (and seemingly by himself) as a 'computer whiz'. In the course of the first meeting, when one of the principal researchers was explaining to the lads the general gist of the project, Stuart commented that, 'The only person who would understand this is Jarrod, 'cause he's the computer whiz!' There was a hint of resentment, however, in the ways that the boys spoke of Jarrod's confidence. This may have explained what appeared to be an intriguing mix of tentativeness and arrogance that he displayed in the sessions. While quick to talk about any computer or technologically related subject, Jarrod was slow to offer his opinions on other issues, and seemed at first to find it difficult to relate easily to the other boys. He seemed comfortable using computers from the outset of the project and recounted how he had done a short course on Basic programming language when he lived in the state capital city two years previously. Indeed, Jarrod almost fitted the caricature of 'computer nerds', and he certainly did not cultivate as tough an image as Stuart and Kyle. Nonetheless, Jarrod was adamant that he preferred hands-on subjects at school like woodwork, metalwork, art and physical education, because 'you're learning trades'.

Explaining the project rationale

The researchers explained the formal project and the students' participation in terms of teachers wanting to learn from students how to teach computing effectively to *their* students. In Pedro's words, 'We want to learn from you how to teach you computers'. This went with a request from Lucy that the four boys help her run a Year 9 subject the following semester on 'Tools and Technology'. The boys seemed to accept the rationale given for the project, but initially resisted the idea of acting as aides for Lucy, claiming that they'd be called 'squares' by the other students.

The group worked on their collaborative project – a website devoted to motorbikes and based on their magazine work – for approximately 30 hours. There were 14 sessions with researchers (approximately 20 hours in total, including a visit to the university). In addition, there were eight 'researcher-free' sessions coordinated by Lucy, totaling 10 hours. During these times, the boys continued working on the website and on completing their motorbike magazine project with Lucy.

The webpage project was decided during the first meeting of the network (21 April 1999). The catalyst was a comment by Lynn, the research assistant, following a lively discussion of motorbike properties.

> *Lynn*: So we could actually have this really cool motorbike magazine and maybe even a motorbike website, the way you guys are talking now.
>
> *Stuart*: I reckon we should. We've got the magazine, might as well do the website.
>
> *Jarrod*: We could put the magazine on the website.
>
> *Lynn*: Yeah, you could and make an online magazine. That'd be great. How would you all feel about using computers to do that?

The four students all nod and say 'Yeah'. In the second part of the session, which was designed to be a warm-up session with the boys generating an animated movie using the Microsoft's *3-D Moviemaker* software, all four as a group wanted to double-check that they would indeed be working on a set of webpages for the project proper. Stuart even spontaneously took a quick vote from the boys to ensure that they all did indeed want to work on a webpage about motorbikes.

The question of 'disadvantage'

Notwithstanding the study's formal interest in disadvantage, neither Lucy nor the school principal described the four boys taking part in this project as 'disadvantaged'. Indeed, Lucy was concerned that other students might see them as privileged in light of their 'special classes' and the outings associated with it (including a visit to McDonald's). Nonetheless, the boys' assessed literacy levels (and their designation as underachievers in the literacy field by their teachers) locate them within a particular segment of the Australian secondary school population – boys described as having literacy problems (Martino, 1995) – that is increasingly being treated in the manner of a disadvantaged group. In this project, the boys and Lucy unquestioningly spoke in terms of the lads' 'inability' to carry out the kinds of literacy-based activities regarded as mainstream for Year 9 English.

In working with this group of boys, the researchers were committed to collaboratively designing a programme that was able to respond to their (the boys') personal needs as well as their literacy skills. This involved indentifying the relationship between the kind of masculinity the boys identified with and their literacy achievements in and out of school. Literacy ability seemingly does not mesh well with influential constructions of masculinity (Browne, 1995; Gilbert and Gilbert, 1998). In Australia at least, an association between boys, high achievement and English is commonly discounted by boys and teachers alike. In working to introduce these Yanga Headlands boys to a range of literacy and technology activities, the researchers were conscious of the need to be aware of and responsive to the investment these particular boys had in 'acting like (real) boys'. The researchers were also committed, however, to working against some of the consequences of 'being' the particular kind of boys the members of this network most commonly portrayed themselves as being (non-academic, not fluently literate, and so on – see Rowan *et al.*, 2002).

The sessions responded to the identified (and fairly stereotypically masculine) interests of the boys – like their shared passion for motorbikes and video gaming – but also provided the boys with non-stereotypical opportunities and experiences (like the teacher's request that they act as assistants in later classroom activities). A particular perspective on disadvantage underpinned these goals. This was a perspective that sees disadvantage as something produced within particular social, cultural and historical contexts and comes to be attached to certain physical markers (like gender, or race, or class). Recognizing the *constructed* nature of disadvantage is an important starting point for any innovative study since it admits the possibility of challenging particular categories of disadvantage and their material consequences.

A note on the learning process

The look and feel of the sessions at Yanga Headlands matched the ideal envisaged in the project proposal. With the exception of Lucy – who, in any event was often on call elsewhere – the adults were all on a first name basis with the boys. The researchers were gently firm at times, as in Leonie's 'It's not going to happen' (see below). Their general mode, however, was informal, open, attentive, and highly encouraging. The boys worked in pairs, overwhelmingly with good humour and mutual support. The group was small and intimate. To some extent it could be seen as a luxury, in the sense that the typical adult–student ratio was 1:1 or better. By the same token, given contemporary trends toward classrooms welcoming multiple parents and/or teacher aides, and the growth of partnerships between schools, community and other educational institutions, the possibilities for at least approximating to a ratio more like that found in the Yanga group are promising for many schools in more mainstream settings.

The 'unschool-like' character of the sessions was perhaps most apparent around the presence of Pedro's baby daughter at most of the sessions. The researchers were

> … surprised at the extent to which these tough, trouble-making boys welcomed Holly into the group. Every session they would stop by her pram first thing and hold her hand, pull funny faces, speak in gentle, baby like voices and generally show that they liked her and were glad she was there.
>
> (Rowan *et al.*, 2002: 152)

The researchers also found that giving the boys responsibility for setting up the research video- and audio-recording equipment helped minimize the development of a researcher–subject relationship. From the second or third session, the researchers were effectively sidelined from setting up. The boys took over and became dab hands at using the equipment.

The warm-up session began with having the boys work with Microsoft's *3D Moviemaker* so that a common base of computing knowledge could be established. This was followed by exploring *FrontPage,* which was the school's software for constructing webpages.

Some of the boys already knew how to use scanners, which was another key application used in the project. Thereafter, it was a matter of all the participants becoming more proficient with the different functions and applications as they went along. None of the researchers was familiar with PC applications – all were Mac users. Given the differences between the operating logics of the two platforms, the researchers were often as deeply involved in learning unfamiliar software as the students were. Learning by doing and learning as you go became the norm for all except Chris who, although unfamiliar with PCs, was at least familiar with webpage and website design and construction. Once the software had been introduced in the initial warming-up phase of the first session, subsequent sessions settled into a familiar pattern. After the research and project gear was set up, the days were based around working on tasks related to 'designing, trying out and testing their webpages. The style of work was based upon mutual support and sharing in which young and old, experienced and inexperienced worked together to solve problems that arose from … building … the four sets of web pages, one for each student' (Rowan *et al.*, 2002: 150). In addition, semi-structured conversations and discussions of issues to be recorded for research purposes were built into the regular pattern. While these were primarily conceived and enacted as facets of the research, they became *bona fide* pedagogical situations in their own right, as questions presented scaffolded opportunities for all the participants to reflect on their understandings and viewpoints, and to consider things from other perspectives. The following excerpts from recorded session transcripts and researcher notes capture much of the flavour of the sessions.

Excerpt 1

Leonie: Okay, guys. We've only got until ten past 11, which means the sooner we get this done the sooner we can get onto other activities, so we kinda need to get a bit better at getting started.

Jarrod: What's the idea of the Moviemaker?

Leonie: Well, the idea of the Moviemaker is to get used to working with each other, and get you guys working with each other, and get you thinking about what it's like to actually learn something and what it's like to try and teach somebody else. So it's like really easy to say ….

Jarrod: With the game in my bag [*Carmaggedon*], we could take turns with that.

Leonie: You people have already put time into getting Moviemaker skills, so we thought it would be a better idea if we focused on that. Otherwise we mightn't get to the webpage activity.

Jarrod: *Carmageddon* skills are good.

Leonie: No. It's not going to happen.

Lynn: It's sort of a different type of thing aren't they? If you are going to be like a teacher and you're going to help other students and other teachers, then you need a few different kinds of skills.

Jarrod: Yep.

(Transcript, 3 May 1999)

[…]

Some general features of the learning processes

A kind of transcendence

The approach to learning that occurred in the Yanga site and the results or consequences of that approach reflect a form of *transcendence* that we think is important
under contemporary conditions within performativity-oriented education systems.
Teachers are often faced with statements of learning outcomes, competencies, and the
like to be demonstrated by learners within a given time frame. In some cases teachers
have to generate their own statements of learning outcomes for which they are
accountable.

Under such conditions, it is common for teachers to adopt the learning outcomes as the
focus or 'top line' for their pedagogy: the goals to be pursued. This is not unreasonable,
given the official and public scrutiny under which schooling has fallen during the past two
decades. This has been accompanied by pressures on funding, the increasing linguistic,
ethnic and cultural diversity of students, increased class sizes, the retrogressive policy
directives of conservative governments, pressures on employment, criticism of the profession based on allegations of falling standards, and so on. Under such conditions, meeting
required learning outcomes starts to look like both a necessary and a considerable achievement. At the same time, many teachers still believe there is more than this to education,
and experience doubts, frustration and diminished career satisfaction.

The experience at Yanga Headlands suggests a different logic and different metaphors.
The boys learned a lot of new skills and acquired a lot of new knowledge related to web-
page construction specifically and computing more generally in the course of the project.
Much of this can be seen better in terms of learning consequences than learning *outcomes*.
This is because what the boys acquired in the way of capabilities was far greater and richer
than the kinds of specific skill and knowledge mastery 'items' that appear on checklists of
learning outcomes. Moreover, from the outset, the pedagogical aims were set much higher.
It was intended that the participants produced some substantial artefact that encapsulated
technical, cultural and critical dimensions of awareness and proficiency. A high proportion
of this had little directly to do with computing or webpage construction, but might be seen
as nonetheless deeply educational and indeed, central to becoming a good citizen, worker,
community person, and family member. The case of Yanga headlands illustrates a logic of
'transcendence' where, in many ways, the kinds of capabilities that appear as items on a
list of required learning outcomes had a status much closer to a *base* line than a top line.
It was more as if these capacities emerged as by-products of a much more rounded pedagogical approach and learning experience.

This logic is hardly novel. We call it a logic of transcendence because the pedagogical
approach wittingly transcended the pursuit of atomized competencies of learning outcomes that have been abstracted from larger social practices and taught in decontextual-
ized or disembodied ways. At Yanga Headlands, the participants engaged in diverse and
complex processes that coalesced around a broad task. In the context of pursuing this task,
there was wide-ranging discussion, skill sharing, wanderings into unanticipated areas of
conversation, negotiation, and sustained hands-on activity. The boys were continually

challenged to think, anticipate, compare and contrast, evaluate, reflect on aspects from very different areas of their lives, and to bring their varied experiences together in ways that promoted significant cultural and critical understandings of computer-based social practices and, indeed, of learning and the institution of school itself. Numerous illustrations of this logic of transcendence will be apparent in the section on learning consequences, where we present typical slices of data from the learning sessions.

A kind of purposefully decentred learning

The kind of learning that occurred in the network context was much less *centred* and *bounded* than that of the subject-based fixed content approach of conventional approaches to curriculum and pedagogy. The traditional epistemology of school has resulted in the idea of learning being organized around bodies of content to be covered in line with a guiding syllabus. Teaching focuses on covering the quota for a particular period following a mapped out programme and keeping within pre-established bounds. It is, precisely, the job of syllabus developers and curriculum planners to map out the learning terrain and put fences around the content.

In the project, however, there was a broad *task* that provided the catalyst for learning to occur. There were also genuine research purposes operating, in the sense that the researchers wanted to collect data and had put mechanisms in place for doing this. These included recording (in both audio and video formats) conversations instigated and loosely structured by the researchers to tap into the boys' ideas, understandings, thought processes, and perspectives. In addition, the interests, purposes, and subjectivities of the boys themselves established a degree of structuring of the learning contexts. These included their shared interest in motorbikes and motorcycling, but also included entrenched forms of masculinity which permeated the sessions and with which the researchers were prepared to engage. Within the loose structure established by these conditions, the highly dialogical nature of the pedagogy allowed for threads and trails of learning to take off in different directions. This is the kind of situation that Michael Doneman (1997) has referred to as 'curriculum on the fly', where things that arise in the moment become stimuli and catalysts for new, unplanned and unanticipated learning and knowledge. And while much of this is incidental, it is not random or unhinged. It winds its way out from broad identifiable learning purposes and tasks, to which it remains linked. But it is not preplanned, and it does not *cover* predetermined ground. Rather, it *uncovers* new ground that produces 'coverage' of an entirely different kind from the conventional curriculum coverage, and that can be extremely rich and fruitful. This is the kind of thing that happened, for example, when Pedro seized on what he saw as the boys' 'games-oriented' view of computing (see below). He prompted them to clarify their understanding of games and programs respectively, where they saw particular kinds of software fitting into this categorization, and how they thought the games and programs taxonomy related to websites and webpages.

Learning consequences

Pedagogical contexts look backwards as well as forwards. They project learners into new areas of capability and understanding, while drawing on what they have previously experienced, learned and understood. The project at Yanga Headlands resulted in very significant *new* learnings for the four boys (as well as for the adult participants). At the same time, however – and very importantly – the sessions provided ample opportunities for the boys to demonstrate literacy- and technology-related cultural knowledge that belied their reputations as poor literacy and English students. The sessions drew out demonstrations of knowledge and understanding that included many examples of language awareness that the state English syllabus identified as necessary conditions for effective and powerful language use. Two of these that we will look at in detail below are an understanding of the importance of context in language use and the ability to use the genre of persuasion effectively.

In this section, we consider examples of both new forms of proficiency and significant demonstrations of extant knowledge and capability that challenge the dominant conceptions of these boys within the school. These examples indicate the extent to which the four lads, and other learners more or less like them, are constituted by approaches to curriculum and pedagogy that presuppose conventional economies of attention and class-room space that have outlived whatever 'use by' date they may once have had. The following sections consider aspects of *technical* and *cultural* proficiency relevant to engaging effectively in new and conventional forms of literacy. They also look at changes in the ways the boys regarded and talked about themselves, and how they oriented themselves toward being capable. Finally, we look at some of the ways the project prompted new ways of thinking about the economics of attention within a school by reference to ideas developed by Chris Bigum and Leonie Rowan. [...]

Jarrod's webpage building 'tour' conducted for Lucy and described below demonstrates many of the elements of the metalanguage that had developed by the end of the project, and which was shared to a great extent by all group members.

Pedro: What might help, Jarrod, is if you put the webpage up on the computer and then talk [to Lucy] about the webpage.

Jarrod: Okay, then.

Lucy: Now, *Front page Express*.

Jarrod: Or we could go straight into 'running draft'.

Lucy: No, let's go through *Front Page Express*.

Jarrod: Okay, then. That's different from –

Lucy: Yeath, this scan is scanning the document; it's a virus scanner put on a couple of days ago.

Jarrod: Looks different – *Front Page Express*. Now we were doing a page on the ... Yesterday you and I were doing the page on the English Department and now we're going into 'file' [clicks on menu].

Lucy: We could go in today to the English Page on the Internet, couldn't we?

Jarrod: Yep. Now 'file', 'open', 'browse', and 'go to' – press down and go up, scroll upwards, go into three-quarter floppy and go into nineteen-ninety-nine, and there's your page.

Lucy: Beautiful. Okay, so what are we doing now? How about we have a look at the English one, the English Department one and then maybe we'll make it a bit fancy.

Jarrod: Just 'E' here; just double click on there.

Lucy: What's 'E' stand for?

Jarrod: Internet Explorer. It's a short cut.

(Transcript, 15 June 1999)

[...]

In the area of how the boys spoke about and regarded themselves as learners

Over the eight-week period in which the network met, there were some notable shifts in the ways the boys regarded and spoke about themselves in terms of being learners. They moved palpably from describing themselves as students in negative ways to being much more willing to recognize and own their strengths and abilities in situations where these were apparent. Early on, and even well into the sessions, they affirmed the view held by the principal, other teachers and, seemingly, by Lucy herself, that they were not 'good' students. They were often critical of themselves and their abilities, and were quick to point out when they had made mistakes.

> *Ben*: Then I went to that picture [pointing to an icon on the screen], then I went to that Word Art.
> *Leonie*: Excellent. Now you pick another one.
> *Ben*: That one [he clicks on a word art icon, but it doesn't open]. Oh, I'm so stupid.
> *Leonie*: It's not stupid.
>
> (Transcript, 18 May 1999)

Commenting on their concerns about recording their audiotape journals, Jarrod and Kyle make the following points:

> *Jarrod*: It's got ours and Miss Marshall [on it]. I hate doing that. You're sitting there talking and you muck it up, so you have to tape over it.
> *Leonie*: But why? How do you muck something up?
> *Ben*: You forget what to say.
> *Jarrod*: You talk into it …
> *Leonie*: But that's okay. We don't expect you to be talking as though you've done a big speech.
>
> (Transcript, 19 May 1999)

[…]

Rethinking the economics of attention

[…] As argued in the original project report (Rowan *et al.*, 2000), schools and teaching have always worked on the assumption that attention is in scarce supply. An economics of attention has always operated in schools. Unlike the deregulated contemporary attention economy that operates in public domains outside school, and that has burgeoned and become highly sophisticated in concert with the growth and development in mass media and communications technologies, the attention economy of school is highly regulated and controlled.

> There are well-established patterns of student behaviour that attract the attention of teachers and there are well-established practices of teachers that attract the attention of colleagues, principals and other administrators. In attention terms then, the school is a *closed* economy.
>
> (Rowan *et al.*, 2000: 301)

That is, attention flows within the school are shaped and regulated by rules of giving and receiving attention that are well established, albeit largely *unwritten*. We also find a kind of economy of attention operating in schools that is analogous to what is referred to as the black or informal economy found in highly controlled and regulated material goods economies. This involves what the boys in the study referred to as their 'brat level', where seeking and gaining attention by illegitimate means constitute resistance to the tight controls of the school attention economy.

[…] Modern mass media and communications technologies, reaching their current high point in the explosion of the Internet, provide enormous capacity for individuals, groups and institutions in the world outside school to seek and pay attention across wide gulfs of time and space (Rowan *et al.*, 2000: 301). This is largely a deregulated economy so far as formal rules and controls are concerned. […] There certainly are *criteria* (e.g. originality) and *standards* that work like the purported invisible hand of the free market to mediate supply and demand of attention in this external attention economy. But almost anything goes so far as competing for and allocating attention against these criteria and standards are concerned. […]

As a consequence, there is a tension between the attention economy operating outside school and the economics of attention within school. Outside school, students have wide freedom of choice as to how and where to pursue and allocate attention. Within school, however, the constraints are tight. Moreover, the means and strategies for seeking and allocating attention outside school have no recognized place inside school. Conversely, the nature of attention flows – including who is permitted to be a 'star' – and ' the quaint rules' that define the school attention economy 'appear to have little relevance in the external economy' beyond equipping a small proportion of students to subsequently acquire credentials (after they leave school) that have the potential to attract attention (see Rowan *et al.*, 2000: 302). […]

Moreover, it is important to note that apart from a small number of tightly delineated spaces, like prefect systems and the sports arena, the attention economy of school largely withholds from students the option to be 'stars'. Schools do not 'position students as "stars": rather they are rewarded most commonly for their ability to act as devoted "fans" – for their attendance, their enthusiasm, their allegiance, their adoption of "star" behaviours and interests etc.' (Rowan *et al.*, 2000: 304).

Given the research goal and the personal interests of the researchers in addressing issues of disadvantage at the interface of literacy and new technologies, the research team aimed at providing the boys with the kinds and qualities of attention that would help them to be able to participate on more equal terms with other students in the 'regular' attention economy of the school. Indeed, by trying to help get them on the inside of various technological capabilities that had kudos in the school, the researchers hoped that from time to time and within particular spaces, the boys might actually be able to participate on a better than equal footing with other students (Rowan *et al.*, 2000: 304).

To this end the researchers developed a series of activities that were designed to give students the attention of the researchers. We sat them down in round table-like discussions and listened to them. We drew on their interests and resources in negotiating a project using computer technology. We developed a rapport with them that was probably outside their experience in schools. In these ways, the researchers 'passed on' their interest in the students to other teachers and students – this served to disrupt at least partially the dominant models for understanding these four boys that circulated within the school.

In addition to this, we worked to provide students with the kinds of skills in web-page construction that they could then use in teaching other students in a standard classroom. This positioned the students as the experts – the people whose attention was required by other students. This inversion of their role from fans to stars has, in our opinion, the greatest potential for allowing the boys themselves, and those who studied with and taught them, to recognise that their position as 'failures' was not a fixed, permanent, and natural position but rather something that could be challenged, disrupted, and rejected.

(Rowan *et al.*, 2000: 303–4)

This approach had interesting consequences in terms of harnessing the boys' persuasive abilities and performances to a new way of relating to being perceived as competent and to new ways of participating in the school attention economy.

Transcripts of the network sessions provide excellent examples of the boys using strategies of persuasion that had the potential to be used constructively and to their benefit in the school's attention economy. Early on in the project, however, the boys tended to use persuasion in order to *deflect* certain kinds of attention way from themselves. During the inaugural session, for instance, Lucy prompted discussion around the fact that when the project was over, she would like the boys to be able to help teachers with the 'Tools and Technology' curriculum subject. The boys resisted the prospect vehemently. Stuart protested that he would 'get called a square by all my friends'. In a kind of ensuing negotiation, the boys persuaded the adults *not* to refer to them as 'experts' or 'teachers'. Eventually, the boys agreed to 'editor' and 'coordinator', and everybody agreed, in Lucy's words, to have 'nothing to do with the word "teach"'. An interesting facet of the attention flows in this situation is that at first glance it might appear that Lucy finally persuaded *the boys* to agree with her idea. On the other hand, she *needed* them to agree, otherwise they would not have helped the teachers in Tools and Technology. Hence, it can be seen that unlike their normal classroom situations, the *boys were receiving the full attention of a teacher* (Rowan *et al.*, 2000: 313).

This situation contrasts markedly with a number of open reflections the boys made about the kind and quality of attention they received in class, and how these differed from what they got in the project setting. Ben provided two examples of what he saw as common experiences.

Yep. There's like teachers here [in the learning group] that listen to you, not like the ones in class. 'Miss, Miss!', 'Yeah I'll be there in a minute'. Half an hour later [still no help]. Here you just have to call out a name and they come.

and

Mr Y … just tells me to sit there and do nothing if I don't know how to do it. So I just sit there and get my Walkman out … […]

When Lucy, near the end of the final session, again asks the boys about helping in the tools and technology subject, they replied with, 'Sure', and 'Easy'. Encouraged, Lucy asked how they thought the logistics could be handled in terms of available computers, number of tutors, numbers of groups, and so on. During the 'brainstorm' that ensued, the boys

effectively moved the discussion away from Lucy being the focus of attention as the one controlling the conversation. Instead, *they* became the focus of attention. This represents a marked
change in the boys' confidence and strategies with respect to competing for attention. It also
reflects a very different personal orientation on the part of the boys toward being competent –
which was now something they could 'own', despite other trappings of their commitment to
a version of masculinity remaining securely intact (cf. Rowan *et al.*, 2002: 146–69). [...]

Bigum and Rowan identify an interesting implication here with respect to the state's
English syllabus that shaped the English programme at Yanga Headlands. The syllabus was
strongly informed by genre theory, and mastery of a designated range of genres was a key
aim of language and literacy education at all levels of schooling. Persuasion was among
the genres identified in the syllabus as integral to language operating as 'a powerful social
instrument' that helps people to 'negotiate their places in social groups' (DEQ, 1994: 8).
In the exchange between Lucy and the boys transcribed here, the boys *do* approximate to
using language in a socially powerful way within the regulated attention economy of the
revamped school setting in which the network operated. Interestingly, what we have here
are insights into the role of persuasion, *not as texts to be studied or produced in a classroom*, but as 'a practice central to the flows of attention within schools and classrooms'
(Rowan *et al.*, 2000: 316). [...]

End notes: between rocks and hard places

The position we have argued for in this chapter is increasingly *not* the kind of position
being taken up by state schools in North America, Britain, and Australasia. A definite
direction has emerged under the powerful impetus of state guidelines, policies, and funding arrangements. This is toward defining literacy in terms of state mandated standardized
tests and proficiency statements and knowledge in terms of the content of a national curriculum. It emphasizes meeting teacher and student technology proficiency standards and
performance indicators, and favours incorporating new ICTs into homework activities and
the kinds of experiences offered by the Grid and similar initiatives. [...]

Our top line is that formal education can be so much more, and make far better, more
direct, and more enabling connections between what students learn now and what they will
do and be later, and this is what we should be struggling for. Our bottom line is addressed
more to teachers and the very real complexities they face on a day-to-day basis. These are
teachers who may [...] say: 'Oh yeah, right! Like I could really practise new literacies and
operate off a new epistemology in my classroom given everything else I'm expected to
deliver on!' To such teachers we would extend solidarity. More than this, we would say
that even if teachers feel too beleaguered and encumbered to incorporate new literacies and
new ways of learning and knowing into their teaching, it is nonetheless important for them
to know and acknowledge the kinds of things young people are doing and being *outside*
school in order to make effective pedagogical connections to them in class. In the final
analysis, however, we believe that examples like that provided at Yanga Headlands support
the view that not only is our top line viable, but that holding out for it is in the best interests of the education profession and students alike.

References

Browne, R. (1995) Schools and the construction of masculinity, in R. Browne and R. Fletcher (eds) *Boys in Schools: Addressing the Real Issues*. Lane Cove, NSW: Finch Publishing.

DEQ (Department of Education, Queensland) (1994) *English in Years 1 to 10. Queensland Syllabus Materials: English Syllabus for Years 1 to 10*. Brisbane: Department of Education.

Doneman, M. (1997) Multimediating, in C. Lankshear, C. Bigum, C. Durrant *et al.* (investigators) *Digital Rhetorics: Literacies and Technologies in Education – Current Practices and Future Directions*, Vol. 3. Children's Literacy National Projects, pp. 131–48. Brisbane: QUT/DEETYA.

Gilbert, R. and Gilbert, P. (1998) *Masculinity Goes to School*. St Leonards, NSW: Allen and Unwin.

Lankshear, C. and Bigum, C. (1999) Literacies and new technologies in school settings, *Pedagogy, Culture and Society*, 7(3): 445–65.

Martino, W. (1995) Gendered learning practices: exploring the costs of hegemonic masculinity for girls and boys in schools, in Ministerial Council for Education Training and Youth Affairs, *Proceedings of the Promoting Gender Equity Conference*. Canberra: ACT Department of Education and Training.

Rowan, L., Knobel, M., Bigum, C. and Lankshear, C. (2002) *Boys, Literacies and Schooling: The Dangerous Territories of Gender Based Literacy Reform*. Buckingham: Open University Press.

Rowan, L., Knobel, M., Lankshear, C., Bigum, C. and Doneman, M. (2000) *Confronting Disadvantage in Literacy Education: New Technologies, Classroom Pedagogy and Networks of Practice*. Rockhampton: Central Queensland University.

Rushkoff, D. (1996) *Playing the Future: How Kids' Culture Can Teach Us How to Thrive in an Age of Chaos*. New York: HarperCollins.

Tunbridge, N. (1995) The cyberspace cowboy. *Australian Personal Computer*, December: 2–4.

Ulmer, G. (1987) The object of post-criticism, in H. Foster (ed.) *Postmodern Culture*, pp. 57–82. London: Pluto Press.

12

Constructing and Deconstructing Masculinities through Critical Literacy

Bronwyn Davies

[…]

The construction of gender through discourse

Gender is constructed, through language, as two binary categories hierarchically arranged in relation to each other. This construction operates in a variety of intersecting ways, most of which are neither conscious nor intended. They are more like an effect of what we might call 'speaking-as-usual'; they are inherent in the structures of the language and the storylines through which our culture is constructed and maintained. The structure of the language and the dominant storylines combine, with powerful effect, to operate on our conscious and unconscious minds and to shape our desire. The male–female binary is held in place because we come to see it as the way the world *is* and therefore *ought* to be—what is constructed as truth becomes an (apparently) absolute unconstructed truth. Foucault, in analysing this process, coins the term 'regime of truth'. […]

A particularly powerful regime of truth emerged in the seventeenth and eighteenth centuries, a time often referred to as the Enlightenment. This new regime of truth caught us up in the glorification of science with its domination of the rational (male) mind over (usually female) matter. In the scientific regime of truth there are two sexes. The differences between them are scientifically established as absolute, or essential. The two-sex model is one in which each sex takes its meaning in opposition to the other, and any deviations are understood as aberrations, deviations from what *is*, and what *ought to be*.

Enlightenment thought encapsulates much of what is understood as 'modernism' and is also fundamental to 'humanism'. Post-modern and post-structuralist discourses take delight in showing the discursively constructed nature of much that was taken in these discourses to be the fundamental unquestionable base on which argument could be built and 'truth' established. Through deconstructing those binaries which form the unquestioned base of knowledge and re-visioning them as 'metaphysical', rather than physical, old binaries become multiples, and the human body becomes something capable of manifesting itself in any number of ways.

But the concept of sex as not fixed, and indisputably 'opposite' to the other sex, is difficult to grasp because we have taken up our own physical and psychic being within regimes of truth that have, as an unexamined base, the male–female binary. The evidence

From: *Gender and Education,* 9 (1), 1997, pp. 9–30. Reprinted by permission of the publisher (Taylor & Francis Ltd, http://www.informaworld.com).

of our own minds and bodies tells us that we are indelibly one or the other, shaped and shaping ourselves within a truth which we do not understand as a 'regime of truth', but the firsthand, unquestionable truth of our own experience.

As Grosz (1990) points out, the culture cannot simply be understood as shaping and constraining individuals from outside themselves. Their patterns of desire, or 'inner bodies', are shaped, and in that shaping, come to desire and thus actively create the culture in which they are continuously being inserted, and through which their actions and desires are read as meaningful. [...]

The active taking up of oneself as male or female, dominant or passive, is a complex process that must be understood if we are to recognise and deconstruct the binaries in our own lived experience of them. That is, if we want to read the ways in which the culture inscribes itself on the inner and outer body, and if we want to read against the grain, that is, discover other than dominant truths embedded in our experience and in the possibilities the culture holds open to us, we must look again, and more closely, at how discourse works to shape us as beings within the two-sex model.

There are three stories from my pre-school study (Davies, 1989) which pick up and illustrate the complex interplay between linguistic structure, cultural storylines and the formation of the inner/outer body with its powerfully embedded patterns of desire. These are stories of subjection and transgression. They illustrate the fluidity of gender and its socially or discursively constructed nature. At the same time, they reveal the power of rational binary thought to hold identity in place inside the binary systems it imposes.

The first story is of George. I retell it here to demonstrate the force of linguistic structures. George was often to be seen running around the pre-school yard with swirling skirts and a cape flying out behind him. As he flew down the slope one morning, dressed in yellow butterfly cape and skirt, he shouted 'I am the power!' Later, he came over to talk to me, as I sat in the pre-school yard, writing down my observations and recording conversations with the children. I asked him how it felt to have a skirt on. He said, 'I feel powerful'. Then another boy came over and punched George very hard in the chest. George took off his skirt, folded it up neatly, tucked it under his arm and punched the boy back. As the other boy ran away, I asked George why, if the skirt made him feel powerful, had he taken it off to punch the boy. He said 'no, I didn't' and ran away.

George's denial completely baffled me. What did he mean when he said 'no, I didn't'? Only much later, when I was engaging with the text of our talk in written form and beginning to make sense of how children become sexed/gendered, did I see what I had done. I had made George's claim of feeling powerful meaningless, or at least contradictory, and therefore unacceptable within the terms of rational discourse. I had done this by assuming that the power he spoke of was the same power as that involved in punching another boy. The binary male–female coincided in my interpretation of George's actions with the binary powerful–powerless. But the power George spoke of was obviously not the same thing as male, dominant, forceful power nor, for him, compatible with it. My inability to see, at that point, beyond the conceptual traps of the language and its binary structure, with the powerful habitual links between one binary and another, meant that his attempt to speak something different into existence was denied him. The force of rational thought with its dualistic hierarchical structures was inadvertently used by me to hold the gender order in place. But it was also partly being held in place by George. He had to divest himself of one form of (female) power in order to use another (male) form of power. For him, in some sense, they were already coded in some form of binary, as oppositional and incompatible.

My second story is of Joanne. I retell it here to demonstrate the force of dominant cultural storylines. Joanne loved to play with the dominant macho boys. But they rarely allowed her into their games as an equal, and she would not consider playing with them if they allocated her the position of victim. Their inclusion of 'outsiders' was often to use them as victims, since they themselves preferred heroic positions. Joanne looked like a boy, she ran and talked like a boy. She was also unusually socially accomplished and knew that people were offended if they were caught out in 'misrecognising' her as male. She wore tracksuits the same as the boys, but signalled her positioning as 'girl' with a girlish topknot.

On the particular morning of this story, a new tree house had just been built in the pre-school yard. The dominant boys had attempted to make it their own place but this had been disallowed by the teachers, who were at that time becoming more conscious of the strategies these boys used to dominate the playground. Joanne and her friend Tony climbed into the tree house as soon as it was vacated and developed a brilliant strategy for keeping the others out. As other small children climbed tentatively up the ladder, Joanne or Tony would lean out over the balcony and discreetly drop sawdust in their eyes as they looked up. The would-be intruders would start to cry and climb down the ladder. Tony and Joanne were ecstatic as they had successfully claimed this desirable leafy space without any form of violence visible to the teachers.

At one point Tony saw me watching. He probably decided I had no real power in the context of this place and turned rapidly back to the game, to his immersion in the excitement of it. Then Joanne saw me watching. She stood and looked at me, seeing herself through what she took to be my (adult, enculturated) eyes. She said to me, 'we are just cleaning up all this sawdust that the carpenters have left on the floor'. Her moment of power, in contrast to Tony's, was gone as she repositioned herself in an acceptable storyline for her sex/gender. No matter how exciting the moment, she lost it when she saw herself from outside herself. And of course she was exercising another kind of power in doing so, that is the power to be convincing to others, to ensure she was recognised as a legitimate member of the culture. Such recognition is probably essential for those who want to transgress the boundaries of the dominant culture or to deconstruct old patterns and speak into existence new ones. At the same time, her experience of power in the taking over of the tree house was not one she could simply take pleasure in as Tony did. [...]

Two aspects of post-structuralist discourse have remained more or less implicit in my discussion so far. One is a focus on the imaginative construction of worlds other than the ones we already inhabit, and the other is the deconstructive work we might do to undo the bonds of already existing, discursively constructed worlds. To find and make visible the detail of how one's specificity is put in place and maintained in place, as I have done so far, can be seen as a fundamental first step in any post-structuralist analysis. To see within that process the power of binary thought to constitute you as one, and not the other, in any binary pair, and thus to make you separate from the other, yet taking your meaning and value in relation to the other in that binary pair, is where the really radical work of post-structuralist practice begins. Binary thought is revealed as metaphysical, that is, not the result of observations of natural pairs which exist in the world, but as ways of seeing built around an unquestioned assumption of opposition and difference—an opposition and difference that are built into the language and thus into the worlds constituted through that language.

These binaries are particularly difficult for those located in the ascendant half of the binary pair to see. They take their category membership to be normal, and normative, and those located in the other category to be marked by their difference. People inhabiting such ascendant categories, such as male, heterosexual, white, middle-class, able-bodied, adult or sane, often wonder what all the fuss is about, and doubt even the relevance of their own category membership in determining who they might be. Their privileged, unmarked membership positions give them the illusion of being simply human, a representative of the human race, able to speak authoritatively for those in all categories, not just their own (Davies, 1993, pp. 89–90).

What deconstruction does is to make visible the dependence of the persons inhabiting the *ascendant categories* on the existence of the *subordinate category* for their own privileged, unmarked location. [...]

The dependence of the ascendant term on the subordinate term robs it of its unmarked position and its illusion of being the unmarked category, otherness to which is what constitutes 'difference'. Membership of any category becomes visible as a story, a fictive locating of oneself (by oneself and others) through this or that discourse, within one context or another and in specific relations of power.

In the work I undertook with Chas Banks for *Shards of Glass* (Davies, 1993), we worked with primary school children to make the power of discourse visible to them. In the following transcript, Chas is talking to 11-yar-old Zac about the ways he stories his life. He has taken photographs of his mother and father and arranged them such that the photographs of his mother, all taken inside the house, are in the middle of the page, and the photographs of his father, all taken outside the house, are arranged around the outside of the page. When Chas questions him about whether his mother ever plays with him in the garden, the following conversation ensues:

Zac: ... she does try, she tries playing cricket or soccer or hockey and we play all them out in the back garden.

Chas: Do you play games with your dad? Does he ever play with you?

Zac: Oh, he usually, he doesn't now 'cause he's always usually working but and he's getting older and but he used to muck around with soccer and play cricket. He still plays cricket, his grandfather was A-Grade and he used to play for Dungowan and everything.

Chas: Really?

Zac: He teaches me strokes and everything.

Chas: Right, but he spends quite a lot of his time working and earning money to keep the house repayments up [*referring back to an earlier conversation*] and ...

Zac: Yeah ...

Chas: But she's looking for a job?

Zac: Oh, she isn't really now.

Chas: Has she always stayed at home?

Zac: Yep.

Chas: She has?

Zac: Oh, When we were young, about 1, 2, 3 she used, she worked at a stock station agents.

Chas: Mm. Notice that these shots of your dad are outside?

Zac: Yeah ...

Chas: And these ones of your mum are inside. Is that fairly typical of the way they operate?

Zac: Yep.

Chas: It is?

Zac: Oh, but mum really, usually does help outside with the garden, she does the gardening a lot.

Chas: Does she?

Zac: Yeah.

Chas: Does she do the flower part of the garden or the vegetable part or …

Zac: All.

Chas: She does all of it does she?

Zac: She mows, and does things.

Chas: Right, so she's very capable?

Zac: Yep.

Chas: Do you get on well with your mum?

Zac: Yeah.

Chas: Are you as close to your mum, closer to your mum or closer to your dad do you reckon?

Zac: Oh, [I'd be] closer to dad if he was at home more probably.

Chas: Would you?

Zac: Yeah.

Chas: Why do you think that is?

Zac: Oh, because I like working outside on cars and that sort of thing. Not really sitting inside doing nothing.

(Davies, 1993, pp. 54–55)

Zac constructs his mother as not *really* playing with them, she only 'tries', as 'not really' working, or looking for work, not really being responsible for the garden, but 'helping' in the garden, and ultimately as a boring inside person doing nothing. He (correctly) positions himself inside the culture, as he knows he must; with his absent father. His father is constructed as correctly male through family myths (of his grandfather) and memories (of his father teaching him strokes). Zac understands himself as a (male) person in relation to these, rather than a person who is close to, or like, his much present mother. He understands the binary male–female as it operates in the discourses of the culture and speaks himself and his parents into existence through them.

Zac's capacity to use language to force the world into a pattern that maintains him and his father and grandfather in the ascendant term can be seen as a very powerful discursive move. In entering into the realm of boys and literacy, we should not underestimate the desirability and joyful sense of power that boys can gain from being positioned within dominant forms of discourse which hand them ascendancy over others.

The following story, for example, was written by a boy whose usual textual productions, both before and after the writing of this story, would have suggested he was virtually illiterate. Derek's teacher asked the students to write a pirate story following a reading of a feminist pirate story in which the male and female pirate did not know what it really meant, in his reading, to be proper pirates, that is, properly violent. Derek asked whether he could write a Ken and Barbie story and his teacher said no. So this is what he wrote:

Barbie and Ken in Pirates

One day when Ken was sailing along with Barbie they saw another ship in the distance. Barbie said to Ken 'What's that?' Ken said 'Its some saught of ship. Wait untill it gets closer. They found out they were pirates. The pirats came on bord and Ken got an axe. The pirate fired a warning shot in the air. Ken put the axe down, they took Barbie hostedege. While Ken had a few beers. It was a set up. Ken worked for the pirates and was the captens first mate. Three weeks later Ken came into Barbies room and said to Barbie 'lie down babe I'v got a surprise for you'. So Barbie lay down. Ken pulled an axe off the wall. Barbie said 'What are you going to do with that?' Ken said 'I I I have to kill you' then he raised the axe and cut off Barbies head then arms then legs. Then they threw her head to the sharks and ate the rest of her for dinner.

THE END

The teacher was totally unnerved by this story, so much so that she could not even discuss it with him. He had totally silenced her. Of course, we do not know Derek's intentions. He may have been angry with her, or he may just have been revealing that, whatever feminist discourse she might introduce to the class, he was clear about how real masculinity was done.

In working with boys and literacy, there is a pressing need to extend them beyond this kind of hegemonic masculine literacy, and to disrupt usual assumptions about power and the illusions and fictions that hold it in place. Derek's primary strategy in class was to present himself as illiterate. The strategy he reveals here is one in which he reveals a great facility with words. Layering one genre over another, Derek creates a complex tissue of masculinity, the power and dominance of which would be difficult to call into question. He stitches together a range of discursive strategies which reinstate proper dominant masculinity, even revealing with Ken's stuttered 'I I I' how difficult the attainment of it may sometimes be. In working with boys and literacy, we need to make visible the constitutive force of discourse if we are to create fissures in the absoluteness of the apparent naturalness of dominant masculinity. Through the process of deconstruction, we can make the dependence of the dominant category on the subordinate category visible, and we can show the oppositional and exclusionary nature of the metaphysically based binary. In making it visible as a fiction, it loses its apparent inevitability and thus some of its power to hold current relations in place. The work of putting binary categories under erasure nevertheless remains as work that needs to be done, again and again, since the unspeaking of something can only ever be overlaid on the experience of being spoken into existence through the binary, and each previous speaking is inscribed on the body like writing on a page that can only ever be partially erased. [...]

Multiple masculinities in the classroom

In this section, I provide an analysis of one teacher's move towards multiplicity for the boys in his class. He does not deconstruct binaries, nor provide the possibility of reflexive awareness of the multiplicity he makes available to them in the ways I discuss in the third part of this chapter. His strategies are to do with *envisioning* and *experiencing* another set of possibilities, work that necessarily goes hand in hand with deconstructive work.

The following transcripts are from one morning in the classroom of a primary school teacher in a small Australian rural school. The teacher begins the day with a class discussion about current affairs. The students then divide into groups and do mathematics work followed by story-writing. The whole class then goes down to the river and writes poetic prose about what they see. On their return, they listen to a story about the past in Australia and then Mr Good cooks a rabbit stew. The particular excerpts chosen here track some of the possibilities being made available to the boys in taking themselves up as oral and literate beings. The excerpts are chosen because they focus on the boys. This should not be read as the entirety of the life of this classroom. The interactions with the girls are not highlighted here. If the selection of excerpts is read to mean that the girls are being ignored by Mr Good, this would be an entirely inappropriate reading. The boys are not being taught that girls are able to be ignored, though Mr Good's gentle charm and charismatic style, which he adopts with the girls (alongside his recognition of their intellectual prowess) is quite possibly significant in the achievement of Mr Good as a competent (heterosexual) male in the eyes of the boys.

There are several points to observe in the transcripts I have chosen:

- Mr Good does not negate the range of possible masculinities available to the boys; he does not constitute literate masculinity as incompatible with other forms of masculinity but, rather, celebrates a wide range of performances that might be called masculine;
- at the same time as showing he acknowledges and even celebrates some forms of dominant masculinity, Mr Good reveals himself in his talk as sensitive and emotional;
- Mr Good invites the students to connect what they are learning about the world to their own emotions and their own moral location in the world; that is, he does not abstract truth from embodied knowledge;
- Mr Good has a particular fascination with physical environments and invites the students to share that fascination and connectedness, and to express that connection through spoken and written words.

The first excerpt begins when the class has been looking at the world map in relation to a letter they have just received:

Mr Good: Okay. [*Mr Good claps hands quietly*] Anything else before we move on? Yes? [*To boy with hand up*]
S(s):   [*Classroom talk*]
Mr Good: Sh sh.
James: Mr Good, has New Zealand and Papua New Guinea, have they broken off as islands off Australia like Tasmania?
Mr Good: They, they think so. They think so. At at one stage [*Mr Good gets up and goes to map*] James, that's a [*pause*] that's a really good observation. At one stage, they think, that all this was connected, [*Mr Good is pointing out areas on map*] … it was a great land mass, and there was some sort of …
James: (   ) um, they, they showed you, do you know how they, they think, do you know how they make, thought they done that, they joined them all together and …

Mr Good:	[*To James*] Yes? [*To Tracey, turning to her and putting a hand on the top of her head*] Just (one moment) [*Mr Good looks at James*]
James:	like see Australia and ur Tasmania, looks like it can just join together?
Mr Good:	[*Mr Good turns to map*] Good boy. [*Mr Good, with hand on map, turns back to class*] There you go. [*Gesticulating with other hand*] Do you know why they think that, that these big, what's, what's the word that describes these that starts with 'c'?
S:	[*Whisper*] (Continent) [*Mr Good makes an expectant body and hand movement as if he has heard the right answer but wants it said so all can hear*]
(Boy):	Continent?
Mr Good:	C
Ss:	(Continent [s])
Mr Good:	These continents were joined together. You know there is some evidence to show that they were joined together.
S(s):	They um they looked…
Mr Good:	[*Mr Good makes a downward motion with his hands*] You know how I'm really wrapped in—what am I really wrapped in when we go into rainforests?
S(s):	[*Chorus answer*] Buttress roots.
Mr Good:	That's right yeh the buttress roots of the Ant, the Antarctic Beeches, those giant trees with big buttress roots that are [*pause*] very very important as far as rainforests are concerned and saving rainforests. They are found, of course, in that part of Australia and do you know those Antarctic Beeches are found in this part of the world also [*speaking slowly and pointing to map*]. So it's thought from that sort of evidence …
S:	they were joined …
Mr Good:	… that it was they were joined together. A sort of one giant continent …
Boy:	[*Boy puts hand up*] Mr Good, can I show …
Mr Good:	yes yes, you can [*Mr Good steps back*]
Boy:	[*Goes to map*] See that bit there? [*Points to map. Mr Good steps forward and looks*]
Mr Good:	Yes.
Boy:	it looks like it can just go in there.
S:	Yeh looks like it fits in there.
Mr Good:	Still that's, that's fair enough.
S:	and that looks like it can join to that.
Mr Good:	Yeh.
S:	and that … can look like it can join to that and things like that.
Mr Good:	… What's that [one]?
S:	It's like a jigsaw.
Mr Good:	Yes it's sort of like a jigsaw isn't it? … Yes
S:	Mr Good …
Mr Good:	Yes?
S:	Like Greenland joining onto North America.
Mr Good:	Right.
Boy:	[*Still standing near map*] Mr Good, it's like a big earthquake happened.

Mr Good: Right, it sort of split them …

Boy: Yeh.

Mr Good: split them all all apart. [*Boy goes to sit down. Mr Good's attention has turned to James bringing a book over. Mr Good looks towards James*] What have you found there [James]? [*James leans across and gives Mr Good the opened encyclopaedia. James steps back. Mr Good holds up the book for the class to see*]

Mr Good: Aahh right. Now look at this. Our own place on the earth. It's showing here how things may have joined together.

S: Where's Australia?

S(s): [*Overlaid conversation. Several students near Mr Good stand up to look at encyclopaedia*]

Mr Good: OK. Give him a clap. That was a that was a great bit of research. [*Students remain standing and clap, other(s) stand too*].

What are the options taken up by the boys here? James *initiates a discussion* about land masses through a question addressed to Mr Good. This is taken up with interest. Mr Good directs attention to the map as a focal point to the conversation as he elaborates the theory, with *assistance* from the students. He invites the students to *observe* the map, to *articulate* the appropriate words but then *connects their discussion to their experience* of trips to the rainforest, *to Mr Good's passion* for buttress roots and *to the moral issue* of saving the environment. The issue is thus not discussed in the abstract but connected to language, to the students' experiences, to emotions and to moral issues. In the meantime, James has gone looking for the book he was talking about and shows it to Mr Good. He is acknowledged as a *researcher* and receives public acclamation. In this the students are both *acknowledged as skilful in accessing knowledge resources, and able to recognise and applaud each other*.

The students then initiate a discussion about the war in Iraq, which was occurring at the time, and talk about a plane that was unable to land. Mr Good turns the discussion to the plight of the Kurds and to the way in which they can find no safe haven:

Mr Good: Yes, but why why not let them come in, [*pause*] 'cause they're starving?

James: Because if they harboured the Kurds, the Iraqis might have a go at them.

Mr Good: Good, that's, that's possibly one reason that that they're worried … about the Iraqis, the Iraqis attacking.

Joey: It could start another war.

Mr Good: Yes. It could start another war. It could, um, but what about a country being prepared to look after all those refugees? You know there are about, half a million, half a million refugees.

Boy: That's a lot of people.

Mr Good: It is, and people, it's really distressing us. It makes me sort of feel very very sad, that, these people are actually dying of starvation right now. They're dying of starvation and *large* planes are coming in and dropping food. What are the air aircraft called that ah come from the airports that are transports that drop lots of food? [*pause—Rodney's hand goes up*] I know you know Rodney. You're an expert. [*pause*] Um

S: not a Caribou, is it?

Mr Good:	No. [*Mr Good waits but probably as there are no volunteers he nods to Rodney*] Go on.
Rodney:	Galaxy?
Mr Good:	No.
S (s):	Oh Rodney.
Mr Good:	Not a Galaxy.
Rodney:	Hercules?
Mr Good:	Sorry?
Rodney:	Hercules?
Mr Good:	Good boy.
Tracey:	Oh good on ya.
Mr Good:	Hercules. Big, lots and lots and lots of Hercules. What are they called, a whole group of planes?
S:	Squadron.
Boy:	[*Mr Good does not respond to previous answer but nods at a boy with his hand up*] Flight. [Mr *Good looks to someone else*]
S:	A squadron.
Mr Good:	Good on you.
S (s):	Squadron, squadron.
Mr Good:	A squadron, a squadron of planes.

In this excerpt, Mr Good again invites the students to connect their observations of events in other parts of the world to *reason* (why is this happening), to *feelings* (in this case, his), and then to *language* and the *particular interests* of the boys who started the conversation. The details of what planes and the jargon of war are discussed alongside the concern they might feel for the refugees and the political issues that might lead to this plight. Mr Good goes on to invite the students to express their own feelings about the war. This they find difficult. The first response is 'I don't know', to which Mr Good responds 'That's fair. You, you don't know. That's cool'. They then offer, 'it's like suicide' and 'ridiculous'. Mr Good picks up on 'ridiculous' and proceeds as follows:

Mr Good:	(Okay) Right. No reason for it. You know we just read about people dying and we we see it on TV but, if you can just sort of imagine [*pause*] if that happened here, [*pause*] because life life is very precious isn't it? Hmm. Life is very precious and when we think of little Kurdish children or Kuwaiti children or Saudi Arabian children or Iraqi children [*pause*] sort of dying. [*pause*] That's sort of [*pause*] how do you feel about that? [*Mr Good turns head towards Tracey, apparently gets no reply and turns to front*]
S:	[*pause*] Feels awful.
Mr Good:	[*Mr Good turns to another student*] How do you feel about that? [*Mr Good turns head towards a student*]
S (s):	… scared, scared.
Mr Good:	[*Mr Good says another child's name and touches (her) hair*]
S:	Distressed.
Mr Good:	Distressed.
S:	Distressed.
Mr Good:	Yeh, so do you think there's another way around having wars? [*pause*] What's a what's another …

Jane: … started the war (front).
S: Yeh.
Mr Good: Is there another way than sort of shooting at each other? [*Overlaid quiet talk by students*]. You're a very wise and knowledgable person. [*Students laugh*]
S: It's not going to solve anything.
Mr Good: Sorry? [*Mr Good didn't hear student's answer*]
S: It's not going to solve anything.
Mr Good: How, how else, how else can we sort of sort out these disputes? [*Students talk while Mr Good is speaking*]
Boy: Kill someone.
Mr Good: But that's killing someone, mate, that's not much good. Yes. [*Overlaid talk from children, Mr Good indicates boy with hand up*]
Laurie: Co-operate.
Mr Good: Ah ah, [*Mr Good indicates he wants quiet*] Just listen to this.
Laurie: Co-operate.
Mr Good: What does that mean?
Tracey: [*Pause*] Oh Mr Good.
S(s):   Oh [*Students call out and several hands go up*]
Mr Good: Yeh.
Laurie: We all work together.
Mr Good: Stand stand. That's it come here [*Mr Good softly asks Laurie to stand and come out to the front of the group*]. That's a that's a superb superb answer Laurie. [*Mr Good puts arm around Laurie's back*] Just just say that again.
Laurie: We all work together.
Mr Good: Just working together, people sitting down and talking and perhaps…
Tracey: Don't we already do that though?
Mr Good: Well we do most of the time. Yeh, but there are some times, some times when we don't. Let's face it, there are some times when we don't.

Mr Good thus invites the students again to think about their emotions and to express them. He then connects the negative feelings they have about war to a discussion about problem-solving in their own lives. When a boy offers 'killing' as a way of solving problems, Mr Good does not accept the answer, but is friendly towards the boy: 'But that's killing someone, mate, that's not much good'. It is as if the answer is recognisably hegemonic, and what observably does go on, but it's 'not much good' for them. He thus accepts the boy's display of hege-monic knowledge, but accords greater value to something else in this context for this group of students.

In the story-writing lesson that follows later in the morning, one group of boys writes a dominant hegemonic story called 'danger football' in which they represent themselves as heroic. While the girls are playing football with them in the story, it is the girl who falls and breaks her arm. Mr Good does not comment on the content of the story, as he is intent on persuading this group of boys that they can actually write. Thus, they do engage in writ-ing and at the same time display themselves as hegemonic in terms celebrated outside this classroom. The class is then divided up into writing groups for the trip to the river:

Mr Good: In a in a moment we're going to go down for a walk to the river. Now, I went out fishing last Saturday and I noticed so many things along the

	river that really, really sort of impressed me [*Josh's hand goes up*] were just so lovely. What's happening at the moment sort of, [*Few hands go up*] yes [*To boy/Joey who first had hand up*]
Joey:	The leaves are falling off the tree and they go in the river and and …
Tracey:	[*Mr Good points at Tracey*] Change of season.
Mr Good:	Yes that's right. It's a change of season. What, what region of the of the state do we live in? It's called [*pause—points and nods*] Yes. [*Points again but probably not at same child*]
S:	Northern Tableland.
Mr Good:	Well its Northern Tablelands, also more specifically The New England … do you know that the New England is just so famous for its change of seasons? Now what season have we just come from? [*Several hands go up. Mr good points at one*]
S:	The New England
S(s):	Summer, summer.
Mr Good:	What season are we going into?
S:	Oh.
S:	Autumn.
Mr Good:	Good. [*Points at someone else*] Spell Autumn please.
S:	a-u-t-u-m-n [*Mr Good has nodded as each letter is said, and when child hesitated before 'm', Mr Good half mouths it*]
Mr Good:	… We're just going into autumn so there's really lovely [*Girl learning on T's knees looks round then gets up and goes off camera*] sort of change and as I, as I was walking along the bank there as I was walking along the bank, [*pause—Mr Good looks at girl*] is that the phone or something?
S:	No.
Mr Good:	Don't worry. [*pause—girl returns and sits down away from Mr Good*] As I was walking along the bank I, I saw all sorts of tremendous things, all sorts of tremendous things and, I really, I really thought of of putting down ah …
S:	the rod.
Mr Good:	The fishing rod [*pause*] and painting. And I can't, I can't paint [*pause*] pretty hopeless at that, but I also thought of, you know, keeping, keeping a record because it was just it was so so lovely. Well in a moment we're going to go take full advantage of that and perhaps I can share with you a little bit … Right, what do you think a a good way of sort of recording rather than [*Mr Good points*] yeh
S:	Writing, writing.
Mr Good:	Yes, good one.
Tracey:	Writing.
Mr Good:	yeh [*Mr Good points to another child*]
S:	Memory.
Mr Good:	We'll keep [*Mr Good taps his forehead*] all those sorts of things in mind. I'm going to take a camera down with me.

Mr Good thus sets the scene for the writing by describing his own emotional response to the beauty of the landscape, and by inviting the students to articulate the kinds of words that will connect the experience with one kind of literacy: season, autumn, summer, Northern Tablelands. He then moves on to the experience he had of seeing so many wonderful things that he wanted to record them. At this point, interestingly, he talks about his own inability to paint, and 'gives permission' to the experience of being unable to do something artistic. He then invites the students to think about the records they might make. As they set off for the river, he explains to them that he wants them to look for words that will enable them to describe what they see, and points out that they have to listen to their own minds for good words as well as look to see what they see:

S: [*Boy stands, Mr Good stands*] Laurie, [*pause while boy looks around*] Andrew.

Mr Good: [*Talking to someone off camera*] Now you've got a good team, you've got a good team. You you two can work it out. Do you want to work by yourself? You and … can work together. Okay. [*Students talk*] Now let's have your attention again please. [*Mr Good clicks fingers and children 'freeze' and are silent. Mr Good is standing in the middle of the room with children around him*] When I walked along the river bank I sort of didn't look at a tree and say, you know, the tree looks magnificent as the sun shines through its sort of sparking leaves, I just looked, I saw, I just, words …

Boy: Came into your head.

Mr Good: [*Mr Good looks at boy*] Yeh, they did, words just sort of came into my head and I sort of, words like sparkling and, rather lovely worlds. So that might be the way to go about things. Just look at the words that ah, that leap into your mind when we, when we get down to the river.

Later, on returning from the river:

Mr Good: I've seen a couple of examples of what has come from the groups but um, Laurie, could we hear yours first, from your group? Would you like to read it?

Laurie: Ah, I'll read it, Mr Good.

Mr Good: Right, okay. We'll just leave what (you're doing for a minute).

Mr Good: [*Jane gets up, crosses room and returns with sheets of paper to sit in same place. Mr Good talks to someone at his feet*] As ah just wait until he …

Laurie: Dead limbs sit on the still.

Mr Good: Wait a moment. Actually we might read just in a really really really loud, a loud voice so we can get some ideas from it.

Laurie: [*Kneeling at edge of group*] Dead limbs sit on the still water as the cool wind blows gently through the trees. Trout and other fish jump harmlessly through the water. Insects swim around in the calm water. Platypus bob up and down like a yo-yo looking for food. Birds sing happily in the trees.

In these various excerpts from this one morning in the classroom, we see how Mr Good invites and makes possible for the boys a connection between language, valued forms of school knowledge, their embodied being in the world, themselves as people with responsibility and agency, their emotions, their connectedness with the landscape around them and the connection of these to wider geographical, political and moral landscapes. The connection between these and spoken language is continually sought, and the further connection to others' writing and then to their own is successfully established. Laurie reads without apparent self-consciousness a poetic piece of prose that sits comfortably with the range of other masculinities available to him in the classroom: mates with the teacher, one who knows and learns from books, one who plays football dangerously, one who knows about war and planes and killing, one who considers moral and philosophical issues and emotional issues, and one who can speak about these.

Mr Good reveals his own preferences, and does not censor the boy's reading of how to be masculine. Rather, he invites them to broaden their range and celebrates their achievements in articulating a range of possibilities. What he does not offer them is the kind of reflexive knowledge that would allow them to see what is happening and to critique the various discourses that are made available to them. They practise a range of masculinities but are offered no discursive tools for articulating their movement across that range or for choosing between one or another (Davies, 1994). In the final section, I will discuss the importance of that kind of reflexive awareness in the development of literacy programmes for boys.

Critical literacy

What critical literacy opens up is the possibility of students and teachers becoming reflexively aware of the way in which speaking-as-usual constructs themselves and others. And it also opens up the possibility of thinking/writing/speaking in quite different ways, ways that enable boys to position themselves in multiple subjectivities which they can recognise and claim as their own, despite regimes of truth that dictate otherwise. Much of the impetus for critical literacy comes from feminist post-structuralist theory and post-colonial theory. In these theories, there is a strong move away from the automatic privileging of dominant colonising discourses and a move towards multiple voices, multiple perspectives, multiple ways of seeing the world.

Colonising discourses have provided the conceptual frameworks through which we do much of our teaching and through which we have done most of our learning. One effect of this is that even when we were or are positioned in the margins, we saw/see from the point of view of the centre. As women we saw ourselves negatively through men's eyes, as homosexuals we saw ourselves negatively through heterosexual eyes, as 'ethnic' we saw ourselves negatively through Anglo eyes, as 'disabled' we saw ourselves through 'able-bodied' eyes, and so on. Post-structuralism and post-colonialism have begun to disrupt that particular violence. Such negative, discursive constructions can no longer so easily go unnoticed nor seem a normal part of the way things are and ought to be.

A second shift in perceptions, following that original disruption, is to recognise (and own) the qualities that give us our particular ethnic or sexual or cultural identity. These are no longer experienced as 'other' to an ascendant category but as a rich, shifting, complex set of possibilities which may or may not take their meaning in relation to the once ascendant 'other' category. Having disrupted the apparently natural ascendancy and rightness of the ascendant term, the binary begins to lose its original meaning and force. This then takes us into the third (or post-structuralist) tier of feminism. Each person comes to see the multiple ways they are positioned and in which they position each other. Old notions of identity are disrupted, new discursive possibilities are opened up through a play on language, and the unconscious, the body, desire and emotions are made relevant in the playful construction of new identities and new meanings (Davies, 1994). [...]

While those inhabiting an ascendant category have difficulty recognising their dependence on the subordinate term for their own meaning, the imagination of the person who is not in the ascendant category is trained in an education system which takes those in the ascendant category to be the major source of meaning making, those who are used to being ascribed 'the status of ... saying what counts as true' (Foucault, 1980, p. 131). From the negative or subordinate category, we discover both the ways of making meaning from those who are positioned as ascendant, and our simultaneous (though partial) exclusion from them. In a fundamental sense, those who inhabit subordinate categories are bi-cognitive, or bi-modal, and as such are more likely to see the shifting, fluid and precarious, discursively constituted nature of identity. [...]

The definition of critical literacy that I am currently working on and have derived from my work with children and in observing classrooms such as Mr Good's, is the capacity to make language live, to bring oneself to life through language and, *at the same time,* bring to bear on language a critique which makes visible the powerful force of rationality and of linear patterns of thought, of usual speech patterns and usual metaphors, and a recognition of their constraints and limitations. Critical literacy enables one to understand how culture(s) and discourse(s) shape the body, desire and deeply felt personal knowledges. This involves developing the capacity to:

- move beyond the constraints of rational linear thought and to recognise and even celebrate multiple and contradictory patterns of thought, to embrace multiple ways of knowing and of coming to know (only one of which is rational argument);
- read oneself and its possibilities in different discourses and contexts;
- engage in moral/philosophical critique; and
- recognise the 'inherent limits to critique and transformation within any and all Discourses' (Gee & Lankshear, 1995, p.17). This is necessary because discourse enchants us, drawing us into the magic of the possibilities it opens up and at the same time places us under a spell which blinds us to its power and its effects (Gee & Lankshear, 1995). [...]

The development of reflexive strategies which reveal and provide strategies for undermining 'dead language' implies the ability to immerse oneself in each discourse (to be enchanted by it—to know the possibilities of oneself through it—to make language live) *and* the ability to break its spell. This requires the capacity to:

- know how to read oneself bodily/emotionally and to know the power of dominant discourses to seep into the unconscious and shape desire;
- know the pleasure of the power language gives and also its dangers; and
- engage in moral reasoning which is far more than the imposition of one morally ascendant discourse over another; it is the capacity to engage in reflexive thought in which the discourse through which one ascertains what is taken to be a truth at any one point in time is always open to revision, to the kind of revision that might lead to a different truth.

Through such skills we come to know how enchanting language is, and we learn to revel in the enchantment of knowing ourselves in the world through language. At the same time as we learn to be transgressive, we develop the skills of critical imagination through which we open up new possibilities, think the as yet unthinkable, beyond and outside dead language.

With *critical social literacy* oneself becomes a shifting, multiple text to be read. The construction of that self through discourse, through positioning within particular contexts and moments and through relations of power, is both recognised and made revisable. Critical social literacy involves the development of a playful ability to move between and amongst discourses, to move in and out of them, to mix them, to break their spell when necessary. It involves the capacity reflexively to critique text and context and to act on that reflection. It involves the capacity to make sense of the discursive shift, to articulate it, and to make it 'sensible' in terms of the cultural/discursive patterns one is speaking/writing into existence. It breaks the enchantment of the compulsory struggle towards dominant and hegemonic forms of masculinity and balances this with an understanding of the effects of that struggle and the freedom to enter into other regimes of truth, understanding at the same time their enchantment and their limitations.

Critical literacy and critical social literacy are not aimed at replacing one dominant discourse with another morally ascendant discourse. They are not 'reformist' in the sense of re-forming the bodies and minds of the students in a different and specific mould dictated by those with authority. Rather, they are aimed at giving students some skill in catching language in the act of formation and in recognising and assessing the effects of that formation. In a critically and socially literate classroom, language is no longer a dead tool for the maintenance of old certainties, but a life-giving set of possibilities for shaping and reshaping a complex, rich, fluid social world. A critically and socially literate classroom would not be caught up, as some might fear, in a mindless, relativist spiral. Rather, in the very visibility and analysability of language, and its effects, lies the possibility of being open to a philosophical and moral critique of the many and multiple meanings and modes of being embedded in and created through different uses of language.

References

Davies, B. (1989) *Frogs and Snails and Feminist Tales: preschool children and gender* (Sydney, Allen & Unwin).

Davies, B. (1993) *Shards of Glass: children reading and writing beyond gendered identities* (Sydney, Allen & Unwin).

Davies, B. (1994) *Poststructuralist Theory and Classroom Practice* (Geelong, Deakin University Press).

Foucault, M. (1980) Truth and power, in: C. Gordon (Ed.) *Power/Knowledge: selected interviews and other writings 1972–1977, Michel Foucault*, pp. 109–133 (Brighton, Harvester).

Gee, J. P. & Lankshear, C. (1995) The new work order, *Discourse*, 16, pp. 5–20.

Grosz, E. (1990) *Jacques Lacan: a feminist introduction* (London, Routledge).

13

Assessment *as* Learning? How the Use of Explicit Learning Objectives, Assessment Criteria and Feedback in Post-secondary Education and Training Can Come to Dominate Learning

Harry Torrance

[…]

Introduction

Claims for the educational value and effectiveness of formative assessment in the mainstream compulsory school system have been made for a number of years, in the UK and elsewhere. It is argued that assessment has to move from 'assessment of learning' to 'assessment for learning', whereby assessment procedures and practices are developed to support learning and underpin rather than undermine student confidence, achievement and progress (Black & Wiliam, 1998; Torrance & Pryor, 1998; Gipps, 1999; Shepard, 2000). Indeed, so commonplace have these claims become that research and development attention has shifted to the dissemination and implementation of formative approaches to assessment on a wide scale, integrating work on formative assessment with that deriving from the school improvement movement and addressing the problem of 'scaling up' across the maintained school system. In England, a Teaching and Learning Research Programme (TLRP) project was funded by the Economic and Social Research Council (ESRC) for just this purpose (James *et al.*, 2006). Key elements of formative assessment practice, which it is claimed implementation should involve, include 'feedback focused on helping students to improve [and] sharing criteria of quality' (James & Pedder, 2006, p. 110; see also Marshall & Drummond, 2006, p. 134). However, the research project on which this chapter reports, which investigated assessment in post-secondary education and training in England, has discovered that these key elements of formative assessment are already widespread in the post-secondary sector, but are interpreted very narrowly, with an overwhelming focus

From: *Assessment in Education*, 14 (3), 2007, pp. 281–294. Reprinted by permission of the publisher (Taylor & Francis Ltd, http://www.informaworld.com).

on criteria compliance and award achievement. Far from promoting an orientation towards student autonomy and 'Learning How To Learn' (Black *et al.*, 2006; James *et al.*, 2006), such practices are interpreted as techniques to assure award achievement and probably help to produce students who are *more* dependent on their tutors and assessors rather than less dependent.

There has been a significant move over the last 20 years towards criterion-referenced assessment and competence-based assessment in post-compulsory education and training, including in the UK modularization of the Advanced Level General Certificate of Education (A-level) and the Advanced Vocational Certificate of Education (AVCE) in the context of 'Curriculum 2000' (Burke, 1989; Jessup, 1991; Wolf, 1995; Hodgson & Spours, 2003; see also Hayward & McNicholl, 2007). This has involved a greater transparency of intended learning outcomes and the criteria by which they are judged, and has benefited learners in terms of the increasing numbers of learners retained in formal education and training and the range and numbers of awards which they achieve (for a discussion of recent figures, see Raffe *et al.*, 2001; Savory *et al.*, 2003). Clarity in assessment procedures, processes and criteria has underpinned the widespread use of coaching, practice and the provision of formative feedback to boost individual and institutional achievement. Detailed tutor and assessor support, in the form of exam coaching and practice, the drafting and redrafting of assignments, asking 'leading questions' during workplace observations, and identifying appropriate evidence to record in portfolios, is widespread throughout the sector and is effective in facilitating learner achievement and progression.

However, research evidence reported below suggests that such transparency encourages instrumentalism. The clearer the task of how to achieve a grade or award becomes, and the more detailed the assistance given by tutors, supervisors and assessors, the more likely candidates are to succeed. But transparency of objectives coupled with the extensive use of coaching and practice to help learners meet them are in danger of removing the challenge of learning and reducing the quality and validity of outcomes achieved. This might be characterized as a move from assessment *of* learning, through the currently popular idea of assessment *for* learning, to *assessment as learning*, where assessment procedures and practices come to dominate completely the learning experience, and 'criteria compliance' comes to replace 'learning'.

The research

The findings on which this chapter is based derive from a Learning and Skills Research Centre (LSRC) funded research project, 'The impact of different modes and methods of assessment on achievement and progress in the learning and skills sector' (additional support was provided by City & Guilds and the 'University for Industry', UfI). The project was commissioned to investigate whether or not, and if so, how, the use of different assessment methods makes a difference to learner achievement and progress in post-compulsory education and training. A review of the literature on assessment in post-compulsory education noted the scarcity of studies in the sector (Torrance & Coultas, 2004), while other recent research reviews such as Stasz *et al.* (2004) note a similar paucity of evidence with respect to what teaching and learning approaches might actually make a difference to achievement and outcomes in the sector. Thus, the project was commissioned to address the need for a comprehensive overview of assessment procedures and practices in the post-compulsory Learning and Skills Sector (LSS) in England, especially at the level of impact on the learner. It sought to compare and contrast the assessment experiences of learners in different settings and is the first comprehensive study of assessment procedures and practices employed across the full range of LSS contexts—school sixth-forms, further education colleges, workplaces and adult learning environments.

Data have been gathered by conducting a series of parallel case studies of assessment 'in action' across a wide variety of LSS settings, and by a questionnaire distributed to a larger sample of learners derived from the case study settings. Case studies were conducted of assessment across the post-compulsory Learning and Skills Sector:

- School sixth-form and college-based A-levels and AVCEs in physical education, sport & leisure and business studies;
- Work-based National Vocational Qualifications (NVQs) in social care, motor vehicle engineering (MVE) and sport & recreation;
- College-based Access to Higher Education (HE) courses;
- College-based Adult Basic Skills testing;
- and an informal Community Education and Accreditation programme conducted under the auspices of a government-funded community 'SureStart' project.

The boundaries of each case were established with respect to particular qualifications and/or awards and the contextual and regional factors which influence the assessment of awards in practice, including awarding body procedures and processes. Thus, the case studies were designed as 'vertical' investigations, exploring a particular qualification such as an AVCE or NVQ from an awarding body through to a learner, though with the emphasis on learner experience. In total, 237 learners/candidates were interviewed, along with 95 'assessors' (i.e. all those involved in operating and conducting assessment within the case studies including the full range of senior awarding body staff, chief and lead verifiers, internal assessors and external verifiers, employers, supervisors, college and school heads of department, tutors, etc.) Completed questionnaire returns were also received from 260 respondents out of the 890 distributed (34% return).

Findings: supporting candidates to achieve awards

The full findings of the research are reported in Torrance *et al.* (2005). This chapter focuses on the key issues of how achievement is defined and how formative feedback is used to support achievement.

Achievement is routinely defined in fairly narrow and instrumental terms. It is interpreted as securing the evidence to complete a portfolio and/or the 'necessary' or 'expected' grades to accomplish an award; these are not necessarily the highest grades available or even directly related to competent practice.

> Achievement would mean getting a C or above; I'd be happy to get a C but I know I could do better. (AVCE student)

> I've got quite a lot of experience as a mechanic because I've worked in a garage for a while but I've just got no papers so … if anything goes wrong if I've got qualifications I can say well I've been in college and I've done that. (MVE trainee)

> I've had four years' experience now since being with SureStart. I can do it—I know what I'm doing … but … I just want all of that on paper… you know I want me bit of paper now to prove that I can do it … . (Adult learner involved in SureStart programme accredited by the Open College Network, OCN)

Failure is defined as *non-completion* (of a portfolio, or of sufficient credits in a course of study) or not securing the *expected and necessary* grades (e.g. for progression to a particular HE course). Provided the work is (eventually) completed, the award will be achieved:

> You can fail if you just don't do the work on time, or you don't take any notice of the teachers' advice … [but] you can drop a couple of the option units if your marks aren't any good and you can still pass the course. (AVCE student)

> They don't fail, they can be withdrawn. For example, if an assessor observes bad practice or if somebody doesn't seem competent in their work, then … they are mentored within the workplace until such time as their manager feels that they are ready to continue. (Lead verifier, social care NVQ)

> Essentially there's no fail as such at NVQ—they're referred. Obviously if they're referred they get another opportunity to update their portfolio to get it to a pass standard or to demonstrate that they've met the units of competence. (External assessor, sport & recreation NVQ)

Even at A-level (i.e. an academic programme preparatory to university entrance), students can resit modular tests to improve grades or retrieve fails (see Hayward & McNicholl, 2007). Students take tests and exam papers in the first year (the 'AS' qualification) but can retake poorly graded papers or simply not progress to the second year (A2) if grades are too poor, focusing instead on those subjects in which they think they will do best. Thus, for example, in one of the case study colleges, students could opt to do one unit of a business studies course as either a coursework project or a modular test, and one student chose both options so that she could pick her higher mark to go forward for final grading.

The process in action

In addition to this overall orientation towards the pursuit of achievement, and the structural properties of awards such as modularization which can facilitate this, there is a significant, even overwhelming, culture of support for learners/candidates at every level and across every sub-sector of the LSS. Even in A-level teaching, beyond modularization, support is provided by tutors through the breaking down and interpreting of assessment criteria and the involvement of tutors in formal examining and moderating roles for awarding bodies (ABs, i.e. what were previously known as examination boards). Such involvement helps to develop teachers' understanding of the assessment process and criteria which they will, in turn, pass on to students through exam coaching.

AVCE and A-level

This culture of support is apparent in choices of awards and awarding bodies even before tutors begin to provide detailed guidance on assessment tasks and criteria.

> We have changed exam board—from [AB1 to AB2]. The practical with the former was too long-winded and complicated, and the moderation system was complicated ... [the AB2 syllabus] is also a little bit more compartmentalized ... which seems to suit our pupils. With [AB1] the questions went down the synoptic line, which our kids found confusing ... (AVCE Sp&L tutor)

ABs also came in for considerable criticism about a lack of responsiveness to queries and clearly this will influence the choice of AB. In some colleges in the study, curriculum managers have been returning to BTEC programmes (that is, older vocational preparation programmes) which they feel are more genuinely vocationally oriented, rather than AVCEs. Additionally, BTEC students are not counted in national achievement data for 'Level 3' (i.e. an A-level equivalent for government statistics), so moving to BTEC and taking vocational students out of college level data could obscure a college's attainment of fewer higher grades in AVCE compared to general A-level. Savory *et al.* (2003) similarly report a move away from AVCE towards offering BTEC Nationals, and note widespread dissatisfaction with ABs' responses to queries. They quote one respondent complaining that:

> The exam boards have become so big that they are drowning and we find it almost impossible to find a real person to talk to about new specification problems. (Savory *et al.*, 2003, p. 16)

Once ABs and syllabuses are selected, detailed grade criteria are articulated for learners at A-level and AVCE—the breaking down of awarding body guidelines and instructions into detailed mark schemes, assignment plans, etc., for students to follow.

> At A-level [the examining boards] want to hear technical terms and expanded vocabulary ... [students] need to be a little more analytical at A-level ... So we have drafted a crib sheet with words, explanations. (A-level PE tutor)

> We have spent a lot of time ... coming up with a sort of a template to issue to our students as a starting point to give them something to work on ... writing frames, templates to fill in, bullet points to follow ... . (AVCE Sp&L tutor)

In turn, students can draft and redraft assignments, receiving feedback on strengths and weaknesses and what needs to be done to improve the grade. They can also retake unit and modular tests as necessary to improve grades. Sometimes tutors operate with the 'straight' AVCE/BTEC nomenclature of Pass, Merit and Distinction; sometimes they operate with a range of grades which parallel AS and A2 (grades E–A) and which in turn 'map onto' AVCE, thus 'D/E' refer to 'describing and identifying' and would correspond with a Pass; 'B/C' involve 'understanding' and 'bringing together' and correspond with a Merit;

'A' must include 'critical evaluation and analysis' and corresponds with a Distinction. When asked what an A grade meant in AVCE Business Studies, one student responded:

> It's analyse, evaluate, and stuff like that. You have to explain things but more in-depth. Instead of just summarizing, you have to extend it and make it relevant and link it to what you've already put, it's clear and it flows and it's fully described.

Other students were equally well tuned to the criteria and drafting process:

> At the start of each module we get like a sheet of paper, it's got 'for an E you have to do this, for a D you have to do that' … they tell you what you have to do to get a good mark. (AVCE student)

Tutors worked very hard to make their feedback as detailed as possible:

> I see a draft, read through it, make notes, talk to each one, show the good areas in relation to the criteria and explain why and how if they have met them, saying things like 'you've missed out M2' … . (AVCE BS tutor)

> I assess continuously … Also there are summative assessments [written tasks that respond to a specific question and a set of criteria]. These are always worked on in a way where they can improve their grades, and they get a lot more than one chance … you can see a piece of work three times. If there is a large group this gets out of hand. But I want to get the best I can for my students. (AVCE Sp&L tutor)

Thus, 'good teachers' are those who can handle this workload and schedule this formative feedback within realistic timescales, offering clear guidance that students feel they can follow. A-level and AVCE alike involve a great deal of criteria-focused 'coaching' of students. The potential downside of such activity is that achievement can come to be seen as little more than criteria compliance in pursuit of grades. Moreover, while the pressure of coursework assignments can become intense, the responsibility for putting in the 'hard work' of assessment in pursuit of achievement might now be said to fall as much on the shoulders of tutors as on the learners, and a great deal of 'hidden work' is undertaken according to tutor disposition (cf. also James & Diment, 2003).

Support in the workplace

Just as ACVE and A-level students get support from their tutors, so, it transpires, do learners in the workplace. NVQ assessment is intended to be largely based on observation of competence in action, *in situ*. It is designed to be conducted when candidates are ready to demonstrate competence, by assessors who either have an interest in ensuring that learners are indeed competent (e.g. supervisors and line managers) and so are unlikely to pass poor candidates, or by assessors who are external to the workplace and are therefore intended to be completely disinterested (external verifiers). In practice, however, assessors get drawn into a much more pedagogical relationship with candidates:

Our primary form of assessment is through observation and questioning, if … I'm not satisfied that the learner has met the standards, I will make reference to it in the feedback that I give to the learner, obviously I'll try to be as positive and encouraging as I can; I'll say that there's been missed opportunities here, therefore I cannot use this piece of evidence … If they need additional support I will make every effort to make a weekly visit as opposed to a fortnightly visit for that learner, to give them the encouragement, to give them whatever training needs are necessary, and to encourage them to get through, and obviously I'll liaise with their managers … . (External assessor, Sp&Rec NVQ)

In other workplace settings, support can be observed in the way 'leading questions' are asked of candidates to help them through observations of workshop practice and in compiling portfolio evidence. In the example below, where an MVE apprentice is cleaning and adjusting brake drums and shoes, the interaction is more like a traditional 'teacher–pupil' pedagogic encounter than a workplace assessment.

[Fieldwork observation:]

Assessor: What were the drums like?

MVE trainee: They had a bit of rust on them so we cleaned the drums out and cleaned the shoes out … [ ] …

A: I'm trying to think of something I haven't asked you before. Yes, what causes the rust on a brake pipe?

MVE tr: Corrosion.

A: So you get outside corrosion, yes, from the weather and then what about the inside corrosion? How does a brake pipe get rusted on the inside which you can't see?

MVE tr: The brake fluid gets warm.

A: No.

MVE tr: It's something in the brake fluid isn't it?

A: Yes, what causes rust?

MVE tr: Water.

A: So if it's rusty on the inside, what do we say the brake fluid does? Why do we have to change the brake fluid? If I say hydroscopic to you, I'm not swearing. Have you heard of it?

MVE tr: I've heard it now.

A: Do you know what it means? Can you remember what it means? It absorbs moisture. So that's why you have to change the fluid so that the brake pipes don't become rusty on the inside.

MVE tr: I knew it was something in the fluid.

A: Well now you know don't you. Don't forget next time will you?

[…]

Adult learning

In Access courses and adult basic education settings, similar levels of support, coaching and practice were observed. Exercises and assignments were drafted, read, commented upon and then resubmitted:

I tend to layout fairly clearly what I want … I've broken it down into four discrete sections and lay out exactly what they have to do for each and then they get handouts which will support them. (Access tutor)

[…]

In Basic Skills programmes, there are continual efforts made to relate literacy and numeracy tasks to relevant social and vocational activities, and render the Adult Basic Skills Unit (ABSU) national curriculum into 'small chunks', but with the addition that in college-based settings as much testing as possible was embedded in ordinary classroom activities.

We all have small chunks for the students to cover and so they are doing activities in the classroom and they can self-assess. They can peer-assess as well. They are doing group work and they are doing listening as well, so they are assessing all these skills as we go along. (Adult Basic Skills tutor)

Right now I have been working through units, I am just working through the units each time … I tend to do them one by one, make sure they are OK, and get them out of the way … you do one paper, and if you get it all right, then you can move on to the next one … It is the set-up to work through each unit and you take your time going through it, make sure it is correct, and you get to the end and do the final test. (Basic Skills learner)

In this respect it is a moot point if some candidates even realized they were taking a test. A number of learners had progressed from one level to another without being able to remember that they had taken tests:

… the English teacher is quite clever, she's given me a few tests without me [realizing]. When I go on the computer she says 'well that's level 1 or level 2', so she says 'you passed that'. I don't know … which is kind of good because of the psychology of it … . (Basic Skills learner)

Significant levels of tutor 'hidden work' were also observed in this sub-sector as in others:

If you've got problems you know who to talk to. You haven't got to go hunting for somebody … I think [tutor] R feels like the mother of the group. She's the mother hen that goes round and worries about everybody … If you need help or you need extra time, you go and talk to R and it's sorted. (Access student)

Last year [named tutor] had them from [village] and it's quite a way out, I mean it's right up in the hills really. And they don't have cars because it's a poorer area … And she brought them down in her car. She went up, collected them all, brought them all back. They did their exams and she took them back again. Because you do worry about them. Well, I worry about them. I know it's stupid. (Basic Skills tutor)

Equity and quality in learner support

It can be argued that none of this support, even exam coaching, is necessarily inappropriate or unfair in and of itself. Such practices are at the heart of professional judgements about the performance/competence interface which tutors and assessors must make. They are also very understandable in the current context of results-driven accountability and the financial viability of programmes and institutions. But the provision of such detailed support raises issues of equity if it is not pursued uniformly. College level provision of support varies with local policies and the level of tutor knowledge of the system (e.g. as noted above, through individual tutors becoming examiners in order to understand better the procedures and assessment criteria of their course).

More broadly, the questionnaire data suggest that there can be wide variations in the frequency and length of assessor visits to workplaces. Thus, for example, while the most frequently reported timing of assessor visits amongst the NVQ-takers was 1–2 hours every 4–6 weeks, one reported that they saw their assessor once a week for 2–3 hours, while four reported that they saw their assessors only every three months or less *and* for one hour or less. There is also evidence that discrepancies may derive from the different cultures that develop in colleges and private training agencies, with college tutors not only seeing apprentices in college (for day-release classes) but also often visiting them in their workplaces to conduct assessments, and thus developing a much closer pedagogical relationship than that of training agency staff who simply travel round workplaces assessing full time.

Helping candidates 'complete the paperwork' is also an important element of the assessor's role in workplace assessment interactions. For example, in garages, it appeared to be a very common practice for MVE apprentices simply to keep their garage 'job-sheets' up to date and filled in with brief descriptions of the jobs undertaken and completed. The assessor then 'deconstructs' this basic information into the relevant 'competences' and maps and transfers the detail into the apprentice's evidence portfolio. Such practices also accord with the findings of other recent studies of portfolio completion in the workplace which indicate that younger workers do not usually take responsibility for portfolio completion (Kodz *et al.*, 1998; Tolley *et al.*, 2003). Indeed, Fuller and Unwin (2003), in their study of apprenticeship in various sectors of the steel industry, note, almost in passing, that:

> Responsibility for recording the apprentices' progress towards the achievements of the qualifications was taken by the external training provider at the regular review sessions. An important part of his job was to help apprentices identify how the day-to-day task in which they were engaged could be used to generate evidence that they were meeting the competence standards codified in the NVQ... . (Fuller & Unwin, 2003, p. 422)

Policy-makers may be tempted to try to reassert the disinterested observational nature of NVQ assessment by defining working practices, including the number and length of assessment occasions, in ever more detail. But even if this is effective (which, given the evidence reported above, is unlikely) it will simply disadvantage work-based NVQ takers against college-based A-level and AVCE takers. Giving clear instructions to assessors that the *quality of the assessment interaction* is likely to be as important to 'fair' and motivating workplace assessment as the accuracy of the observational record may be more helpful. Stasz *et al.* (2004) and Fuller and Unwin (2003) similarly note the importance of the vitality and range of workplace relationships for the quality of trainee learning.

Transparency promotes instrumentalism

A corollary of the level of support provided is that not only is it both demanded and expected by learners, it is also expected to be very specifically focused on achieving the qualification:

> Sometimes we have to do other tasks but the bottom line is 'is it relevant' … [there's] no time to do irrelevant stuff. (AVCE student)

> We're all there for one reason. We're all there at the end of the day to pass it … I just want to get it over and done with. Get it passed and carry on. (Access student)

> I've got to get my papers … so I can walk into any job in the future. (MVE trainee)

In turn, the instrumentalism of learners both drives and validates the level of tutor support. Similarly, institutions themselves are target-oriented and instrumentally driven. Thus, learners seek and expect details of assessment specifications, evidence requirements and so forth. They want support and appreciate it when they get it; but their instrumentalism reinforces tutor moves to focus on grade criteria, the elucidation of evidence, etc. As a consequence, assignments and portfolios from some institutions can often look very similar— in structure, format, types of evidence included, etc.—so it seems that some institutions are becoming very adept at 'coaching' cohorts through assignment completion; exam cramming by another means. In a very real sense, we seem to have moved from 'assessment of learning' through 'assessment for learning' to *'assessment as learning'*, for both learners and tutors alike, with assessment procedures and processes completely dominating the teaching and learning experience. In saying this I am not necessarily suggesting that each and every tutor or supervisor has made this transition empirically, but rather that the field of practice as a whole seems to have made the transition conceptually. Indeed, empirically, it might be argued that in post-compulsory education and training, practice has moved directly from assessment *of* learning to assessment *as* learning, but this is justified and explained in the language of assessment for learning: providing feedback, communicating criteria to the learner, and so forth. Thus, the supposedly educative formative process of identifying and sharing assessment criteria, and providing feedback on strengths and weaknesses to learners, is ensconced at the heart of the learning experience in the post-secondary sector, infusing every aspect of the learner experience. But it is a process which appears to weaken rather than strengthen the development of learner autonomy.

This finding of extensive support, manifest across all sub-sectors of the LSS through coaching, practice, drafting and the elicitation of evidence, coupled with an associated learner instrumentalism, seems to derive in large part from the move towards transparency in assessment processes and criteria. The more clearly requirements are stated, the easier it would appear for them to be pursued and accomplished. Equally, however, the imperative to compliance and the 'expulsion of failure' from the post-secondary sector (except with respect to non-completion) beg questions about what should now constitute a legitimate learning *challenge* in the context of post-secondary education and training. The danger is that as the number of enrolments and awards achieved increases, the underlying purpose of such expansion—increasing the numbers in *and* improving the standards achieved in further education and training—is compromised. Making learning objectives and instructional processes more explicit calls into question the validity and worthwhileness of the outcomes achieved.

Conclusion

Previous studies of formative assessment in the compulsory school sector have noted that broad recommendations to 'share criteria' and 'provide criteria-focused feedback' can be interpreted in different ways. Torrance and Pryor (1998) report that formative assessment can be 'convergent', with teachers focusing on identifying and reporting whether or not students achieve extant curriculum-derived objectives, or 'divergent' which is much more oriented towards identifying what students can do in an open-ended and exploratory fashion. Similarly, Marshall and Drummond (2006) note that while some teachers in the 'Learning How to Learn' study attempted to implement the 'spirit' of formative assessment with respect to developing student autonomy, most simply followed the 'letter' and used formative assessment techniques to facilitate short-term lesson planning and teaching, and promote short-term grade accomplishment. It would appear that not much has changed in the compulsory sector in the eight years between the two studies. Certainly, it would seem that formative assessment is not necessarily or inevitably a benign or expansive process, or one that will always promote 'learning autonomy' (Black et al., 2006).

Perhaps the more interesting point to note in the context of post-compulsory education and training, however, is the widespread use of convergent formative assessment in the sector, without the aid of a 'rolling out' programme (James et al., 2006). Why is it so widespread and why is practice so convergent? The answer would appear to lie partly in the long-term advocacy and development of criterion referencing and competence-based assessment in the post-compulsory sector, and partly in the attainment-oriented culture of the sector.

Criterion referencing involves establishing aims and objectives for a course, along with clear criteria for deciding whether or not the aims and objectives have been achieved, and then identifying what candidates know and can do in relation to those criteria. Competence-based assessment is a particularly strong form of criterion referencing practised in vocational and especially work-based learning environments. What the learner can do, and can be seen to do, in relation to the tasks required of them for competent practice, are paramount. It is of little interest to the learner or assessor to identify what *else* the learner can do (i.e. engage in divergent assessment) although this may be of considerable importance to their longer-term development. Clearly, this overall orientation of the post-compulsory system has an enormously powerful convergent impact. Moreover, the majority of the sector is operating within a strong 'second best but second chance' culture. Vocational routes are still perceived as second best to academic achievement and progression, and tutors are often dealing with learners who have experienced previous school failure. They are determined to maximize the possibilities of success for this 'second chance' client group. In addition, the more general policy trend towards widening participation and improving achievement levels at 19 ('level 3') and in higher education means related practices are also influencing A-levels. This, together with the high stakes accountability and financial insecurity of the sector, will also inevitably drive a convergent focus on criterion attainment and award accrual.

Does it matter? More learners are staying on in post-compulsory education and training, or returning to it in later life, and are achieving more awards than even before. But the trade-off, which would now appear to be a major issue for policy, is that the content of the awards and of learners' overall learning experience may be overly narrowed. To reiterate, we seem to have moved from 'assessment of learning' through 'assessment for learning' to '*assessment as learning*'. If formative assessment is to develop more positively in post-compulsory education and training, attention must be paid to the development of tutors' and assessors' judgement at local level, and the nature of their relationships with learners, so that learners are inducted into 'communities of practice' (Wenger, 1998) which explore and interrogate criteria, rather than accept them as given. The provision of clear national programmes of study, and the criteria by which success can be judged, have certainly led to increasing numbers of learners achieving awards; but this very process has led to too narrow a reliance on accumulating marks, or elements of competence, and a narrowing of the quality of the learning experience. What is required now is an acknowledgement that local communities of practice are the context in which all meaningful judgements are made, and thus should be the level of the system at which most efforts at capacity building are directed. This may start to reinstate the challenge of learning in the post-compulsory sector and attend to it as an act of social and intellectual development rather than one of acquisition and accumulation.

References

Black, P. & Wiliam, D. (1998) Assessment and classroom learning, *Assessment in Education*, 5(1), 7–74.

Black, P., McCormick, R., James, M. & Pedder, D. (2006) Learning How to Learn and Assessment for Learning: a theoretical inquiry, *Research Papers in Education*, 21(2), 119–132.

Burke, J. (Ed.) (1989) *Competency-based education and training* (London, Falmer Press).

Fuller, A. & Unwin, L. (2003) Learning as apprentices in the contemporary UK workplace: creating and managing expansive and restrictive participation, *Journal of Education and Work*, 16(4), 407–426.

Gipps, C. (1999) Socio-cultural aspects of assessment, *Review of Research in Education*, 24, 355–392.

Hayward, G. and McNicholl, J. (2007) Modular mayhem. A case study of the development of the A-level science curriculum in England, *Assessment in Education*, 14(3), 335–351.

Hodgson, A. & Spours, K. (2003) *Curriculum 2000* (London, Routledge).

James, D. & Diment, K. (2003) Going underground? Learning and assessment in an ambiguous space, *Journal of Vocational Education and Training*, 55(4), 407–422.

James, M. & Pedder, D. (2006) Beyond method: assessment and learning practices and values, *The Curriculum Journal*, 17(2), 109–138.

James, M., Black, P., McCormick, R., Pedder, D. & Wiliam, D. (2006) Learning How to Learn, in classrooms, schools and networks: aims, design and analysis, *Research Papers in Education*, 21(2), 101–118.

Jessup, G. (1991) *Outcomes: NVQs and the emerging model of education and training* (London, Falmer Press).

Kodz, J., Dench, S., Pollard, E. & Evans, C. (1998) *Developing the key skills of young people: an evaluation of initiatives in the former Avon area*, Report 350 (Brighton, Institute for Employment Studies).

Marshall, B. & Drummond, M. J. (2006) How teachers engage with Assessment for Learning: lessons from the classroom, *Research Papers in Education*, 21(2), 133–149.

Raffe, D., Croxford, L. & Brannen, K. (2001) Participation in full time education beyond 16: a 'home international' comparison, *Research Papers in Education*, 16(1), 43–68.

Savory, C., Hodgson, A. & Spours, K. (2003) *The Advanced Vocational Certificate of Education (AVCE): a general or vocational qualification?* (London, IoE/Nuffield Series Number 7).

Shepard, L. (2000) The role of assessment in a learning culture, *Educational Researcher*, 29(7), 4–14.

Stasz, C., Hayward, G., Oh, S. & Wright, S. (2004) *Outcomes and processes in vocational learning: a review of the literature* (London, Learning and Skills Research Centre (LSRC)).

Tolley, H., Greatbatch, D., Bolton, J. & Warmington, P. (2003) *Improving occupational learning: the validity and transferability of NVQs in the workplace, DfES Research Report RR425* (London, DfES).

Torrance, H. & Coultas, J. (2004) *Do summative assessment and testing have a positive or negative effect on post-16 learners' motivation for learning in the learning and skills sector? A review of the research literature on assessment in post-compulsory education in the UK* (London, LSRC).

Torrance, H. & Pryor, J. (1998) *Investigating formative assessment: teaching, learning and assessment in the classroom* (Buckingham, Open University Press).

Torrance, H., Colley, H., Garratt, D., Jarvis, J., Piper, H., Ecclestone, K. & James, D. (2005) *The impact of different modes of assessment on achievement and progress in the learning and skills sector* (London, LSDA for the LSRC).

Wenger, E. (1998) *Communities of practice: learning, meaning and identity* (Cambridge, Cambridge University Press).

Wolf, A. (1995) *Competence-based assessment* (Buckingham, Open University Press).

Index

Page numbers followed by (Figure) or (Table) refer to Figures or Tables
Page numbers shown as roman numerals refer to the Introduction at the front of the book